IDEAS AND IMAGES

IDEAS AND IMAGES

Developing Interpretive History Exhibits

Kenneth L. Ames, Barbara Franco, and L. Thomas Frye
Editors

American Association for State and Local History
Nashville, Tennessee

Funding provided by the National Endowment for the Humanities supported the author research and travel necessary to write the essays and the editorial work for this book.

Published by the American Association for State and Local History, an international nonprofit membership organization. For membership information, please contact Membership Services, (615) 255-2971.

Library of Congress Cataloging-in-Publication Data

Ideas and images: developing interpretive history exhibits / Kenneth L. Ames, Barbara Franco , L. Thomas Frye, editors.
    p. cm.
Includes bibliographical references and index.
ISBN 0-942063-20-1 $24.95
        1. Historical museums--United States. 2. Historic sites—United States— Interpretive programs. 3. United States—History, Local—Exhibitions—Handbooks, manuals, etc. I. Ames, Kenneth L. II Franco, Barbara. III. Frye, L. Thomas.
E172. I34 1992
973 .074—dc20   92-14130
                                                                     CIP

ISBN 0-942063-20-1

Produced for the American Association for State and Local History by Zenda, Inc.

CONTENTS

ACKNOWLEDGMENTS

It seems fitting that the creation of a publication about exhibitions should be as complex as the process it describes. *Ideas and Images: Developing Interpretive History Exhibits* would not have been possible without the ideas, encouragement, support, and hard work of a large number of people who care about history, history museums, and the exhibitions that they produce. The idea for this volume first emerged during discussions at the 1987 Common Agenda Conference. Nicholas Westbrook, author of the conference's working paper on interpretation, Kenneth L. Ames, chairman of the Common Agenda Interdisciplinary Task Force and Tim Meagher, program officer at the National Endowment for the Humanities, all expressed the need to better understand how exhibitions come about. Together they conceived the idea for a case study approach to document and analyze the exhibition process.

When Mary Alexander joined the Common Agenda as coordinator she took on this publication as one of its projects. Under her able supervision, the idea for an exhibition reader became a reality. Her enthusiasm, energy, and good humored persistence kept the project on track. She sought funding, coordinated meetings, contacted authors and institutions, and assembled manuscripts and photographs. The National Museum of American History supported these efforts by providing office facilities and organizational support. Celeste Lopina, an intern from the Museum Studies Program of George Washington University, completed background research on recent exhibitions and assembled a preliminary list of possible candidates for inclusion in the book. Ken Ames assumed the responsibility of editing the fledgling publication and solicited the aid of Barbara Franco and Tom Frye as associate editors.

Throughout the early stages of the project, the staff of the National Endowment for the Humanities provided invaluable guidance and support. Don Gibson, Marsha Semmel, and Tim Meagher met with Mary Alexander and the editors to help refine the criteria for the essays so that the focus remained analytical and served as wide a variety of museums as possible. Under AASLH sponsorship, the Common Agenda received funding from the National Endowment for the Humanities to support the writing and editing of the essays.

The American Association for State and Local History deserves special recognition. The success of the project has been dependent from the outset on the continuing support and involvement of both Council and staff of AASLH. Patricia Gordon Michael, director of AASLH, and her entire staff have continued to support the project and to see it through as an AASLH publication that serves the history museum field. Their commitment to completing this project has never faltered.

The authors of the essays, Lonnie Bunch, Lizabeth Cohen, Michael Frisch, Mary Ellen Hayward, Michael Heisley, Warren Leon and Cynthia Robinson, Candace Matelic, Tom McKay, Clement Price, Carroll Pursell, and Peter Welsh took considerable time to visit exhibits one or more times and to track down and interview staff who worked on the exhibits. They deserve credit for their openness to experiment with a new model of exhibition literature and their willingness to tackle a difficult assignment. We would particularly like to thank the participating institutions: the Brooklyn Historical Society, Henry Ford Museum and Greenfield Village, Indianapolis Children's Museum, Minnesota Historical Society, Museum of Florida History, Museum of International Folk Art, Museum of Our National Heritage, National Afro-American Museum and Cultural Center, Stearns County Historical Society, Strong Museum, and Valentine Museum. These institutions and their staff members took the time to revisit completed projects, despite the demands of current work, and generously shared their experiences for scrutiny and analysis in order to further our profession's knowledge and understanding of history exhibitions.

Finally, our thanks to Zenda, Inc., who edited, produced, and designed the *Ideas and Images*. In particular, we would like to acknowledge the efforts of Patricia Hogan who took a large package of manuscripts, photographs, and computer discs and made it into a book.

Kenneth L. Ames
Barbara Franco
L. Thomas Frye
Editors

PEERING INTO THE PROCESS

An Introduction

Kenneth L. Ames

Not very long ago, I spent an evening with a group of bright and lively history museum professionals. Their animated talk touched on a wide variety of museum related issues and topics. Finally they turned to the subject of exhibitions. I asked them to tell me about the most memorable exhibitions they had seen. I was eager to hear what they had to say. Their response was enthusiastic. Everyone had seen great exhibitions. As it turned out, however, most were about art or science; few were about history. It was difficult for them to draw up much of a list of great history exhibitions. They admitted that although they had seen many, only a few seemed really outstanding.

True excellence in any area of human activity is admittedly rare, but I got the impression that these people thought the average history exhibition—their own included—was not as good as it might be. This news was disappointing, even a little depressing. But it was also exciting. It meant there was room for improvement. After all, you can't deal with problems until you acknowledge they exist. These people saw the quality of history exhibits as a problem. They knew that the process of creating these exhibits was part of the problem, for the experience was often muddy, even muddled, and an occasion for considerable uncertainty, tension, anxiety, and conflict. They knew that the genre needed attention. More to the point, they were deeply committed to solving these problems and were enthusiastic about finding ways to do so.

As I listened to their commentary, it became clear to me that there would be real value in a book that would help people produce better history exhibitions. I confess that I took some covert delight in my colleagues' lamentations about the state of history exhibitions, for on the evening of these discussions this book was already well underway. Their words convinced me once again that this volume would prove beneficial to the large number of people and institutions constantly wrestling with the complex medium of interpretive exhibitions. But, then, this book was not exactly a speculative venture. It had been conceived in response to a long-felt need, a demand that had been loudly and repeatedly articulated within the history community.

The origins of *Images and Ideas* can be traced to the earliest days of the collaborative venture known as the Common Agenda for History Museums, a project administered by the American Association for State and Local History. In late February of 1987, a group of people interested in history museums gathered in Washington D.C. at the invitation of Lonn Taylor and Douglas Evelyn of the Smithsonian Institution's National Museum of American History. At what came to be called "The Common Agenda Conference," these museum professionals and sympathetic academics explored a wide range of issues and problems pertaining to history museums. During the conference and again in his introduction to the conference report, Evelyn noted that history museums of the United States had much in common in the way they formed their collections and made them accessible through research facilities, publications, and, most important, interpretive exhibitions. There were good reasons for history museums to work together rather than in isolation. The common agenda they shared was to present to their publics better history, history that was more accurate, more compelling, more sophisticated, more informed. They had in common the goal of becoming more active participants in cutting edge historical discourse.

Discussions at the conference resulted in a set of concrete recommendations for specific actions. The working group on interpretation identified three areas of need: first, a need to improve the dissemination of information about problems of interpretation and solutions to those problems throughout the history museum community; second, a need to develop mechanisms for closer collaboration with colleagues in other museums and in the college and university world; and, third, a need to create standards of criticism by which history museum exhibitions might be evaluated. In response to these needs, a platform of ten actions was recommended. One of those was the call to national, state, and regional organizations to "develop and disseminate case studies of exemplary exhibits and public educational programs." Over time that action step was reconfigured into a proposal for an exhibition reader that would analyze the process of exhibition development within a cross-section of institutions mounting history exhibitions, ranging from very large to small, from East Coast to West, and including traveling exhibitions, short-term exhibitions, and major long-term reinstallations.

While Common Agenda participants were refining this concept, the Division of General Programs at the National Endowment for the Humanities, long supportive of interpretive history exhibitions, expressed interest in a publication about exhibitions. Although the NEH's long-term interest was in helping to generate quality products, endowment staff members made it clear that the NEH had no interest in funding a narrow how-to-do-it book or technical manual. On the other hand, they indicated NEH willingness to entertain a proposal for a rigorous publication that would "address logistical, intellectual, and institutional processes of exhibition development" and "would analyze key decisions made by the museum and evaluate the choices made during the project's evolution."

The key word in this project description was *analyze*. The NEH emphasized that it could support only an analytical project. As it turned out, that is what the museum field wanted as well. As the idea of an exhibition reader evolved and matured, it was continually tried out on colleagues in the museum field. Responses were overwhelmingly positive. Some of the most helpful feedback came from Nicholas Westbrook, then at the Minnesota Historical Society and now at Fort Ticonderoga in northeastern New York. Westbrook had prepared a paper on interpretation for the Common Agenda Conference and was an early and enthusiastic supporter of the concept of a reader. In a much-circulated letter, he wrote:

> A case study literature would be invaluable to museum studies students, entry-level professionals, and even advanced students of our art. . . . Currently in museum work, one must develop those repertoires through mentor relationships and painful experience. Case-study literature would help entrants to the profession accelerate their skill development and provide collegial "trouble-shooting" advice to those who, for reason of institutional size or geography, lack other sounding boards. . . . Such case studies should take the reader inside a project. . . . For such a literature, we need to develop a typology of situations faced by museum staff and suggest through case study examples a variety of solutions. . . . Developing such case studies will require an unusual approach to authorship. . . . The outsider serves as objective amanuensis in co-authoring the case study.

Westbrook also noted that in the process of this retrospective assessment, museum staff originally responsible for the exhibit would reflect on past projects and learn a good deal. He acknowledged that a book of case studies might be difficult to pull off but would be well worth the effort. Each essay could yield "a potentially eye-opening, inside view of a complex project."

Responding to support in the field, the Common Agenda submitted its application to the NEH and was funded. In the spirit of collaboration endorsed by the Common Agenda, editorial responsibility was shared by three museum professionals with extensive and varied exhibition experience: Barbara Franco, at the time on the staff of the Museum of Our National Heritage in Lexington, Massachusetts, and now at the Minnesota Historical Society; L. Thomas Frye, of California's Oakland Museum; and Kenneth L. Ames, then at the Winterthur Museum, but subsequently at the New York State Museum in Albany. As it turned out, unanticipated moves by Franco and Ames produced a serendipitous geographic symmetry that again reified the programmatic intentions and national purview of the Common Agenda: Ames was from the East Coast; Franco, from the great heartland; and Frye, from the West.

From the inception of the project and through most of its evolution the editors enjoyed and profited from the enthusiastic, dedicated, and capable counsel of Mary Alexander, first coordinator of the Common Agenda and coordinator of this project. Her sound judgment shaped this volume in significant ways. And also from the beginning, the project was embraced and nurtured by the American Association for State and Local History.

More than anyone else, however, Westbrook was the spiritual parent of this volume. And he was absolutely correct when he warned that the project would require an unusual approach to authorship. Taking Westbrook's cautions to heart, the editors worked closely with authors to be sure that they understood the somewhat unorthodox position we were asking them to assume. In our introductory discussions with authors we acknowledged that we were asking them to take on a challenging task. We were frankly attempting to create a ground-breaking volume. We admitted freely that while exhibitions were being reviewed with increasing frequency, reviews were not what we sought. We asked them to resist the seductive impulse to critique the exhibition and turn their attention instead to analyzing the more elusive creative process behind the exhibition. What they shared with reviewers was the responsibility to reveal not only the positive aspects of the process but the negative as well.

To orient authors we sent them a long list of questions to consider. We asked them to find out what the exhibition developers' goals were and how well they were met. We wondered how consciously issues of audience were dealt with. How central were collections to the conception of the exhibition? To its implementation? Did the institution draw primarily on its own holdings or on those of other institutions? What were the critical stages of the development process? Who were the key decision makers? How did they operate? Was the exhibition grounded in an articulated philosophy of exhibitions? Was it clearly related to the institution's stated mission? Where did the exhibition's originators locate this exhibition in scholarly discourse? Was it derivative? Synthetic? Innovative?

Alert to Westbrook's interest in a typology of problem situations, we asked the authors to outline the major difficulties encountered in the course of developing the exhibition. We also wanted to know what the solutions were and how they were arrived at. We asked our authors to find out how consultants and other specialists were used. We wanted to know about the role of the designer. We asked who directed research. Who did the research? What did it cost? How was it funded?

We asked our authors to identify the person or persons who assumed authorship for the exhibitions they analyzed. Was the exhibition the creation of one individual? Of a team? We wondered if any institutions made their own process of creating the exhibition part of that exhibition. We asked if the institution's size or geographic location was relevant in any way to the development process. And we wanted to know if there was anything special— either positive or negative—about the process the authors were investigating.

This was a lot to ask. To complicate the situation even more, we told the authors that they might well find several additional questions of their own to ask, for we said they could feel free to be guided by the spirit of the exhibition process and to follow it wherever it led them. We knew that each case study would be in some ways distinctive. We asked the authors to search out and explicate that distinctiveness.

We required the authors to visit the museum they were studying and, if it was still on view, to examine the exhibition as well. In the case of traveling exhibitions, this sometimes meant trips across the country. We also asked the authors to talk with all key people, and here again this sometimes meant a good deal of travel and long-distance telephone calls, since some of those people had moved on to other institutions. Many authors made a first visit to an institution, crafted their initial accounts, then returned later to confirm their findings. Much of the book's development demanded, as Westbrook had foreseen, an unusual kind of authorship.

We knew that we were putting many of our authors in positions that would be new and possibly uncomfortable for them — and for the museum staffs they would be dealing with. It was important for the authors to retain their personal independence of thought. It was critical for them to maintain their professional objectivity in explicating the process they were examining. They were free to comment on that process once they had traced it, but they needed objectivity to patch together from interviews, documents, and their own observations as factual an account as possible of what had actually taken place in the process of developing the exhibition. We told them that they were not required to adhere to any institutional party line they might encounter, no matter how high a place it emanated from. We charged the authors to be impartial investigative reporters with the authority and responsibility to record accurately and objectively. If they found utopia, they were obligated to tell us about it. And if they found intrigue, scandal, and corruption, that obligation still held.

They found little of the latter. And they did not find utopia. What they did find was many variations on a theme, variations enriched and hobbled by all the blessings and afflictions of real life and people working with other people. In short, they found out how eleven different cultures crafted their exhibits. Each essay is a field study of sorts, an ethnography of an episode in institutional life. For if they were reporters, our authors were also visiting anthropologists. They recognized that to know the exhibition process fully they had to understand the culture from which it sprang and in which it was embedded. Each case study is a discrete anthropological detective story and makes fascinating reading. Taken together, the essays provide a cross-section, a typology, of situations so inclusive that every historical museum in North America should find something of relevance.

In selecting the exhibitions for analysis, the editors first made it clear that their emphasis would be on exhibitions within museums devoted to interpreting history. In order to keep focus sharp, the editors consciously excluded historic houses, living history farms, and many other types of programming not strictly understood as exhibitions. Within the category of exhibitions, the editors tried to identify exhibitions that met two broad criteria. First, the exhibition itself had to be held in relatively high regard by the museum community; otherwise, there was little reason to include it. Second, the exhibition had to be surrounded by a set of circumstances relevant to and preferably even identical to those at other institutions. The editors reasoned that this volume would have little value if it dealt only with unique, nonreplicable conditions.

For example, while there is only one Minnesota Historical Society, there are many state history museums with similar mandates and similar collections. Minnesota's exhibition, "The Way to Independence," had several features we thought were applicable elsewhere. It was the creation of a state agency (actually, a semistate agency) that made novel and imaginative use of collections that had been long owned by the society. The exhibition was shaped with considerable input from native Americans, whose changing culture was the subject of the show. The exhibition brought new voices and new perspectives into the Minnesota Historical Society—and then into other institutions as it traveled around the country.

"Familia y Fe" was also produced by a state agency and also reinstalled collections long in its possession. The exhibition was significantly shaped, even demanded, by changes in demographic, cultural, and political patterns in New Mexico. The lesson is transferable because the challenge of pluralism increasingly confronts museums, particularly those dependent on tax dollars for support. Like Minnesota, the New Mexico example showed how staff guided by new perspectives, new input, and new agendas found new insights in old collections.

Accounts of the peculiar circumstances surrounding each of the nine other exhibitions appear in the essays. Here I want only to suggest some of the variables the editors were attentive to. "From Victory to Freedom" was selected as an exemplar of an exhibition created by a new museum that started its life with a broad mandate but no collections and as an instance of an exhibition curated by a historian on loan from another institution. It also dealt with and was produced by an American ethnic group without a long history of museum interest or tradition of collecting material culture.

"Folk Roots, New Roots" had its origins in dialogues with the academic world; "Fit for America" was in large part the vision of a single academically trained historian. Both were traveling shows. "Minor League, Major Dream" was chosen as a useful example from a smaller organization outside a major metropolis. The case study of the Museum of Florida History was included because of that institution's reputation for working with the team model of exhibition development. "Mysteries in History" exposed some of the peculiar challenges and opportunities that confront children's museums and any history museum that wants to make its exhibits accessible and comprehensible to a young audience.

There is only one Henry Ford Museum, but many other institutions face reinstallation of major collections. And many other institutions are moving from old-time static specimen display of their collections to more sophisticated—and more difficult—interpretive humanities exhibitions. In many cases this change is symptomatic not only of new notions about the educational potential of exhibitions but also of new understandings of the purposes and responsibilities of museums. In this context, the inclusion of the exhibition at the Brooklyn Historical Society makes sense. That institution is in the process of redefining itself. Its exhibitions are both tools for and evidence of its new orientation. Finally, the Valentine Museum, like the Brooklyn Historical Society and, to a lesser extent, the Henry Ford Museum, is an institution that is in dramatic transition, re-examining itself, its mission, and its audiences. The

Valentine's exhibition program is a barometer of its institutional transformation. With its exhibition program, the Valentine challenges not only the institution it used to be but even prevailing orthodoxies about the proper relationship of research and exhibition in a historical museum.

You have before you in one volume the best of current thinking about creating interpretive history exhibits. The eleven innovative case studies gathered together here provide a summary of the processes of developing interpretive history exhibitions within a wide variety of institutional settings. Each study, by focusing on a single exhibition, provides a manageable body of material for readers. The reportorial or ethnographic style provides readers with sufficient data to form their own interpretations and evaluations of the situations and processes described. While each essay has its own distinct features, just as does each exhibition, when read together common patterns of concern emerge. What role should collections play? What is the audience and how should it be involved in developing the exhibition? Who should serve as consultants? How do we find them? How do we fund them? How much do we listen to them? How best to coordinate the many people necessarily involved in the development of these complex productions? How do we document the exhibition? How do we evaluate it?

Here then is a collection of profiles of history museum professionals at work. Here is an ethnography of prominent cultural activity in our time. Here is a profession studying itself with the goal of self-improvement. Here is thoughtful reflection on the central way history museums communicate—the interpretive exhibition. In every act of human creativity there is a part that lies beyond words. You will not find that here, but you will find all that can be put into words.

If you want to know what really happens between the time a museum decides to do an exhibition and the opening, read this book. The process is as fascinating as the product.

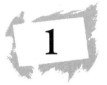

BEEN SO LONG

A Critique of the Process That Shaped "From Victory
to Freedom: Afro-American Life in the Fifties"

Clement Alexander Price

For more than three generations, American historians have substantively reshaped much of what was traditionally believed about the bittersweet experience of Americans of African ancestry. Beginning over a century ago, when George Washington Williams "tracked [his] bleeding countrymen through the widely scattered documents of American history . . . listened to their groans, their clanking chains, and melting prayers . . ." historians have persuasively shown that American blacks endured a unique and often tragic experience in the land of their birth.[1] Such a story, written at a time of growing professionalism in historical literature, led to a larger reassessment of American democracy and emboldened the historical imagination of those seeking social justice. The first generation of scholars of the black experience was comprised largely of blacks, veritable Race Men, whose greatest influence was on the progeny of slaves. They especially had an impact on the thinking and artistry of New Negroes of the early twentieth century, introducing to many a vast body of information and racial reaffirmation that would later revolutionize American race relations.

Yet, during most of the twentieth century, the efforts of black historians and intellectuals to recast the historical image of the race went largely unnoticed. Many Americans, deeply influenced by popular and occasionally racist treatments of historical accounts, clung to the notion that American society was essentially just and that the history of blacks, particularly their bitter experience as slaves, was a distant anomaly.

Not surprisingly, history museums were far more influenced by the traditional approach to the nation's racial past than by the scholarship of blacks and empathetic whites. The deep cleavage that existed between the nation's democratic ideals and its racial practices marked a disturbing and vast contradiction which was not generally incorporated into interpretive exhibitions. Moreover, the exclusionary practices of American museums in collecting, staffing, and exhibiting severely limited the influence of historical scholarship that emphasized the lives of victims. Uncertain of how to interpret the troubling experience of blacks, museums took a pragmatic look at the past: a view of American history that primarily emphasized the achievements of members of the dominant society. What Americans saw in museum exhibitions reinforced a historical vision that many blacks claimed was morally obtuse and a justification for continued racial injustice.[2]

During the years surrounding the modern civil rights era, small community-based museums in black neighborhoods and historically black colleges were among the first institutions to inform their exhibitions with black scholarship. In short, the difficult responsibility of mounting black historical exhibitions continued to be taken up by institutions that were inspired by an important corollary of modern life, the rise of Afro-American consciousness. Not unlike an array of other black institutions during and following the New Negro Era, the efforts of black museums to exhibit what the race had accomplished were emblematic of a long quest for group respectability, driven by the belief that in time black worth would be recognized by white Americans. They sought, with some success, to promote racial pride and to show how blacks, in the face of exceptional racial and economic obstacles, had contributed to American democracy and culture.

Nonetheless, during the 1960s, when the scholarship on black life and history surfaced as a national phenomenon, many major museums that had traditionally promoted a consensus, Anglo-American influenced view of the past garnered the lion's share of attention when they sought, finally, to bring the black experience center stage. In 1968, the Metropolitan Museum of Art mounted a highly publicized, if somewhat controversial, exhibit, "Harlem On My Mind: Cultural Capital of Black America, 1900–1968." It signaled a new interest in black subjects by established museums.

Some years later in 1981 and 1982, the Afro-American Historical and Cultural Museum in Philadelphia mounted "Of Color, Humanitas and Statehood: The Black Experience in Pennsylvania over Three Centuries, 1681–1981," followed by the Atlanta Public Library exhibit, "Homecoming: Black Family Life in Georgia." Both were marked by the use of many objects to support broad, synthetic themes. Equally important, they reflected the new emphasis on racial injustices *and* efforts by blacks to withstand those adversities. By the end of the decade, several additional shows on black American life succeeded in placing the new black historiography at the core of historical exhibitions.[3]

"From Victory to Freedom: Afro-American Life in the Fifties," the inaugural exhibit at the National Afro-American Museum and Cultural Center, in Wilberforce, Ohio, also came into being at a time when revisionist interpretations of Afro-American life and history were in vogue. However, in comparison to earlier black exhibitions, it became far more influenced by the new black history's celebratory approach to the past. That approach, which explored African and Afro-American cultural survivals, group strengths and accomplishments, family life, and separatism, was among the most significant imperatives of black scholarship in the years after World War II.[4] Not surprisingly, museums specifically devoted to documenting and articulating the story of Afro-Americans would be increasingly influenced politically and psychologically by this approach to historical interpretation.

The National Afro-American Museum and Cultural Center was started in 1972. The state of Ohio was keenly interested in establishing a major black museum on land having great historical significance for the race. After many years of activity toward that objective by a growing number of black museum professionals, scholars, collectors, and elected officials, their efforts, and those of Ohio, converged in the founding of an institution "to encourage and promote an understanding and appreciation of African-American history and culture."[5] A bill submitted to the Ohio General Assembly by State Representative C.J. McLin established Wilberforce as the site of the new museum, which in the mid-nineteenth century had been a stop on the Underground Railroad and since 1856 had been the location of the nation's oldest black institution of higher learning, Wilberforce University. Later in 1980, President Jimmy Carter signed Public Law 96–430, establishing the National Afro-American History and Culture Commission, which was to determine the federal government's role in the museum's future.

Undoubtedly the most important and persistent driving force behind the shaping of both the museum and its inaugural exhibition was the director, John Fleming, whose extraordinary career symbolizes at once the emergence of black museum expertise in the years between the modern civil rights and the Reagan eras and the triumph of the new black history in American museums. A professionally trained historian with a Ph.D. from Howard University, Fleming has for many years been active on the national museum scene. He is a long-standing member of the African-American Museums Association and currently serves as that organization's president. He is also the president of the Ohio

Museums Association. Before assuming the directorship of NAAMCC, Fleming was division chief of the Afro-American Museum Project at the Ohio Historical Society. NAAMCC grew out of the project. The early support given to the museum throughout Ohio remained steadfast; over the years in which the exhibition took form, the state contributed $1.2 million to the project.

"From Victory to Freedom" was initially planned as a part of an ambitious, comprehensive examination of Afro-Americans in the history of United States. Toward that end, Benjamin Quarles, Rayford Logan, and Charles Wesley, pioneering and elder luminaries in black historiography, were asked by museum officials to provide advice on collection development and the appropriate ways to present historical issues in exhibitions. It soon became clear, however, that the museum, which had not been constructed and was only in the planning stages of building a collection, could not take on such a daunting task. Moreover, as Fleming has noted, the scarcity of artifacts from the early years of black life in the United States could well have made it difficult for the institution to open with a major exhibition.

As a result of this concern, Fleming decided that the opening exhibit, conceived as a permanent installation, should focus on a modern theme, specifically the 1950s, "the last decade in which American society was segregated."[6] It may be true, too, that the spirit of the fifties, which survived longer in the Midwest than in other regions of the nation, was especially relevant to the new institution. Museum officials also decided that the exhibit would embrace themes that transcend, yet shed light upon, the modern civil rights movement, the foremost accomplishment of the fifties. Toward that end, family life, domesticity, the development of religious and economic institutions, political aspirations, leisure, and music were chosen as concurrent themes for the period, inasmuch as each reflected the momentous changes wrought by the postwar years. An emerging scholarly interest in the 1950s also made the decade an appropriate theme for the exhibit. By the 1980s, popular interest in black accomplishments during the racially segregated fifties, and its larger romantic appeal, had made the decade, according to Juanita Moore, the museum's director of education, "a hot issue."[7]

The multifaceted tasks inherent in building a collection from scratch, developing a staff, and mounting a major exhibition in time for the museum's grand opening presented challenges that all participants now freely acknowledge. While new museums, their cultural and racial sensibilities notwithstanding, may face similar difficulties, the early history of NAAMCC was in many ways unique. Museum aficionados throughout the nation were taking great interest in the process by which an arts and humanities institution largely managed by blacks defined itself—how it, in contrast to other museums, would depict the race's past. Hence, "From Victory to Freedom" was destined to serve not only as a signature piece for the Museum, but also as a symbol and vehicle for the full emergence of black museum professionalism in the United States.

In retrospect, despite the difficulties experienced in building a collection, raising funds, and conceptualizing and mounting the exhibition in time for the grand opening, the museum benefited from a long tradition of voluntary organizational work and institutional development in black American society. After the end of slavery, racial segregation in the United States fostered a strong sense of ethnic identification, interdependence, and institutional development among blacks that over time led to a viable network of sacred and secular organizations promoting service to the race and group uplift. Although museums were not pivotal institutions in traditional black American communities, they nonetheless benefited from the emerging ethic of black group betterment and voluntary service. Among its most salient features are individual responsibility and service to the race and community support for organizations and institutions emblematic of black progress.[8] By comparison, another major non-European racial group in the United States, the native Americans, have until recently experienced much greater difficulty in preserving and controlling their heritage through collective group action.[9]

The museum was also the beneficiary of an aroused scholarly interest in Afro-American history and culture, which, since the 1960s, had informed political and cultural advocacy. Although Negro history gained popularity during the World War I years, when Carter G. Woodson established the Association for the Study of Negro Life and History, not until the 1960s, during the most momentous years of the modern civil rights era, did the study of black life and history become "fashionable, a 'hot' subject finally legitimated as a scholarly specialty," having enduring importance in political, cultural, and social affairs.[10]

The tradition of black interdependence and the aroused sense of urgency about what blacks had accomplished in the nation's past, however, had to be harnessed and directed toward the museum's interests and its inaugural exhibit. As Fleming has observed, most black communities were without a long tradition of collecting objects and donating to museums. Many individuals, believing their possessions lacked value, were reluctant to contribute artifacts, a problem reinforced by the museum's "infant" status.[11] Dominant culture museums, on the other hand, were seldom interested in the lives of common folk, which may have reinforced the notion that the history of the so-called inarticulate was of dubious value. "From Victory to Freedom" was envisioned by Fleming and his staff as a challenge to traditional assumptions about the relative value of historical artifacts and those who had used them.[12]

Although the museum's importance to the future exhibitions informed by the so-called new black history was recognized by many, financial support for its first opus was initially hard to come by. The first request for funds to the National Endowment for the Humanities was denied because the project was insufficiently developed. Subsequent requests for funding from the endowment were also denied, which in hindsight is rather surprising given the ambitious objectives and significance of "From Victory to Freedom." Consequently, the museum asked Roger Kennedy, director of the National Museum of American History at the Smithsonian Institution, for assistance. That assistance came in 1986, with Kennedy's recommendation of Fath Davis Ruffins, a curator at the Smithsonian, as guest curator of the exhibition. She served in that capacity for eighteen months.

Ruffins, not unlike Fleming, is emblematic of the emergence of black professionalism in the museum field. A graduate of Radcliffe College and a social and cultural historian, she is the head of the Collection of Advertising History at the Archives Center of the National Museum of American History, where she has been for eleven years. Prior to her curatorial role at NAAMCC, Ruffins obtained valuable experience as project director of the Smithsonian's 1985 exhibition, "Everyday Life in America: After the Revolution, 1780–1800." As a scholar and practitioner in the field of black material culture and exhibit development, Ruffins brought to the Wilberforce project a keen understanding of how revisionist historiography could be incorporated in a museum setting.

Assisting Ruffins as associate curator was Marian Moore, then a graduate student at the University of Toledo, a past fellow at NEH and a former intern at the Smithsonian Institution. The exhibition was to become for her, and other members of the staff, an exceptional opportunity to learn how to shape a compelling view of the Afro-American history into a major exhibition.[13]

Obviously, when Ruffins assumed leadership of the exhibition, then tentatively and curiously entitled, "The Other Side of Happy Days: Afro-American Life in the 1950s," she faced a considerable challenge. The museum was without a system for determining the kinds of materials needed for the exhibit, and its small collection was organized by donor rather than by subject. Most members of the staff, it was recently remembered, were "new and nervous," although the arduous task of building a collection was to become their responsibility.[14] That may have been a blessing in the most beguiling of disguises: during the early stages of the project, the museum's professional staff was not tied to traditional roles. Most were involved in promoting the institution's mission and helping, often through personal affiliations, to build the collection. They created what Fleming has called a national plan for collecting. That plan included the identification of desired objects and the development of literature specifically targeted to potential donors, many of whom knew little if anything about the new museum.

The museum's direct and personal approach to collection building, in that it was unfettered by bureaucracy, proved to be remarkably successful. It enabled the museum to acquire objects from all parts of the country as well as from various economic and social levels. All the more, it helped to establish a national network for collecting in black communities and a future audience that saw the value of donating the artifacts of black life to a new museum of significant historical importance. Nearly all of the objects—99.4 percent as Fleming remembers—acquired from the public were donated, and since the exhibition was envisioned as a permanent installation, only a few objects were borrowed from other museums. As one member of the staff has observed about the collecting efforts of her colleagues: "*We* demonstrated all the attributes of the *other* museums while not necessarily going about it *their* way."[15]

Ruffins, who was given a wide berth by the director in conceptualizing the exhibition, helped to guide the fledgling curators in collection building. They were asked to collect photographs of black family life, documents, selected books, old copies of *Ebony* magazine, and other materials illustrative of black religious life and labor. Donations included letters, financial papers, photographs, and periodicals as well as three-dimensional materials, although some of the items given to the museum were of little value to the exhibit.[16]

To supplement the collecting being done by the staff, the museum launched an innovative marketing strategy that encouraged donations and support. A public service announcement, televised in fourteen metropolitan areas with sizeable black populations, urged viewers with artifacts relevant to the black experience from the 1940s through the 1960s to contact the museum. The campaign turned out to be most effective in reaching upwardly mobile black families.[17] Against a visual backdrop of objects of twentieth-century Afro-American life, the advertisement announced: "The National Afro-American Museum in Wilberforce, Ohio, is preserving American history as it was lived by black people in the 1940s, fifties and sixties. Please call the museum toll free: 1-800-BLK-HIST. If you have anything to donate from the 1940s through the sixties, call us." Viewers saw the museum's logo, followed by an assemblage of artifacts, a cover picture of Billie Holiday from the July 1949 issue of *Ebony* magazine and a photograph of a late 1950's white Cadillac coupe. Items solicited through the advertisement included clothing, furniture, farm items, magazines, school books, automobiles, "and more." The advertisement was one of the first attempts by a black museum, or any museum, to build a collection through the medium of television. When the museum opened on 15 April 1988, Fleming, in acknowledging the success of its innovative efforts in collection building, commended those who responded to the call. "The men and women across the nation who donated artifacts, manuscripts, and other memorabilia are true preservers of Afro-American history and culture," he observed. "Without the support of these individuals, we would be opening an empty building, instead of a national museum and cultural center." [18]

Throughout the many months in which the exhibit took on its unique interpretive framework and design, the museum used a team approach which involved the director and curator, academic scholars, educators, museum staff, community representatives, and designers. Over the course of the planning stage this approach, marked at many junctures by the excitement and tensions of a scholarly debate, was especially beneficial to museum staff members. It helped to sharpen the conceptual framework of the entire project and gave to a remarkably large and diverse group of individuals a sense of ownership of the final product. Moreover, the array of scholars who came to Wilberforce during the course of the exhibit's planning further demonstrated the singular importance of the project as a potential stimulant for further research on black life. Indeed, the scarcity of scholarly interest in the larger social and institutional life of blacks during the 1950s encouraged staff and consultants to envision the exhibit as a way to underscore the pivotal importance of that decade to an understanding of contemporary black history.

The work of those forty-six nationally recognized scholars, whose modest honoraria, travel expenses, and accommodations were covered by the Museum, began in the fall of 1986 and lasted a year. They met in small, round table discussion groups which explored various aspects of the fifties. A comprehensive bibliography on the era was completed and appropriate themes were refined and expanded to include music, family life, economics and labor, the work of the NAACP and Urban League, the civil rights movement, sports, African and Afro-American relations, education, visual arts, military service, films and entertainment, Afro-American values and cultural identity, women's history, and religion. These were, to be sure, a profusion of issues; however, Ruffins believed the subject matter warranted such a comprehensive approach. Also, since few of the 120 black museums in nation had incorporated overarching historical and cultural issues in their exhibits, she envisioned the round table discussions as a way to encourage stronger themes in the field through the involvement of scholars in exhibition development. [19]

Such a large number of scholars, with sharply different perspectives on the period, did indeed enhance the exhibition's interpretive framework by placing the era's most notable achievement, the civil rights movement, within the larger context of major changes in modern black society, including the consequences of the great migration, family and urban life, and the growing incorporation of blacks into American popular culture. In that sense, the round table discussions helped the staff to better appreciate revisionist history. Moreover, inasmuch as the exhibit would ultimately deal with a multiplicity of themes in modern black life, the round table discussions set the stage for an unprecedented attempt by a museum to shed light on the complexity of the 1950s.

A fervent desire to make the exhibit accessible to a broadly based and largely uninitiated patronage also helped to shape the exhibit's development. From the outset, the team of scholars and the staff wanted the exhibit to project various symbols of Negro respectability without simplifying or romanticizing the past. In short, they wanted to avoid an overindulgence in the achievements of black middle-class life. The museum's curatorial staff, especially, wanted to show that blacks were a distinct, if not separate, group in American life during the 1950s, a group with attributes distinctively American and inherently positive.

To reach that objective the team decided that black music would be an integral feature of the exhibit because, among the many aspects of race life, it dramatized the great diversity of midcentury black Americans. Donna Lawrence, a film maker, and Portia K. Maultsby, a professor at Indiana University, were brought onto the team. As a major consultant, Maultsby assumed responsibility for conceptualizing the music component, directing the research, identifying interviewees, selecting music, and editing the script.[20] The final product, "Music as Metaphor," a twenty-seven-minute multimedia film produced by Donna Lawrence Productions, became the centerpiece for the exhibit.

"Music As Metaphor" uses still photographs, film, sound, and oral history techniques to examine black music "as a functional dimension of culture."[21] Beginning with the African roots of Afro-American sacred music, the film juxtaposes historical photography and genre music in a brief survey of black musical expression before the twentieth century, followed by a quickly paced tracing of the modern, derivative styles found between 1945 and 1965 in gospel music, be-bop jazz, urban blues, rhythm and blues, black involvement in the European classical tradition, and songs inspired by the modern civil rights movement. Drawing upon the exhibit themes of group optimism, migration, urban life, and community development, the film shows how the gospel, urban blues, be-bop, and rhythm and blues music of the period were emblematic of black life and how that music "brought unity to post–World War II urban black communities."[22] Screened in a small theater at the center of the exhibition space, "Music As Metaphor," in its compelling images, stirring musical selections, interviews, and eloquent narration delivered by Yvonne Kersey, provides "From Victory to Freedom" with a powerful emotional experience rarely found in historical exhibitions.

In order to mount a deeply textured exhibit that would both dramatize the confluence of forces of modern black life in a coherent, educational context and to make a powerful visual presentation, the museum required the services of an exhibit design firm experienced in the mounting of innovative historical presentations. After a call for proposals was sent to design firms across the nation, the museum chose ten of the thirty respondents for further consideration. It finally selected Gerard Hilferty and Associates of Athens, Ohio, which, despite its lack of experience in mounting an ethnic oriented exhibition, demonstrated a keen sensitivity for helping the museum mount a compelling exhibition on modern black life. In keeping with that objective, the firm was willing to subcontract important aspects of the project to minority vendors. The museum involved the project and graphic designers, respectively David W. Fox and Janis Miller-Fox, in the early developmental stages of the exhibit, including the round table discussions with the team of scholars.

From the beginning of the project, the curator and the designers disagreed on an appropriate scale for the exhibit. The curator aimed to demonstrate the inherent complexity and thickly textured quality of black life through a profusion of objects (approximately eleven hundred). Ruffins sought a design that encouraged the visitor to feel a sense of intimacy with the objects, a design that fostered careful examination of the artifacts and thoughtful contemplation of their meanings. The designers, on the other hand, wanted to keep the exhibit orderly, to avoid a profusion of artifacts that might contribute more to visitor confusion than to visitor contemplation. The conflict between curator and designers was exacerbated by the exhibit gallery's twenty-five-foot ceiling height, which everyone considered too high for an exhibition space of fifty-two-hundred square feet. Ruffins wanted a design that kept the artifacts close to the visitor; the designers wanted a design that was not dwarfed by the gallery's size. The role of the designers was further complicated by the museum's ongoing construction, the constraints on staff resources, and the ambitious objectives of the curator. Ultimately, Ruffins's vision, and Fleming's support of her objectives, led to an artifact rich show that sought to stir the visitor's memory of the period as much as it challenged the notion that history exhibitions should not be infused with an overabundance of things to see.[23]

To give the exhibition a vibrant character in keeping with the period, the curator and designers conceptualized it as an environmental piece that would invoke memories of the recent past. To accomplish this, and to imbue the exhibit with the rich quality of modern black life the scholars desired, they re-created commonly shared aspects of race life in six period rooms. Social historians, whose work has significantly influenced the way we now look at the past, have emphasized the private lives of anonymous historical actors and actresses. In keeping with that major conceptual change in historical imagination, the period rooms, which include a beauty salon and barber shop, a church, a saloon, and regional living rooms from the South and western states, provide an insight into

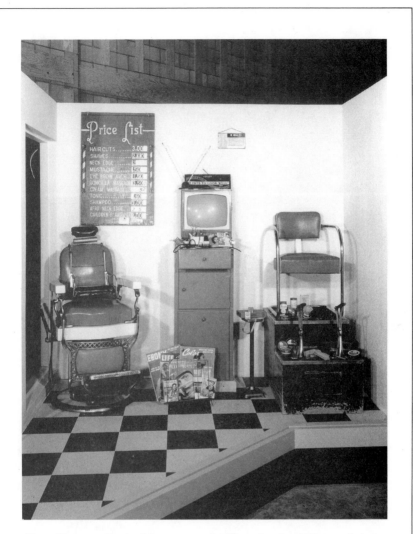

"From Victory to Freedom" features several well-appointed period rooms depicting the living environments found throughout Afro-American communities in the 1950s. Reflecting recent scholarly interest in social history, particularly the private lives of anonymous Americans, the period settings, such as the barber shop, recall daily activities, the penchant for personal grooming, and the rich quality of life of many Afro-Americans during a period of heightened consumerism.

Photo by Greg Sailor.
Courtesy National Afro-American Museum and Cultural Center.

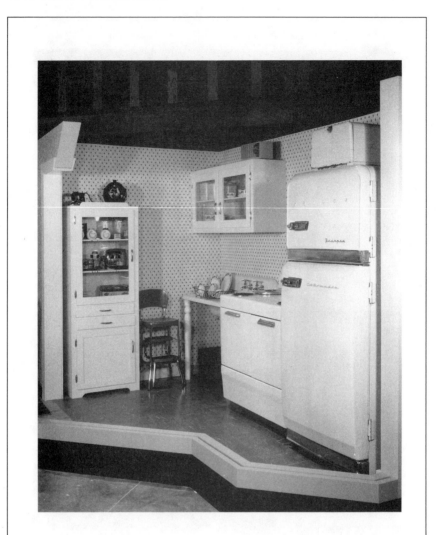

The fifties brought modern conveniences in cooking, home entertainment, and personal hygiene within the reach of some black families. The kitchen period room reflects domestic living during the period when black families, especially women, were able to utilize time-saving appliances in culinary arts.

Photo by Greg Sailor.
Courtesy National Afro-American Museum and Cultural Center.

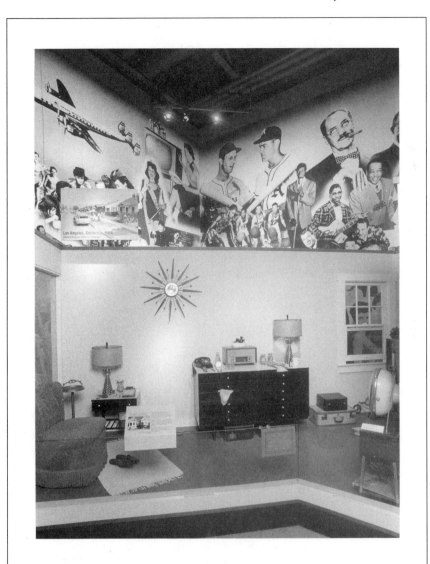

A stylishly appointed living room of a black family in the western states of the 1950s is indicative of the upward mobility of a growing number of black who, despite continued racial discrimination, shared in the nation's postwar prosperity. Images and events of the fifties as seen through the eyes of Afro-Americans appear in the dramatic photomural above the period room.

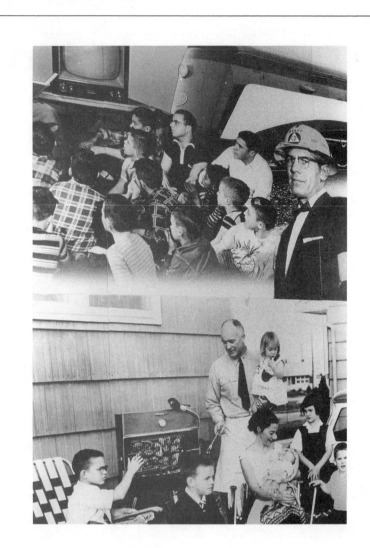

A twenty-two-foot photomural featuring images of black American achievements in politics, social advocacy, sports, entertainment, and the arts, envelop the "From Victory to Freedom" gallery, evoking memories of a mass culture in which blacks were for the first time prominent figures. The artist of the mural, Dan Williams of Ohio University, sought "to select and artistically assemble images that convey a sense of the diversity and complexity of American society during the fifties."

Photo by Greg Sailor.
Courtesy National Afro-American Museum and Cultural Center.

the way black Americans lived unscrutinized by white society. In the rooms, the visitor sees a wealth of objects that in their profusion leave the impression that blacks were avidly stylish and race conscious consumers. While some museum purists could easily criticize the grand indulgence in objects within the period rooms, in fact the abundance of curios, knickknacks, photographs, records, and magazines vividly replicates the living environment of many black American homes during a period of increasing consumerism.

The sense that modern life is best represented through an array of objects also informs the way the exhibit treats black public life and its impact on American society. The exterior walls of the period rooms serve as a veritable gallery of larger than life photographs and text that explores such developments as black America's participation in World War II, the ascendancy of the Negro press, revisionist scholarship on race relations, black luminaries, civil rights organizations, and the struggle for full citizenship rights. These exhibit sections are interspersed with cases and object platforms for artifacts that symbolize the diversity and complexity of black life.

At the center of the exhibition space a small theater constructed for the screening of "Music As Metaphor" presents the popular sounds and musical artists of modern black America, interwoven on film with the imagery and settings of everyday life in the period rooms.

Moreover, the exhibit's synergism, so avidly sought by Ruffins, is enhanced by a dramatic twenty-two-feet high photomural collage that envelopes the room with compelling images unique to the optimism of the fifties and the sharper, and somewhat harsher, symbols of a race and a nation that by the early sixties had seemingly lost their innocence. The many images in the mural dramatize a powerful feature of the postwar years: the rapid emergence in the popular media of a succession of black images in American life from the arenas of sports, entertainment, politics, social advocacy, and the arts. This indeed was the objective of the artist, Dan Williams, an associate professor of art at Ohio University, who sought "to select and artistically assemble images that convey a sense of the diversity and complexity of American society during the fifties."[24] The effect is quite stunning: a visual representation of modern America through the prism of its black population. The mural's visual prominence also minimizes some of the spatial problems inherent in the room's height. It is not merely a design conceit.

Notwithstanding the cooperative spirit that was encouraged by the team approach to the exhibit, there remained some disagreement on the appropriate way to discuss the complexities of black life at midcentury. At the heart of that disagreement, found so often in major historical exhibits, was the extent to which historical interpretation should be embodied in the wall text and labels.

Ruffins, whose views probably reflect those of other academically trained historians, believed that the exhibition's text should be written at a level higher than is often found in comparable presentations. To do otherwise, she has argued, "might encourage a misunderstanding of black history as a simplistic genre."[25] That view was in sharp contrast to the approach of members of the museum's education department and the designers. They maintained that the text should be written at a seventh-grade reading level. "Although writing is important," Gerard Hilferty and Associates observe in its handbook, *Museum Exhibition Development, Research, & Writing*, "it may be the least effective communication technique in an exhibit. Exhibits are a three-dimensional, multi-sensory medium."[26]

In the end, the curator, with the support of Fleming, prevailed: the text was written at a level above the seventh grade and, because of its length, required from patrons more time and historical insight than might be customarily found in museum exhibits. The text also features vernacular expressions of the period, which may make the exhibit difficult for younger patrons and others unfamiliar with contemporary black speech.

If a mature literary style was intended to elevate the stature of the exhibition, enhancing its value to scholars as well as the general public, that objective was also served by the curator's decision to include a profusion of objects from black institutional and domestic life. Museum visitors encounter hundreds of objects ranging from the spectacular photomural surrounding the exhibition space to a varied assortment of artifacts in period rooms that provide a sense of both the similarity and diversity in black American life during the 1950s and the present.

On entering the exhibition space, the museum visitor sees the title of the exhibition rendered in a period-style neon sign hoisted above a gleaming 1957 Chevy Bel Air, suggestive of the ability of growing numbers of upwardly mobile blacks to purchase new cars by the fifties. The themes of black consumerism and transportation are the first encountered, but soon it becomes clear that many more—represented by the abundance of artifacts—are to follow. If the curator sought to impress the visitor with the sheer momentum of events, sounds, and images, her objective was successful. In fact, the visitor is challenged to identify immediately with the period through the questions raised in the introductory wall labels: "When Were the Fifties?" "What Were the Fifties Like for Afro-Americans?" and "Why Study the Fifties?" The explanations given to these questions help establish the pivotal themes explored in the exhibition.

Moving left along the exhibition space, the visitor, perhaps overwhelmed by the sudden impact of images and sounds, sees the beginning of the surrounding photomural's array of images of American life from the late 1940s and early

1950s, and to the right, the vista through the period rooms. The exhibition space is immediately enlivened by the energetic sound of contemporary black music, mostly rhythm and blues, coming from a jukebox at the end of the corridor, while in the distance one can hear faint gospel music from the black church period room.

Obviously, there is much to see and ponder in "From Victory to Freedom," and for some visitors there may be, at first, too much. It would seem that individuals born in the interwar years might find the exhibit more accessible than those born after the period. The same may be said based on a visitor's understanding of modern American history: those familiar with the underlying issues of federally enforced social and political reform, national demographic trends, and ethnic group articulation would find the exhibit far more useful than the uninformed.

Yet the exhibition, in its emphasis upon the concrete and symbolic linkages that exist between the postwar years and the present, has a near universal appeal. The vast majority of patrons, representing a cross section of the nation's cultural mosaic, have given extremely positive responses to the exhibition on questionnaires provided for all patrons as they leave the space. Some were stirred by the music and images reminiscent of their youth, while others benefited from the exhibition's historical information. One important visitor, President George Bush, told Fleming that many items in the period rooms brought back memories of his own home.

The Museum has also published a guide to the exhibition, "Let's Go on a Treasure Hunt," that encourages young visitors to carefully identify objects of enduring cultural and economic value. The guide supplements an ambitious effort to train docents for the hundreds of area school children of many cultures, who are encouraged through the museum's education department to tour the exhibit. For adult visitors there is a four-color brochure which includes the exhibit's floor plan and a description of the major themes.

There have been too few critical reviews of "From Victory to Freedom," but those published to date are laudatory, emphasizing the exhibit's pivotal importance among contemporary exhibitions that seek to explore black American life from a social historical context. "The overall exhibition design," Thomas J. Davis observed in his review for *American Quarterly*, "invites visitors into the era, not so much to examine artifacts as to experience or re-experience the texture of life and to compare and contrast how things were in the 1950s and 1960s with how they are today." Davis's review also noted that the early objective of the exhibition was met, since "It shows blacks moving further into the mainstream of American life while at the same time moving further into their own Afro-American heritage."[27] Local newspaper coverage of the show

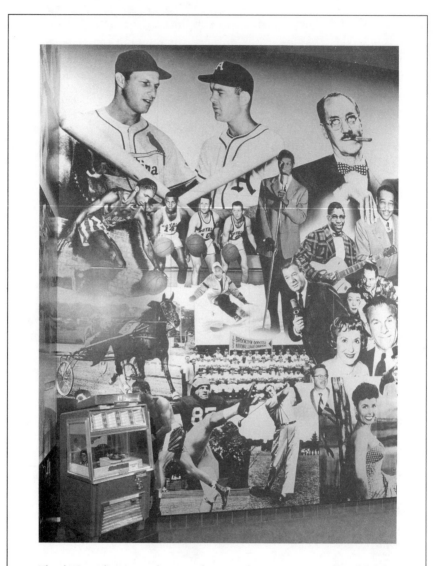

The photomural's interracial images of sports and entertainment in the 1950s recall an easier mixing of black and white cultures than was found in other sectors of society. The juke box's constant playing of contemporary black music contributes to the abundance of popular sounds, images, and events that are featured in the exhibit and that, in fact, characterized the ascendancy of blacks in American life in the fifties.

Photo by Greg Sailor.
Courtesy National Afro-American Museum and Cultural Center.

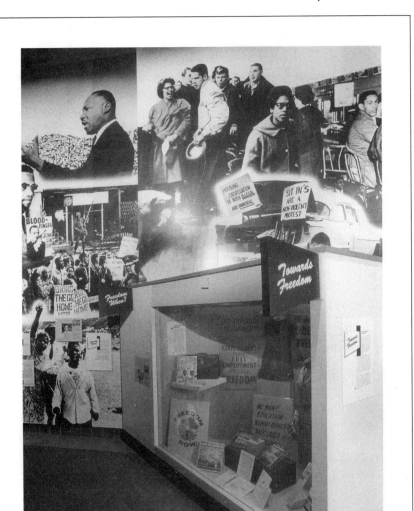

Social and political reforms marked America's postwar years. In "From Victory to Freedom," the photomural's images of the tumultuous 1950s and sixties recall black Americans's struggle for racial justice and equal opportunity during the modern civil rights era. Combined with an array of artifacts, the larger than life images stir strong memories in older visitors and raise many questions about the past among younger ones.

Photo by Greg Sailor.
Courtesy National Afro-American Museum and Cultural Center.

took a less perceptive look, but nonetheless emphasized the importance of the exhibit to the continuing development of the museum's collection and national stature.[28] Fleming notes that donated objects continue to come in from across the nation and that some will be exhibited as the character of the show evolves in the future. Local visitorship to the museum has also increased as a result of the show's popularity, and black organizations regularly tour the museum as a part of their national meetings held in nearby Dayton.

In retrospect, the formidable challenges that faced the many individuals who organized "From Victory to Freedom" may have resulted in two unique qualities, one found in the exhibit, the other embodied in the process of organizing the exhibit. First, the synergistic design of the exhibition is a success. It promotes a unique museum experience, marked at once by an interaction with discrete components of black life and a recognition of their greater collective impact on the future of all Americans. In this sense, "From Victory to Freedom" mirrors the vast emotional and visual terrain of the era it so courageously explores. And, too, the enthusiastic cooperation and optimism that characterized many months of work by scholars, curators, designers, educators, fund raisers, and museum officials harken back to that earlier age—the fifties—when black Americans were most confident, ready once again to move forward.

Institutional Profile

Name: National Afro-American Museum and Cultural Center
Location: 1350 Brush Row Road, Wilberforce, Ohio 45384
Size of institution: 52,000 square feet, including offices
Date of founding: Ohio charter, 1972; U. S. Congress charter, 1980
Number of professional staff: 21

Exhibition Data

Name of exhibition: "From Victory to Freedom: Afro-American Life in the Fifties"
Dates of exhibition: 1988, permanent exhibtion
Size of exhibition: 5,200 square feet
Cost: $1,200,000 (excluding salaries)
Names and titles of exhibition personnel: John Fleming, Director; Fath Davis Ruffins, Guest Curator; Marian Moore, Curator; Edna Harper, Researcher; Juanita Moore, Educator
Date of original conception: 1984
Duration of exhibition development process: four years

Source of funding: State of Ohio

Consultants—Content:

Music: Bernice Johnson Reagon, Horace Boyer, Portia K. Maultsby, Ted McDaniel, Gary Giddons, Geneva Southall, Frederick Tillis; *Family Life:* Micheline Ridley Malson, Deborah Gray White, Linda James Myer; *Economics and Labor:* Dennis Dickerson, Robert Rhodes, Henry Taylor; *NAACP and the Urban League:* August Meier, Jessie Moore; *Civil Rights Movement:* Clayborn Carson, Aldon Morris, Darlene Clark-Hine, Bernice Johnson Reagon, David Garrow, John Ditmer, Phillipa Jackson, David Colburn, Genna Rae McNeil, Mills Thorton; *Sports:* Stanley Warren, William Wiggins, Jr.; *African and Black American Relations:* Sylvia Hill, Sylvia Jacobs; *Education:* Beverly Gordan, Faustine Jones Wilson; *Visual Arts:* Willis Bing Davis, Richard Long; *Afro-Americans and the Military:* Gerald R. Gill, Bernard Nalty; *Film and Entertainment:* Thomas Cripps, Gloria Gibson; *Afro-American Values and Cultural Identity:* Robert Carter, Janet Helms; *Black Women:* Sharon Harley, Elizabeth Clark-Lewis, Rosalyn Terborg-Penn; *Religion:* Cornell West, James Washington, William B. McClain, Arthur P. Stokes

Consultants—Design: Hilferty and Associates

Consultants—Other: Donna Lawrence Associates (audio-visual); Exhibit Concepts (fabrication)

Number of objects exhibited: 1,100

Related Programming: Lectures, workshops, films

Publications—Previsit and postvisit school packages

Gallery talks—docent guided tours

Professional journal reviews:

Thomas J. Davis, "They, Too, Were Here" *American Quarterly* 41 (June 1989): 328-40.

Notes

1. Vincent Harding, "Beyond Chaos: Black History and the Search for the New Land," in John A. Williams and Charles F. Harris ed., *Amistad* 1 (New York: Random House, 1970), 267.

2. For a discussion of the problem in mounting exhibitions informed by new historical perspectives and cultural sensitivities see Spencer R. Crew and James E. Sims, "Locating Authenticity: Fragments of a Dialogue," in Ivan Karp and Steven D. Lavine, eds. *Exhibiting Cultures: The Poetics and Politics of Museum Display* (Washington, D.C.: Smithsonian Institution Press, 1991), 159–75.

3. Thomas J. Davis, "'They, Too, Were Here': The Afro-American Experience and History Museums," in *American Quarterly* 41 (June 1989): 328–40.

4. For a discussion of the rise of the new black history and its impact on American historical scholarship, see August Meier and Elliott Rudwick, *Black History and the Historical Profession, 1915–1980* (Urbana: University of Illinois Press, 1986), 161–238.

5. John Fleming, interview with author, Wilberforce, Ohio, 4 November 1990.

6. Ibid.

7. Juanita Moore, interview with author, Wilberforce, Ohio, 4 November 1990.

8. August Meier, *Negro Thought in America, 1880–1915* (Ann Arbor: The University of Michigan Press, 1968), 256–78; also see David Gordon Nielson, *Black Ethos: Northern Urban Negro Life and Thought, 1890–1930* (Westport, Conn.: Greenwood Press, 1977).

9. Raymond H. Thompson, "Looking to the Future," *Museum News* 70 (January/February 1991): 37–40.

10. August Meier and Elliott Rudwick, *Black History and the Historical Profession*, 161.

11. Curatorial staff, National Afro-American Museum and Cultural Center, interview with author, Wilberforce, Ohio, 4 November 1990.

12. John Fleming, interview, 4 November 1990.

13. Juanita Moore, interview, 4 November 1990.

14. Curatorial staff, interview, 4 November 1990.

15. Juanita Moore, interview, 4 November 1990.

16. Isabel Jasper, staff member, National Afro-American Museum and Cultural Center, and John Fleming, interviews, 4 November 1990.

17. John Fleming, interview, 4 November 1990; National Afro-American Museum and Cultural Center, public service announcement video tape.

18. National Afro-American Museum and Cultural Center, "Grand Opening" booklet, 15–17 April 1988.

19. A list of the scholars consulted for the exhibit's development appears in the Institutional Profile section of this essay.

20. Portia K. Maultsby, "Music as Metaphor," a summary of the project; interview with the author, 8 December 1990.

21. Ibid.

22. Fath Davis Ruffins, guest curator of "From Victory to Freedom: Afro-American Life in the Fifties," interview with author, Washington, D.C., 30 November 1990.

23. Gerald Hilferty, interview with author, Athens, Ohio, 5 November 1990.

24. Fath Davis Ruffins, "From Victory to Freedom: Afro-American Life in the Fifties," (final exhibit script), 10.

25. Fath Davis Ruffins, interview, 30 November 1990.

26. An articulation of the designer's approach to appropriate reading levels in exhibition text is found in Andrew F. Merriell, *Museum Exhibit Development, Research, & Writing* (Athens, Ohio: Gerard Hilferty and Associates, 1987).

27. Thomas J. Davis, "They, Too, Were Here," 330.

28. *Springfield (Ohio) News-Sun*, 11 November 1990, sec. B.

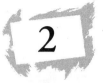

"THE WAY TO INDEPENDENCE"

A New Way to Interpret a Native American Collection

Peter H. Welsh

"The Way to Independence: Memories of a Hidatsa Indian Family, 1840–1920," has been characterized as a landmark exhibition. According to one reviewer, its "sophisticated curatorial approach . . . opens new vistas in the presentation of Native American and other non-Western cultures."[1] Another reviewer stated, "public interpretation of western history has taken a giant step forward" by the "fine melding of new scholarship, magnificent collections, and modern interpretation [that] yields an exhibit with powerful implications, not only for the way that Indian history is interpreted, but also for the entire field of western studies."[2] A third called it "the most subtly complex portrait of an indigenous population that a U.S. museum has ever presented. It is also one of the best history shows of any variety to appear in many years."[3]

The following discussion of "The Way to Independence" will explore the elements of the exhibit that produced such strong reactions. Three aspects of the exhibit contributed most significantly to the success of the whole. The first was the extraordinary material that the curators used as their springboard. The second major element contributing to the exhibit's success was the ongoing commitment of the exhibit team—and their institution—to furthering work originally begun in 1906, particularly by involving Hidatsa individuals from the Ft. Berthold Reservation in the planning and execution of the project. The third feature that led to success, but by no means the least important, was the creativity of the exhibition team in making their concepts concrete and accessible through the exhibit and catalog.[4]

"The Way to Independence" considers a critical period in the history of the Hidatsa Indians. It shows the transition, for two generations of one family, from life with the last prominent trappings of "traditional" ways to that in which the outward appearance of life was more like that of the dominant society. Serving as a metaphor for the transition, and the basis of the exhibit's title, is the most dramatic of the changes—the shift from life in the circular earth lodges concentrated in Like-a-Fishhook Village to the dispersed settlements called Independence, a group of government assigned allotments some thirty miles up the Missouri River.

One of the keys to understanding why this is an important exhibit—and one that deserves close attention—is that one way of life was not simply abandoned for another. While the material culture shifted obviously, other parts of the culture did not change to the same extent. The exhibit challenges the assimilationist's view of Indian history. However, the argument is not a simple one to make in an exhibit displaying object assemblages that indeed *have* changed from one period to the other. Using objects, it is hard to show that the things that matter—culture, values, beliefs—have really stayed much the same, even though everything looks different. Although this problem was not handled with complete success in "The Way to Independence," the extent to which the attempt was successful has led museum exhibition into new territory.

The Hidatsa

The Hidatsa people have made their primary homes along the Missouri River at least since the mid-1600s. They are closely affiliated politically with the Mandans and the Arikaras, with whom they now share the Ft. Berthold Reservation in central North Dakota.

The traditional Hidatsa way of life is one of great antiquity on the Great Plains. Although our minds might first leap, when Plains Indians are mentioned, to images of equestrian, tipi-dwelling, buffalo-hunting warriors, it is important to remember that the equestrian adaptation to the Great Plains environment was historically late and brief. Hidatsas represent a way of life that predated the equestrian adaptation and was based on a mixed economy, heavily—if not primarily—dependent on agriculture. The peoples who successfully occupied the Great Plains for nearly one thousand years concentrated their villages along the fertile river bottoms where they dry-farmed corn, squashes, beans, and other crops. People certainly ventured seasonally onto the uplands—the great open stretches we usually associate with the Great

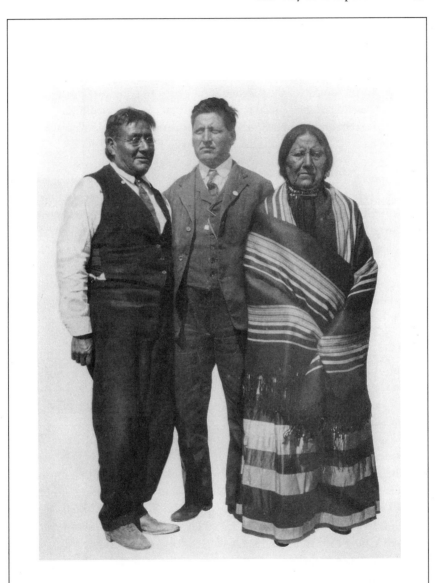

Composite image of Wolf Chief (left, photographed in 1913), Goodbird, and Buffalo Woman (photographed in 1906).

Photographs by Gilbert Wilson.
Courtesy Minnesota Historical Society.

Plains—to exploit the rich resource of buffalo. At these times, they lived in tipis and moved camp often. But it was the threadlike oases formed by the rivers flowing eastward from the Rocky Mountains along which people established permanent settlements—the earth lodge villages. The Hidatsa and the Mandan were the northernmost of these agricultural peoples, living just east of the one hundredth meridian, the general boundary for traditional agriculture.

The Hidatsa and their Mandan allies were well known to traders and travelers on the Northern Plains. Their large earth lodge villages became important hubs in the trading patterns that developed in the eighteenth and early nineteenth centuries. For instance, it was in 1804 at a village of the Awatixa Hidatsa that the American expedition led by Meriwether Lewis and William Clark met the French trader who was married to Sakakawea (or Sacajawea), the Shoshone woman from the eastern slopes of the Rocky Mountains, who had been captured as a girl by the Hidatsa.

The period of prosperity brought by Euro-American trade ended abruptly in the 1830s with a series of devastating smallpox outbreaks. In 1837, nearly half of the Hidatsas and nearly 90 percent of the Mandans died from smallpox. The early nineteenth century also witnessed the tremendous growth in military power of the equestrian Plains tribes—Lakota, Cheyenne, Atsina, Assiniboine, and Piegan—who were challenging one another, as well as the village tribes, for control of hunting areas and access to trade networks. In the early 1840s, the Hidatsa and the Mandan joined together and established Like-a-Fishhook Village,[5] a large settlement surrounded by a defensive ditch and palisade, built directly adjacent to the fur trading post named Ft. Berthold.

In Like-a-Fishhook Village, two of the main characters of "The Way to Independence," Wolf Chief and Buffalo Bird Woman, grew up. The exhibit's story begins here and traces their lives from the period when young men joined war parties and women purchased the religious right to make baskets, to the time when Wolf Chief fought for his right to become an independent shopkeeper, and Buffalo Bird Woman dedicated summers to teaching her skills to anthropologists.

The story is told in several ways. The exhibit itself uses a wide range of objects, documents, photographs, text, and oral narratives. The presentation is complex with many artifacts that reflect, rather than direct, the presentation. It is important to recognize at the outset the philosophy about the objects that guided the exhibit team's interpretation in "The Way to Independence." Much in the spirit of Gilbert Wilson, the original collector, objects serve as the implements for accomplishing a larger task; their presentation is not an end in itself. Thus, in the exhibit, the objects and text together form a connected whole that is not immediately revealed by looking just at the objects, nor is the meaning complete with just the words.

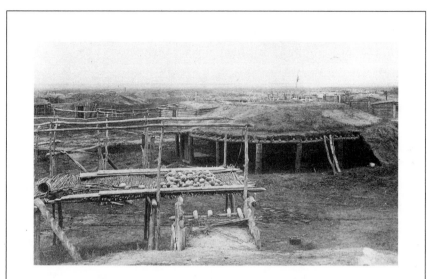

Like-a-Fishhook Village, July 1887. The earth lodge is partially dismantled as the people prepare to leave for Independence and other allotment communities.

Photographed by A. J. Gifford, U. S. Indian Agent. (Neg. No. 15,979)
Courtesy Department of Library Services, American Museum of Natural History.

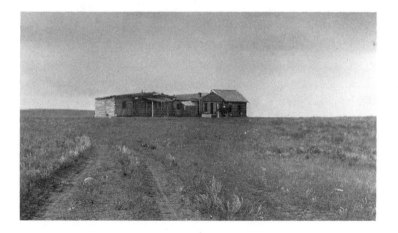

Wolf Chief's store in Independence, 1907.

Photograph by Gilbert Wilson.
Courtesy Minnesota Historical Society.

The exhibit's two major sections concentrate on the principal settings: life in the last of the earth lodge villages, Like-a-Fishhook, and life at Independence. In both sections, cases with thematic unity are arranged in clusters. Each case deals with one topic. For instance, one cluster presents the skills by which Buffalo Bird Woman's status in the community was measured. Cases within that cluster discuss agriculture, daily chores, hide working, wood gathering, and food preparation.

The Wilson Collections

"The Way to Independence" would have been an entirely different exhibit, and unquestionably less significant, had it not been for the earlier work of Gilbert Wilson. The exhibit team was well aware that they stood on the shoulders of a giant. Many features that give the exhibit its distinctive quality—individual biography, objects that bring alive the details of daily life, and even the materials that reflect areas not originally part of the collection—resulted from the diligence, thoroughness, and unsurpassed commitment to documentation that characterized Wilson's work.[6]

The exhibit catalog highlights many details of Wilson's work,[7] so only a few of the special qualities that he brought to his work appear in this essay. Gilbert Wilson was born in 1869. He was ordained as a Presbyterian minister in 1899 and served as pastor of churches in North Dakota and Minnesota until his death in 1930. Wilson's interest in Indians apparently began as a child, but the first evidence of this in his adult life appeared in 1902, when he took the position of pastor of the First Presbyterian Church in Mandan, North Dakota. There, he began working with Lakota people on the Standing Rock Reservation and published his first book in 1903. Wilson's fieldwork with the Hidatsa began in 1906 and spanned twelve summers, until 1918. His work was supported by the Museum of the American Indian in 1906 and 1907, and subsequently by the American Museum of Natural History. In 1910, he became a Ph.D. candidate in anthropology at the University of Minnesota and received his degree in 1916, having written a dissertation on Hidatsa agriculture.[8] In 1920, he accepted a position at Macalester College, where he worked until 1927. In his last years, he served as a pastor in St. Paul, Minnesota.

Many of Wilson's attitudes and approaches seem very modern by today's standards, but they were not completely accepted in his day. His fundamental approach to data collection was summarized in a 1916 letter to Clark Wissler, curator of anthropology at the American Museum of Natural History. He said:

I am quite unwilling to rewrite, on Caucasian method, what is better told in the Indian's own language. I am equally unwilling to jumble accounts. Let each man tell his own story, then we have something truthful. The value of this is having on record something that is *Indian*. We have an abundance of material upon Indian culture from white men, but telling us merely what white men think of the subjects treated. It is of no importance that an Indian's war costume struck the Puritan as the Devil's scheme to frighten the heart out of the Lord's anointed. What we want to know is why the Indian donned the costume, and his reasons for doing it.[9]

He is also quoted in the exhibit catalog from the same letter:

My chief criticism of anthropological material is that it is gathered too much by deductive methods. A collector approaches an Indian informant; takes up a special subject, say the corn dance. He asks the Indian to tell him all about the corn dance, what were its special features, what things in it are to be emphasized etc.; but this is making the Indian generalize, a work to which he is totally untrained. And in essential method, it is reasoning from *a priori*, for it assumes that the Indian has a clear and general idea of the subject, whereas if he is a good informant, he is too ignorant of English ways to even be able to judge what it is you want. The proper and essential way, in my mind, in the study of primitive cultures, is to take a typical and intelligent informant and use him for a type representative on the chief subject. Get from him your major account, out of his own experiences. Then follow with corroborative accounts, also from personal experience, preferably from other members of the same family. Then add miscellaneous corroborating evidence from any source at hand.[10]

Thus, Wilson resisted Wissler's exhortations to "have a theory" to guide his work, but rather saw himself primarily as a transcriber of the accounts of his Hidatsa collaborators. Wissler sent Robert Lowie, who was then his assistant, to Fort Berthold in 1910. Lowie's characterization of Wilson is illustrative:

Among the Hidatsa I was taken down another peg. The Reverend Gilbert L. Wilson was neither particularly cultivated nor in any sense intellectual, but he was a superb observer. In the recording of ethnographic detail—about house building or pottery making or farming customs or the care in infants, for example—I, the trained ethnologist, could not begin to compete with him.[11]

Wilson's approach to ethnography—his commitment to giving authoritative voice to the people whose way of life was the subject of the writing—gives a strong humanistic quality to his work. Wilson was committed to collections of all kinds. He collected objects, botanical specimens, stories, photographs, and songs. His collections were not haphazard, but were coordinated and—while he might not have expressed it this way—governed by a theory about the nature of ethnographic data. That theory emphasized the significance of material culture as process and performance, rather than as a final product or culture trait.

For instance, Wilson often collected, in addition to the object itself, the raw materials as well as the same object in various stages of completion. With his primary collaborators, Buffalo Bird Woman, Goodbird, and Wolf Chief, Wilson had many reproductions and models made. Wilson recorded the manufacturing process in writing and in photographs. Wilson was accompanied on his trips to Independence by his younger brother, Frederick, a commercial artist, who made sketches of many of the processes for use as illustrations in Gilbert's publications and reports. In addition, Wilson had Goodbird make drawings of objects as they would be used by Hidatsa people. His multifaceted approach to collecting went beyond the technological and included recording the use, meaning, and significance of the objects collected. It differed significantly from the approach of many of the university trained ethnographers of that time. Robert Lowie, for instance, often did not even record the name of the person from whom he acquired an object.[12]

One of the key tasks of the exhibit's development was to track down the current locations of Wilson's collections. The American Museum of Natural History, for which Wilson collected, and the Minnesota Historical Society, where Gilbert's and Frederick's personal collections were deposited after their deaths, held some materials. Other collections are at the Museum of the American Indian and the Science Museum of Minnesota. In addition to the hundreds of artifacts, the collections include over twelve hundred photographs, numerous volumes of field notes, formal reports, manuscripts, sketchbooks, and audio recordings.

The history of Gilbert Wilson's collections subsequent to their deposition at the various institutions can serve as an important lesson in collections management. Much of the detailed information that Wilson collected became disassociated from the artifacts once the collections went to museums. For example, Wilson attached a tag to each object he sent to the American Museum of Natural History on which he wrote one or two identifying words. His extensive documentation of the items appeared in a list attached to his formal report. Unfortunately, only the information from the tags was entered into the museum's catalog, without clear reference to the reports. The exhibit's catalog notes that as early as 1931 this led to mistakes. For instance, when Leslie Spier compiled his definitive work on parfleches,[13] he attributed parfleches to the Mandan and Hidatsa even though Wilson's detailed notes show the objects were collected from Lakota people of the Standing Rock Reservation.

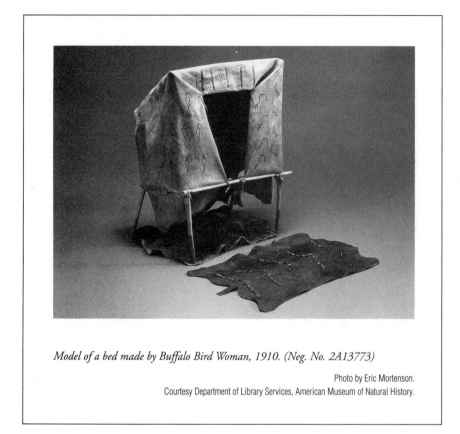

Model of a bed made by Buffalo Bird Woman, 1910. (Neg. No. 2A13773)

Photo by Eric Mortenson.
Courtesy Department of Library Services, American Museum of Natural History.

Discouraging is the sequence of events that led to the loss of information associated with Wilson's personal collection deposited at the Minnesota Historical Society. According to catalog author, Mary Jane Schneider, many of the objects in Gilbert Wilson's own collection were to be models for his brother Frederick's illustrations. In 1915, Wilson wrote to Clark Wissler and offered the collection, along with complete documentation, to the American Museum of Natural History. In his letter to Wissler, he said that he knew the source of every piece and was willing to write it all down. However, the transaction did not take place, and Wilson never recorded the provenience or other field data. Wilson retained the collection until his death in 1930, at which time his widow, Ada M. Wilson, donated his objects, photographs, books, and manuscripts to the Minnesota Historical Society.

At the Minnesota Historical Society, the components of the collection fell under the care of different divisions of the society. As the collection had not

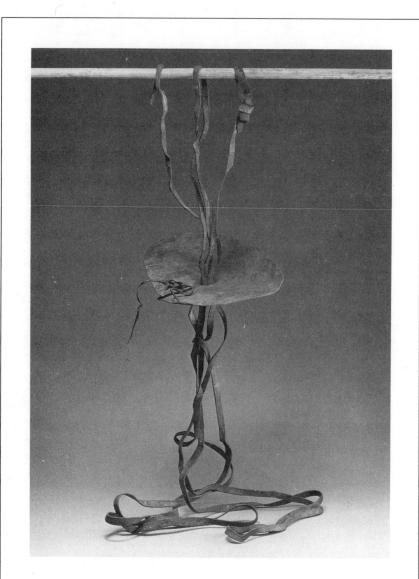

Storage swing, collected in 1912 by Frederick Wilson from its maker, Hairy Coat. Such swings were used to store bags filled with clothes. The leather disc at the top kept mice from crawling down the straps and getting into the bags. (Neg. No. 2A13763)

Photo by Eric Mortenson.
Courtesy Department of Library Services, American Museum of Natural History.

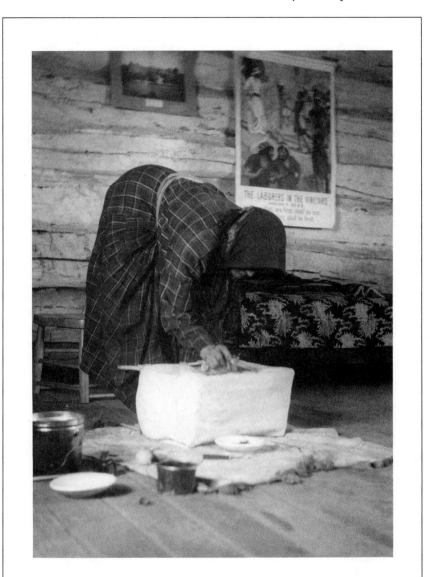

Buffalo Bird Woman making a model bed, 1910.

Photograph by Gilbert Wilson.
Courtesy Minnesota Historical Society.

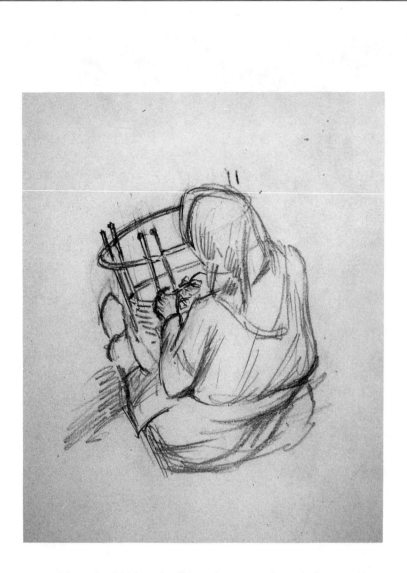

Drawing by Frederick Wilson of Buffalo Bird Woman making a basket, 1912(?).

Courtesy Minnesota Historical Society.

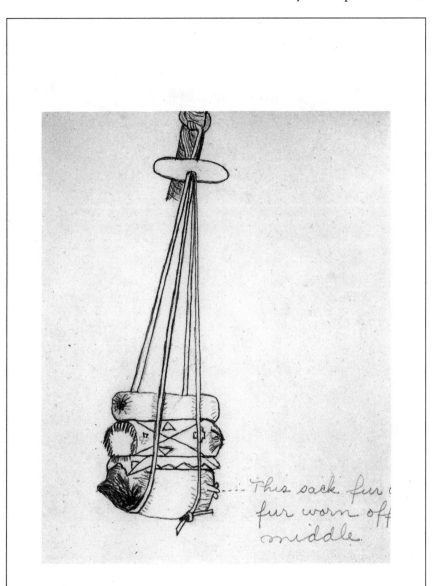

Picture of a storage swing drawn by Goodbird, 1916.

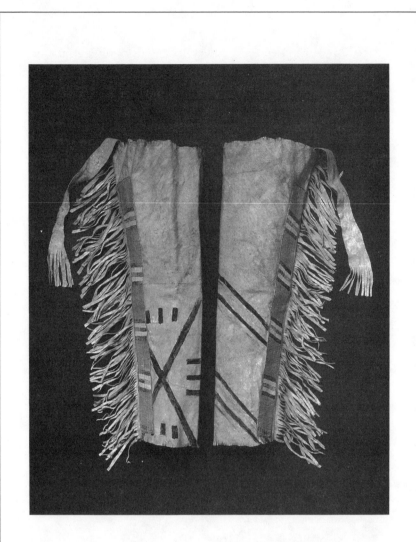

Leggings that had belonged to Lance Owner, a Mandan. When Gilbert Wilson collected these in 1911, he recorded, among other things, that the leggings had been made by Lance Owner's wife, Leader, and that the painting on the leggings had been done by Wolf Ghost, a Hidatsa, and Wounded Face, an Mandan. (Neg. No. 2A13785)

Photo by Eric Mortenson.
Courtesy Department of Library Services, American Museum of Natural History.

originated in Minnesota, it came to be regarded by some personnel as marginal to the society's mission. Over the years, the collection lost its cohesiveness. When "The Way to Independence" project began, the exhibit team knew only about the artifacts. The team became aware of the photographs and manuscripts during the planning process. The negatives had not been identified, and the manuscripts had not been microfilmed. In fact, sometime in the past, certain parts of the collection had been considered for deaccession. Happily, this did not take place, and the curatorial team working on the project was able to reunite the separated components.

Clearly, one of the major contributions of "The Way to Independence" project is the rediscovery of Wilson's unique legacy. The rich collections, now documented and reconnected, will serve as the foundation for many future exhibits, publications, and insights into the life and history of the Hidatsa people. Even if the project had ended with the reuniting of Wilson's collections, the scholarly community could be grateful. "The Way to Independence" went beyond the scholarly community, however, and engaged the public in new discovery.

Institutional context

The Minnesota Historical Society was founded in 1849 to collect, preserve, disseminate, and interpret Minnesota's history. It includes library, manuscript, newspaper, photograph, artifact, and archaeological collections; Minnesota's public archives; a publications program; an education program; museum exhibits; and twenty-two historic sites. Exhibits have been important for interpreting historic sites and the society's collections.

According to Director Nina Archabal, "The Way to Independence" established a new direction for the society's exhibits. Archabal viewed "The Way to Independence" as part of a larger program of interpreting Indian history. The Minnesota Historical Society has a long tradition of representing the tribes of Minnesota in historical publications. However, through projects like "The Way to Independence," it has become more aware that the presentation of Indian history requires the involvement of Indian people. As Archabal noted, the interpretation of a battle or other conflict site in a way that reflects the views of both sides produces a result very different from one that is presented in the more traditional way. "The Way to Independence" was, for the Minnesota Historical Society, a major breakthrough in the presentation of history.

"The Way to Independence" was developed at the society in the context of an ambitious exhibition program under the leadership of Nicholas Westbrook, the curator of exhibits. Westbrook studied with Henry Glassie[14] at the University of Pennsylvania and brought to the society's exhibits an approach to material culture that emphasized the objects' abilities to illustrate historical and social processes. Westbrook's approach built exhibits around themes, with artifacts as their interpretive foundation, and did not emphasize, or have much patience for, presentations stressing connoisseurship or typologies.

"The Way to Independence" had its beginnings in the development of the society's 1982 exhibit, "Where Two Worlds Meet: The Great Lakes Fur Trade." Carolyn Gilman curated "Where Two Worlds Meet," which received an Award of Merit in 1983 from the American Association for State and Local History. In preparing "Where Two Worlds Meet," she first encountered Wilson's collection. It seemed to be an anomaly, and the material intrigued her. What was this collection of North Dakota Indian material doing at the Minnesota Historical Society? According to her recollection in 1990, she approached Westbrook with the tantalizing hints she had seen of the Wilson collection, and Westbrook encouraged her to apply to the National Endowment for the Humanities (NEH) for a planning grant for an exhibit.

The planning grant played a significant role in refining the ideas that fueled the exhibit. In the first place, the grant proposal forced the exhibit developers to decide whether the exhibit was going to be about Gilbert Wilson and his collection, or about Hidatsa history. Gilman remembers clearly that Sally Yerkovich of NEH presented the question in the planning grant proposal's early stages. Staff concluded that the exhibit would emphasize Hidatsa life, rather than Wilson's work.

Other refinements took place during the planning process. The project's perspective shifted from a generalized consideration of acculturation and modernization at the start of the project to a personal and biographical presentation on "the process of minority adaptation." For instance, the planning grant proposal states:

> The cultural transformation that overtook Buffalo Bird Woman and Goodbird in the late 19th century is strikingly revealed in photographs of them from the 1910–1918 period. These portray the material reality of that era: cast iron stoves, frame houses, Euro-American clothing and canned goods sold in the reservation store. Using these photographs along with artifacts and quotations from Goodbird, we hope to create a sense of the choices which faced every Native American family undergoing the same collision with modern white society.[15]

This preliminary theory of Hidatsa culture change resembles the one Gilman later ascribes to the Indian agents who "year after year counted their progress by chronicling the decline of the earth lodge, blanket, and moccasin, and the rise of the frame house, suit coat, and shoe."[16] It differs markedly from the theory presented in the implementation grant proposal that ultimately guided the final exhibit. In the implementation proposal, for instance, Gilman discusses how the Hidatsas's response to missionaries' encouragement to celebrate Decoration Day by placing silk flowers on the graves of family members. She states that:

> Though the concrete evidence—underground burial, stone grave markers, and silk flowers—all suggest acculturation, the *meanings* of those artifacts were still profoundly Hidatsa. The objects of white culture actually bolstered rather than undermined traditional values.[17]

A goal of the project was to "help viewers understand the abstract questions of culture change in compelling individual terms."[18]

From the beginning, the exhibit had an additional goal: to "restore the concept of change over time to the museum presentation of Indian history." As the proposal points out: "Museums frequently portray Indians living anonymously in an idealized, ahistorical moment, their lives affected by seasonal cycles but not by events."[19] The exhibit organizers saw that by using Wilson's collections, they had a rare opportunity to give visitors a chance to "envision particular people caught up in profound social changes at particular moments in time."[20]

The Exhibition Team

The specific roles of individuals involved in the development of the exhibit were well defined. Westbrook had overall administrative responsibility for the project and chaired the staff advisory committee. Gilman, as project curator, coordinated the exhibit's development and implementation. She directed the research, formulated the exhibit strategy, and was the primary author of the catalog text and the exhibit labels. Earl Gutnik and John Palmer Low shared design responsibilities. Gutnik did the preliminary conceptual design of the exhibit as well as the design of the catalog. Low finalized the exhibit design.

Among the outside consultants, Gerard Baker played a key role by advising on contemporary Hidatsa life, facilitating field research, and contributing an essay to the exhibit catalog. Baker, an interpretive ranger-historian for the National Park Service at the Theodore Roosevelt National Monument in North Dakota, joined the project in the planning stages. A Hidatsa, he has been actively involved in learning and teaching Hidatsa traditional ways for a number of years. Baker worked with the exhibit team to ensure that objects were exhibited correctly—seeing that sacred objects either were not displayed, or, if they could be displayed, that they were appropriately presented. He helped other members of the exhibit team understand the relationship between old-time and modern Hidatsa religion. When Baker agreed to write a chapter on Hidatsa religion for the catalog he had Hidatsa elders review his first manuscript.

When Gilman and the project's research associate, Mary Jane Schneider, went to the Ft. Berthold Reservation to conduct interviews, Baker was their primary facilitator for gaining access to elders. Baker coached Gilman and Schneider in appropriate interviewing techniques. The interviews were usually one-on-one, tape recorded, and concentrated on the elders' lives at Independence. Independence had been inundated in the 1950s by the construction of Garrison Dam, displacing, yet again, many of the Hidatsas. Thus, these interviews were an emotional time for many of the elders, as they recollected this traumatic period.[21] Baker's advice for interviewing elders—reminiscent of Wilson's—was: "Just let them go, don't be pushy, and don't try to keep on the subject." He was aware that people's knowledge has value, but that for Hidatsa elders, such value should not be expressed in monetary form. Gifts of blankets, food, or tobacco more appropriately expressed the interviewers' gratitude. People interviewed included Baker's mother and descendants of Goodbird.

Perhaps most fortuitous was the arrival of Mary Jane Schneider on the project scene. When the Minnesota Historical Society received its NEH planning grant, it advertised nationally for a research associate to join the team on a one-year contract. The society expected to hire someone at a junior level. Instead, according to Gilman, Schneider "turned up on our doorstep [and said] 'Hire me.'" At the time, Schneider was associate professor and chair of the Indian Studies Department at the University of North Dakota, from which she was granted a year's leave to work on the exhibit. She brought to the project detailed knowledge of Hidatsa history and culture as well as friendships with many Hidatsa people on the Ft. Berthold Reservation. Through the efforts of Schneider, particularly, relationships among the disconnected and dispersed parts of Gilbert Wilson's collections were reestablished. In Gilman's estimation, Schneider's involvement raised the project's scholarship to a level that had not been contemplated at the outset.

One of Schneider's more important contributions was in reorienting the intellectual framework of the exhibit. Earlier, Gilman had decided to emphasize the Hidatsa history in the exhibit; and with Schneider's arrival, the project's approach toward Hidatsas's historical experience shifted.

Initially, the story line had emphasized Hidatsa cultural assimilation. Gilman remembers struggling as she tried to make the acculturation/change argument when she wrote the NEH implementation grant proposal. Gilman expressed her frustration to Schneider. Schneider pointed out that perhaps assimilation was *not* taking place—an idea that opened Gilman's mind to recognize that simplistic explanations based on assimilation were not tenable. Thus, the exhibit emphasized that "it is necessary to see the difference between the physical artifact and the cultural image that the artifact projects upon people's minds."[22] The exhibit encouraged us to be cautious in projecting perceived changes in material culture to changes in other—less visible—areas. As Gilman notes:

> The story of Buffalo Bird Woman's family shows that the Hidatsa did not follow a one-way street toward acculturation. Their traditional society was not a static, ideal way of life that disappeared without a trace when overwhelmed by whites. The process of change was more complex than that. Individuals reacted in their own idiosyncratic ways to the pressures upon them. They developed strategies for coping with change, and for co-opting aspects of the white world to achieve continuity in their lives. They neither clung without compromise to the old ways, nor accepted the new without question. Instead, they created a new culture within a culture.[23]

This theory of culture change, and the ways that objects can inform us about such change, profoundly affected the exhibit's presentation.

The Exhibit

The exhibit had a number of special features that the project planners felt were key to the presentation of their concepts and to the flexibility of the exhibit, which was destined for several venues. The biographical approach, the focus on everyday things and concerns, the treatment of culture change and continuity, and the selection of objects that carried these messages had particular importance. In addition, the exhibit's physical design incorporated a number of features that reinforced the curatorial elements, facilitating successful travel.

The emphasis on biographies and the focus on everyday things flowed directly from the approach that Gilbert Wilson brought to his work. Wilson allowed the first-person voice of individual Hidatsa people to guide his understanding of Hidatsa culture. Wilson's material suggested and supported the exhibit team's biographical approach, since so many things he collected could be traced to individuals—especially to one family. The exhibit team's recognition of the unusual opportunity offered by Wilson's material enabled them to bring real life into their presentation. Using biographies met one of the exhibit's major goals: to show personalities in the presentation of Indian history. By focusing on real individuals, the exhibit could consider the different ways each person responded to cultural change.

Biography was not selected without careful consideration. One of the main questions asked of consultants during the planning phase had to do with the feasibility of the biographical approach. Gilman knew that the nature of biography could force a sequential presentation onto the exhibit. A biographical approach necessitates an exhibit presentation that directs visitors' movement through it chronologically. She was concerned about such a "coercive" exhibit design. Furthermore, biography is not necessarily visual.

To avoid these problems, the exhibit's installation used a combination of biographical and thematic approaches. In each thematic area, the exhibit team attempted to write text that "looked from the inside out." That is, the story was told from the viewpoint of one of the main characters, using as many direct quotations as possible.

Themes focused mainly on the activities of everyday life. Again, the exhibit reflected the Wilson collections. Wilson assembled as thorough an inventory of the historical Hidatsa way of life as he could. In particular, he researched Hidatsa agriculture for his doctoral dissertation. The exhibit team incorporated these collections into a historically rich presentation of individual lives— completely compatible with Wilson's earlier work. Had the exhibit attempted to explore less-concrete aspects of Hidatsa culture, it would have quickly lost the human connection it so successfully fosters between the Hidatsa subjects and visitors to the exhibit.

Early in the project, staff decided to draw from collections other than Wilson's when necessary. The historical materials necessary to explicate life in Like-a-Fishhook Village, which predated Wilson's time among the Hidatsa people, came from the collections at the State Historical Society of North Dakota (SHSND) that had been excavated from the village site in the early 1950s. Bringing these materials into the exhibit established the historical foundation for tracing the transition into reservation life. The excavated artifacts enabled the presentation to go beyond the memories of Wilson's primary collaborators. For instance, the excavations revealed quantities of patent medicines and other items[24] that Wilson's collaborators did not discuss with him.

The exhibit also included the kinds of Euro-American manufactured items used by Wolf Chief and his family during the time that Wilson was visiting with them, but which Wilson assiduously did not collect. Based on the fundamental goal of the exhibit—to present Hidatsa history—the team decided to include items from the Minnesota Historical Society collections to represent Hidatsa life in the early twentieth century.

Gilman recalled her difficulty in deciding to use objects that were not actually part of the lives of the real people featured in the exhibit. "Think of the

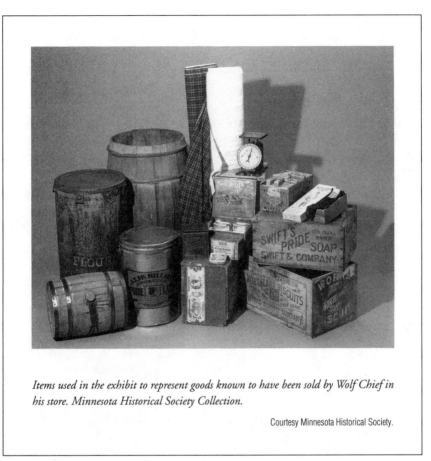

Items used in the exhibit to represent goods known to have been sold by Wolf Chief in his store. Minnesota Historical Society Collection.

Courtesy Minnesota Historical Society.

stories that are connected to the things that are part of our lives," she said. The team reached a compromise that highlighted another aspect of Wilson's work: they chose items that could be seen in Wilson's photographs, often objects that appeared incidentally in the backgrounds. In addition, through the National Archives, the exhibit team acquired an inventory of the merchandise in Wolf Chief's store, making it possible to re-create that setting in the exhibit.

Exhibit Design and Presentation

The exhibit presented real design challenges. It had a complex theme, richly supported by well-documented collections. Curators envisioned a fairly rigid sequence of presentation. The show had to travel. Special lighting effects, as well as audio stations, had to convey particular aspects of the message. Considering these constraints, the exhibit design works well.

The exhibit's two major areas convey the theme of change. The first deals with life in Like-a-Fishhook Village, the second with life at Independence. Within each area, clusters, or "pods," of connected cases present particular topics. The clusters in the earth lodge area are arranged in semi-circles, while those in the Independence area are square. In its original installation at the Minnesota Historical Society, exhibit visitors went from the Like-a-Fishhook area to the Independence area through a passageway that was highlighted by a wagon to suggest the move from one locale to the other.

The transition is crucial. It defines the two major thematic areas and makes the historical transition clear. While the kinds of objects and photographs change from one section to the other, and while there is a distinct, if subtle, change in the design of the cases—from circular to angular—the shift in

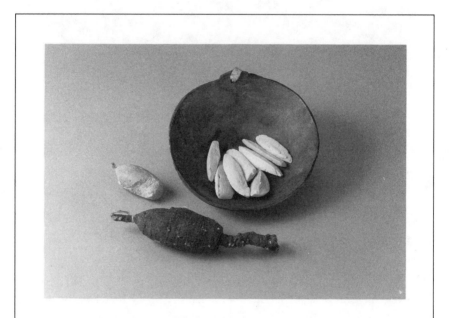

Prairie turnips collected by Gilbert Wilson, 1916. The turnip in the foreground is whole, those in the wooden bowl are sliced and dried. Minnesota Historical Society Collection.

Courtesy Minnesota Historical Society.

perspective required a more obvious expression. That need prompted Gilman to say of the later installation at the State Historical Society of North Dakota: "It breaks my heart." The North Dakota staff decided to place the two sections of the exhibit in different parts of the museum.

Verbal information in three distinct categories, or, as the exhibit team characterized them, "voices," challenged the designers as well. The Narrative Voice carried the primary historical background and themes in silk-screened labels in each case or each cluster. The Character Voice consisted of tape recordings of actors reading directly from the autobiographical narratives of Wolf Chief, Buffalo Bird Woman, and Goodbird. Visitors used small earphones mounted in each of the case clusters to hear to the readings. The Curatorial Voice consisted of elaborate labels for the individual artifacts in the cases. Visitors gained access to the labels by pressing and holding a button that illuminated otherwise darkened panels.

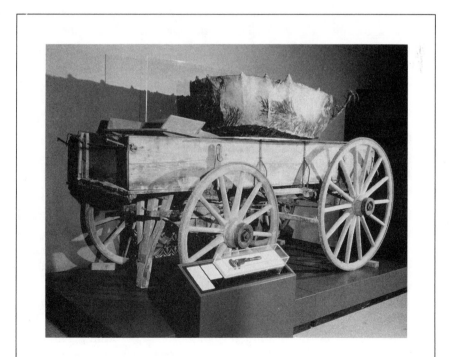

"The Way to Independence" installation at the Minnesota Historical Society.

Courtesy Minnesota Historical Society.

These elements of interactivity gave different priority to the three voices. The primary narrative labels required visitors to read. The recordings, though, offered wonderful insights into the lives of the primary characters of the exhibit, but they also demanded the visitor's patience and commitment. Each tape had two or three readings, requiring the listener to remain standing in one place for as long as ten minutes. They were not for the casual browser. Yet, only from the tapes could the visitor develop a sense of individual personalities and multiple interpretations of similar events. The recordings are the visitor's primary access to an authoritative Indian narrative about cultural change. The exhibit design would have better supported the theme if the recordings had been more accessible. In the exhibit's installation, the primary authority remains with the written narrative, which was not the exhibit team's original intent.

The design also made a clear statement about the role of artifacts in the exhibit. While each case contains many artifacts, identification and descriptions for the objects were of distinctly less importance to the story than one usually encounters in exhibits. The exhibit's design forced the visitor to search for the curatorial significance of an object. The design was a conscious choice on the part of the exhibit team who felt that the artifacts should be treated in depth in the catalog rather than in the exhibit. Even so, since object information appears in the exhibit, the design should have been more accommodating to the visitor. The height at which the buttons were placed and the switches that the visitor had to hold down while reading forced those interested in object information to "inch through the exhibit at a semi-stoop."[25] Though notable, this flaw is minor in light of the significant impact the exhibit has had on its audiences.

Homecoming

Although "The Way to Independence" traveled to New York and Washington, D.C., perhaps the most significant stop on its tour was at the State Historical Society of North Dakota. Several staff members—Chris Dill, curator; Marcia Wolter, educator; and Claudia Berg, exhibit designer—provided insights into the importance of the exhibit for their institution.

For Dill, a major impact of the show has been financial. Most exhibits at the SHSND are budgeted at approximately three to six thousand dollars. "The Way to Independence" cost the institution close to twenty thousand dollars. Still, when the show was offered, Dill felt strongly that "it has to come home."

According to Wolter, the SHSND has seen an increase in the number of native American visitors, following some publicity targeted at nearby reservations. A number of school groups have come from the Standing Rock Reservation (Lakota), located just south of Bismarck. In particular, native

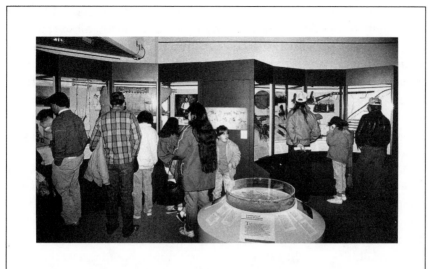

Exhibit installation at the State Historical Society of North Dakota showing individual cases and case clusters.

Courtesy Minnesota Historical Society.

American people have attended the SHSND's education programs in greater numbers. These programs focus on contemporary culture, and approximately one-third of the audience has been Indian people. In sum, Wolter feels that "The Way to Independence" has brought the institution closer to the tribes—to the point that some are asking, "Why wasn't the exhibit about us?" It should be pointed out that simultaneous to the presentation of "The Way to Independence," the SHSND staff was negotiating significant and difficult repatriation action with native Americans.

The installation at the SHSND was a disappointment. The two sections of the exhibit were installed in two different areas of the Museum. The carefully crafted continuity between Like-a-Fishhook and Independence was lost to the vast majority of the visitors. The Like-a-Fishhook section was prominently exhibited adjacent to the main entrance. The Independence section was tucked into the lobby of the auditorium. On leaving the Like-a-Fishhook area, a visitor had to pass the information desk, the entrance to the permanent exhibits, the rest rooms, and a long hallway to reach the Independence gallery. While at the SHSND, I was able to observe visitors' movement through the exhibit, and few made the trek.

"The Way to Independence" clearly affected the Hidatsa people. I had the opportunity to visit with Gerard Baker, the project's primary consultant from the Ft. Berthold community. He observed that, overall, the exhibit had a very positive effect on the reservation. The show, for example, got people thinking about that past time—kids would say, "I wish we could live like it was at Independence." Baker felt that, to a degree, the exhibit stimulated young people to talk to older people. In addition, in the neighboring, non-Indian town of Watford City, the library has acquired the exhibit catalog, and, according to Baker, it has been checked out repeatedly.

Baker did note a few areas of concern. While he felt that the approach of using one family was very effective, he said that it did arouse some jealousy among other families. He also pointed out that in the exhibit there are not many negatives. Like-a-Fishhook Village is idealized, with little reference to the difficulties many of its residents had supporting themselves.

Above all, Baker wished that the exhibit's run had not been so short. He would like it to stay intact forever, and he wished that the State Historical Society of North Dakota would organize such a presentation. He is very encouraged by the plans of the Minnesota Historical Society to donate the casework of the show to the tribal museum on the reservation. He feels that gift is the culmination of the Minnesota Historical Society's commitment to work in partnership with the people represented by the exhibit.

Conclusions

Clearly, "The Way to Independence" has had an important impact on the intellectual community, on the institutions where it has been shown, and on the Indian community connected to its origination. It was, to use Carolyn Gilman's words, "a charmed exhibit, a juggernaut" in which "we were agog most of the time."

Speaking as one of the exhibit's audience, I would have to say that some of the exhibit's messages are communicated better than others. The biographical approach provides an effective core around which the exhibit coalesces. The viewer certainly comes away with a strong feeling of connection with Buffalo Bird Woman, Wolf Chief, and Goodbird. We have a clear sense of three different personalities whose lives offer insight into the historical experience of the Hidatsa people. We need to keep in mind that these individuals are not necessarily typical of all Hidatsas of their time. In fact, the show has been criticized for painting too positive a picture of the cultural transition that the Hidatsas experienced.[26] The criticism was expected, but Gilman felt it was important to show that some Hidatsa people faced the uprooting and upheaval that accompanied a marked shift in lifeways with reasonable success. The exhibit gives an alternative view to that which presents Indian history as one of defeat and victimization. "The Way to Independence" shows how individuals, representative or not, play an active part in responding to historical circumstances. Wolf Chief's tenacity and dedication to becoming a merchant when so many obstacles were placed in his way is a story that would be impressive in any setting.

The story of culture change and continuity that "The Way to Independence" tells is a subtle one that requires the visitor's close attention. Visitors are asked to see beyond the artifacts presented and to discover that although the material assemblages changed radically, the structure of Hidatsa life did not. In this, an exhibit curator is at a disadvantage. Visitors to an exhibit first encounter artifacts, not theories.

For instance, as I moved through the Independence section of the exhibit, I found that I was spending far less time with the artifacts than I had in the area that represented Like-a-Fishhook Village. The objects seemed less compelling, until I realized that *I was responding as if I already knew all about them.* Of course, this was not true. I, as a visitor, no more knew what the coffee grinder (displayed in the "Home Life" case) was *in terms of the experiences of the Hidatsa people of the early twentieth century* than I knew about the large wooden corn mortar and pestle representing an earlier time. I thought I knew a coffee grinder when I saw one, and I could apply plenty of personal experience to the act of making coffee. In short, the artifacts in the Independence section transported me first into the realm of my own experience, which I then had to suppress in order to understand that these familiar artifacts were being used to tell about a much different way of life. In this way, the artifacts in the Independence section actually can impede a visitor's understanding of the story of cultural continuity and change.

Not surprisingly, I experienced a very different kind of reaction to the "traditional" Hidatsa items, with which my experience—like most visitors'—is much more limited. The objects supported the story in this section much more directly.

Visitors are asked—in a very short time—to make a conceptual leap that social scientists and historians have struggled with understanding for decades. Although the Hidatsa people in Independence lived with a material inventory that looks just like what our own grandparents used (especially when it is in a museum display case), the fundamental message is that the Hidatsas remained profoundly different. Assumptions can not be made about values, beliefs, or priorities based on the things that people possess. That similar material assemblages can have different meanings in different cultural contexts is a terribly important truth for understanding our contemporary pluralistic society. However, it is an argument that is extraordinarily difficult to make with objects presented in traditional museological fashion.

A first-person Hidatsa voice presenting authentic and authoritative interpretations of various actual experiences in relation to objects helps convey this complex concept in the exhibit. For example, Wolf Chief's experience with coffee grinders included memories of roasting coffee beans using the same techniques that had been used for parching corn and of pulverizing the beans in a corn mortar. When the first-person account of Hidatsa life is available, as it was in audio recordings throughout both sections of the exhibit, it effectively aids contextualization. However, the authority and dominance of the objects is hard to override. Gilman was fully aware of the objects' power as she struggled with the Independence section of the exhibit, which explains her great reluctance to have included objects "just like" ones that could have been used by Buffalo Bird Woman or Wolf Chief. She recognized the danger of losing the vitality of the message conveyed by things that had actually been part of the life of someone we have come to know—whether that person is our grandfather, or Wolf Chief.[27]

If, somehow, the authority of the objects had been more directly challenged in the exhibit, if their ambiguity had been highlighted, or if their representativeness had been questioned, the coffee grinders and frying pans might have been made to seem as much in need of explanation as strings of dried squash. We can imagine, for instance, the kind of reaction that a visitor would have had if some objects had been arranged in ways that did not suggest familiar, daily experience. It is important to keep in mind, I think, that the connection between museum cases—or case clusters—and the experience exhibit planners are trying to convey in them is not necessarily obvious. We, in museums, have come to see these glass boxes as meaningful, conceptual units that can encapsulate and communicate an event or a realm of experience. But if we listen to ourselves as we stand before a case giving tours, we will notice that the case arrangements are mnemonic cues that we use for extended discourses about the lives represented by the objects and words locked inside. To produce an exhibit is to struggle with condensing complex concepts into tiny spaces.

Perhaps our difficulty comes from trying to use concepts and categories developed in anthropology and history that were adapted to the open plains of the unwritten page. When these approaches are forced into museum cases, much is compromised. Rather than seeing this as a problem, however, we can explore the opportunity that museum presentation offers. With powerfully evocative objects at our disposal, we can explore other kinds of communication beyond linear, verbal exposition. Using object juxtapositions, unfamiliar

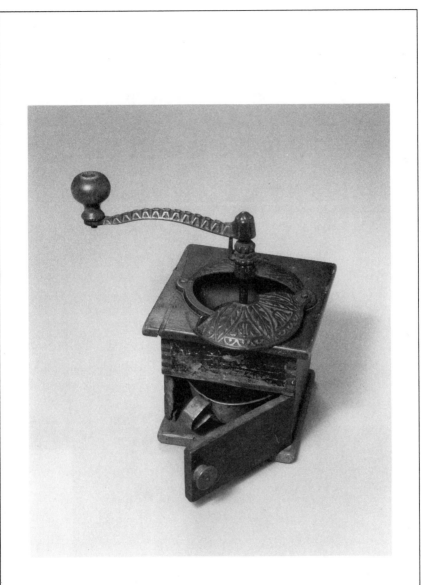

Coffee grinder, ca. 1900. Minnesota Historical Society Collection.

Courtesy Minnesota Historical Society.

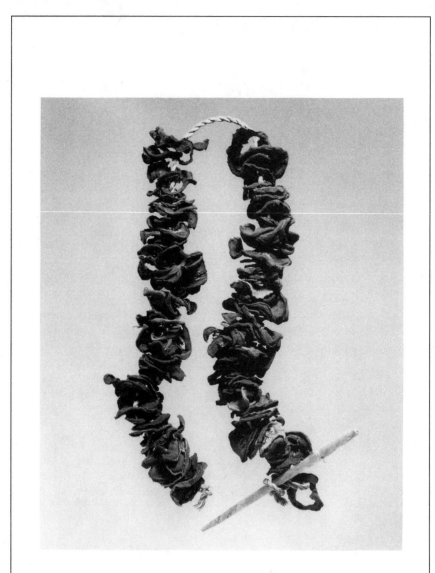

String of dried squash collected by Gilbert Wilson, 1916. Minnesota Historical Society Collection.

Courtesy Minnesota Historical Society.

combinations, or concepts that frame ideas in new ways, museum exhibits can develop a medium of communication of their own.

As Gilman and I spoke about "The Way to Independence," our conversation ranged beyond the immediate exhibit into the process of exhibit creation. We found that likening museum exhibits to written texts was misguided. Although the parallel to a well-illustrated magazine article was a comparison that I had found useful for organizing exhibits in the past, I mentioned that increasingly it was making sense to think of exhibits as akin to performances, in which movement, pacing, and drama were as critical to success as lucid, vivid text, exciting objects, and stimulating themes.

Gilman contributed the extremely important observation that although other media—film, literature, theater, dance—have vocabularies for talking about their genres, no such vocabulary exists for exhibits. We use words like "important" or "blockbuster" or "disappointing" in vague ways, usually to indicate the rarity and appeal of the objects, or the glamour of their display. Such terms do not recognize the intrusive, creative, and interpretive act that is the curatorial effort. Anthropological and historical exhibits include significant levels of interpretation, and curators must no longer regard themselves simply as passive conduits for presenting the creative accomplishments of others.

Institutional Profile

Name: Minnesota Historical Society
Location: 690 Cedar Street, St. Paul, Minnesota 55101
Size of institution: $18,000,000 annual operating budget; programs reach 2,000,000 people annually
Date of founding: 1849
Number of professional staff: 184

Exhibition data

Name of exhibition: "The Way to Independence: Memories of a Hidatsa Indian Family, 1840–1920"
Dates and venues: Minnesota Historical Society, June 1987–1989; National Museum of American History, April–October 1989; State Historical Society of North Dakota, December 1989–September 1990; Western Heritage Museum, October 1990–April 1991; and the American Museum of Natural History, July–October 1991.
Size of Exhibition: Approximately 2,500 square feet
Cost: $450,000 (excluding salaries)

Names and titles of exhibition personnel: Carol Gilman, Project Curator; Mary Jane Schneider, Research Associate; Nicholas Westbrook, Curator of Exhibits; Susan H. Holland, Assistant Curator; Earl Gutnik, Chief Designer; John Palmer Low, Exhibit Designer

Date of original conception: 1982

Duration of exhibition development process: 1983–1987

Sources of funding: National Endowment for the Humanities (planning and implementation grants), Northwest Area Foundation, Northwestern Bell Foundation, Northwestern Bell Telephone, 3M Foundation (educational programs), Otto Bremer Foundation

Consultants: Gerard Baker, Jeffrey Hanson, Roy W. Meyer, W. Raymond Wood, Alan R. Woolworth, Anson Baker, Cora Baker, Jill Gillette, Doreen Long Fight, Alyce Spotted Bear, Tillie Walker

Number of objects exhibited: Approximately 500 artifacts and a number of modern reproductions

Related programming:

Publications: Exhibition catalog—Carolyn Gilman and Mary Jane Schneider, *The Way to Independence: Memories of a Hidatsa Indian Family, 1840–1920,* with essays by W. Raymond Wood, Gerard Baker, Jeffrey Hanson, and Alan R. Woolworth, St. Paul: Minnesota Historical Society Press, 1988.

Museum Lessons Series, with in-gallery classes, levels K–3 and 4–6. Teacher workshops were also offered.

Professional journal reviews:

John C. Ewers, "The Way to Independence: Memories of a Hidatsa Indian Family, 1840–1920," *Minnesota History* 50 (Winter 1987):331–32.

Thomas D. Thiessen, "Carol Gilman and Mary Jane Schneider, 'The Way to Independence,' " *Nebraska History* (Winter 1987): 205–206.

Larry Remele, "'The Way to Independence': An Exhibit Review," *History News* 43 (July/August 1988): 30–33.

Jo Blatti, "Review of 'The Way to Independence," *Oral History Review* 16 (Fall 1988): 121.

Edward Chappell, "Minnesota's 'The Way to Independence,'" *The Nation* 249 (18 December 1989): 763–66.

Donald Garfiled, "This Exhibit is Anchored in History, Saturated with Dignity," *Museum News* 68 (May/June 1989): 26.

Peter Nabokov, "Carol Gilman and Mary Jane Schneider, 'The Way to Independence: Memories of a Hidatsa Indian Family, 1840–1920,' " *North Dakota Quarterly* (Spring 1989): 202–205.

Roger L. Welsch, "Carol Gilman and Mary Jane Schneider, 'The Way to Independence,' " *Winterthur Portfolio* 23 (Winter 1988): 288–89.

Timothy A. Zwink, "The Way to Independence: Memories of a Hidatsa Indian Family, 1840–1920," *Kansas History* (Spring 1988): 146.

Notes

1. Donald Garfield, "This Exhibit is Anchored in History, Saturated with Dignity," *Museum News* 68 (May/June 1989): 26.

2. Larry Remele, "'The Way to Independence': An Exhibit Review," *History News* 43 (July/August 1988): 30–33.

3. Edward Chappell, "Minnesota's 'Way to Independence'" *The Nation* 249 (18 December 1989): 763–66.

4. Carol Gilman and Mary Jane Schneider, *The Way to Independence: Memories of a Hidatsa Indian Family, 1840–1920*, with essays by W. Raymond Wood, Gerard Baker, Jeffrey Hanson, and Alan R. Woolworth, (St. Paul: Minnesota Historical Society Press), 1988.

5. G. Hubert Smith, *Like-a-Fishhook Village and Fort Berthold, Garrison Reservoir, North Dakota*, U.S. Department of the Interior, National Park Service, Anthropological Papers no. 2, (Washington, D.C.: Government Printing Office), 1972.

6. As part of the Common Agenda, Lonn Taylor has issued a contemporary call for a national commitment to the documentation of museum collections. Lonn Taylor, "A Focus for Common Agenda: The Documentation of History Museum Collections," *History News* 44 (May/June 1989): 26–29.

7. See especially pages 285–302, and the essays by Allan R. Woolworth, "Contributions of the Wilsons to the Study of the Hidatsa," 340–47; and Mary Jane Schneider, "A Guide to the Wilson Collections," 348–351.

8. Gilbert L. Wilson, *Agriculture of the Hidatsa Indians: An Indian Interpretation*, Studies in the Social Sciences, no. 9 (Minneapolis: University of Minnesota, 1917; New York: AMS Press, 1979; St. Paul: Minnesota Historical Society Press, 1987).

9. Gilbert Wilson to Clark Wissler, 14 June 1916, Anthropology Department, American Museum of Natural History, New York. Quoted in the exhibit catalog, 287.

10. Ibid. Quoted in the catalog, 346. This approach is completely compatible with modern ethnographic methods. For example, see Oswald Werner and G. Mark Schoeplfe, *Systematic Fieldwork* (Newbury Park, Calif.: Sage Publications, 1987).

11. Quoted in catalog, 347. Original from Robert H. Lowie, *Robert H. Lowie: Ethnologist: A Personal Record* (Berkeley and Los Angeles University of California Press, 1959), 104.

12. Mary Jane Schneider, "A Guide to the Wilson Collections," in *The Way to Independence*, 349. Although, note Lowie's admonitions in 1910 to a potential collector of African materials for the American Museum of Natural History, which follows Wilson's (and Boa's) approaches closely. Quoted in E. Schildkrout, "Art as Evidence: A Brief History of the American Museum of Natural History African Collection," In A. Danto, ed. *ART/artifact: African Art in Anthropology Collections*, (New York: Center for African Art), 153–59.

13. Leslie Spier, *Plains Indian Parfleche Designs*, University of Washington Publications in Anthropology, vol. 4, no. 3 (Seattle: University of Washington Press, 1931).

14. Henry Glassie, *Folk Housing of Middle Virginia: A Structural Analysis of Historic Artifacts* (Knoxville: University of Tennessee Press, 1975); idem, *Patterns in Material Folk Culture of the Eastern United States* (Philadelphia: University of Pennsylvania, 1968).

15. Minnesota Historical Society, "NEH Planning Grant Proposal (1983), 10.

16. *The Way to Independence*, Introduction, xi.

17. Minnesota Historical Society, "NEH Implementation Grant Proposal" (1985), 18. Emphasis in original.

18. Ibid., 15.

19. Ibid., 18.

20. Ibid., 20.

21. For a historical account of the politics that led to the Missouri dams, see Michael L. Lawson, *Damned Indians: The Pick-Sloan Plan and the Missouri River Sioux, 1944–1980* (Norman: University of Oklahoma Press, 1982).

22. *The Way to Independence*, xi.

23. *The Way to Independence*, viii.

24. G. Hubert Smith, *Like-a-Fishhook Village and Fort Berthold, Garrison Reservoir, North Dakota.*

25. Jo Blatti, "Review of 'The Way to Independence' Exhibit," *Oral History Review* 16 (1988): 121.

26. W. Roger Buffalohead "Review of The Way to Independence Catalog," *Oral History Review* 16 (1988): 122–24.

27. See Mihaly Csikszentmihalyi and Eugene Rochberg-Halton, *The Meaning of Things: Domestic Symbols and the Self* (Cambridge: Cambridge University Press, 1981). On page 16 they comment that "the things that surround us are inseparable from who we are. The material objects we use are not just tools we can pick up and discard at our convenience; they constitute the framework of experience that gives order to our otherwise shapeless selves."

COLLECTIONS AND COMMUNITY IN THE GENERATION OF A PERMANENT EXHIBITION
The Hispanic Heritage Wing of the Museum of International Folk Art

Michael Heisley

Author's note. This essay is based on tape-recorded interviews that I conducted with members of the Museum of International Folk Art (MOIFA) staff from 2–5 April 1990, in Santa Fe, New Mexico. From these interviews and subsequent conversations and correspondence, I have attempted to reconstruct the process through which the idea for the Hispanic Heritage Wing evolved from concept to final installation of the "*Familia y Fe*" exhibition in that space. My task was greatly assisted by the willingness of the MOIFA staff and others to share their recollections with me, and I am very grateful to them for their cooperation. I underscore my reliance on oral history as a principal source in order to emphasize two aspects of my information gathering for this essay. First, as with any oral recollections, these sources are subject to the limitations, distortions, and idealizations that are a part of any account based on human memory. This was made especially clear to me by the comments of some with whom I spoke who observed that our interviews were conducted at "a good time" i.e. nine months after the exhibition's opening when memories of the frazzled nerves and frustrations had subsided sufficiently for them to be "objective" about the process of developing the "*Familia y Fe*" exhibition. Such admissions suggest to me that the recollections that I recorded may have been colored by the successful final outcome of the exhibition and the subsequent positive public reaction to it. In short, being a latecomer on the scene has some disadvantages for the reviewer who must comment not just on the finished product in the gallery but also on the dynamic process which brought the exhibition into being. I should also note that this essay is based primarily on conversations with MOIFA curators and administrators. Unfortunately, the time I had available did not allow me to interview the dozens of professional and community consultants and the artists who gave their time to make this exhibition a reality.

The second point which I wish to make is that while I consulted written resources such as memos, grant proposals, and insightful reports by consultants, the recollections of the individuals involved proved to be the most informative sources for understanding how the exhibition evolved. Their memories provide windows into the participants' *perceptions* of the exhibition process. Many decisions are made in face-to-face meetings of which there are no records and—as with most enterprises in the twentieth century—important discussions frequently take place on the telephone and rarely leave the kind of written documents that one would like.

Charlene Cerny interviewed for the position of director of the Museum of International Folk Art in 1984. She remembers from the interview a puzzling but revealing comment made to her by one of the members of the museum's Board of Regents. "He said to me," recalls Cerny, who was at that time a curator at the museum and was later selected for the position of director, "Why is it that you never show your Spanish Colonial or Hispanic collection?" The statement puzzled her, for as she remembered, "At that moment we had three concurrent exhibits of Spanish Colonial arts going on." The trustee's statement, although strictly speaking inaccurate, expressed a perception that Cerny believed many Hispanic New Mexicans held: that, in spite of numerous exhibitions on the subject, the museum had not fully recognized the cultural contributions of the local Hispanic population. Underlying the trustee's statement was the perception that MOIFA had never dedicated a *permanent* space in its galleries for exhibiting and interpreting its extensive collections of New Mexican Hispanic folk art.[1]

Not long after taking the helm at MOIFA in April 1984, Cerny instituted a long-range planning process involving both the museum's staff and the board of trustees of the International Folk Arts Foundation (IFAF), a private non-profit corporation that assists in raising funds for the museum's operations. The plans for the museum's future included the development of a new permanent gallery dedicated to exhibitions of Hispanic folk art from the Spanish Colonial period to the present. This long-range planning process was the initial step leading to the inauguration of the Hispanic Heritage Wing and the "*Familia y Fe*" ("Family and Faith") exhibition, the first long-term exhibition in the space which opened on 7 July 1989.

The idea for such an exhibition did not originate with Cerny's becoming director of the museum. MOIFA, which has long been a center for folk art studies in the region, has over five thousand objects in its extensive Spanish Colonial and Hispanic folk art collections. The collections contain materials dating from the 1700s to the present including religious art, textiles, furniture and household items, tin work, and straw applique. Although MOIFA was founded less than forty years ago, its collections were amassed beginning in the mid-nineteenth century by the Historical Society of New Mexico and subsequently by others such as the Fred Harvey Company in the late 1800s and by private collectors such as the museum's founder Florence Dibell Bartlett in the 1920s. In addition to its own collections, MOIFA (a unit of the state's Museum of New Mexico) also houses on long-term loan the collections of the Spanish Colonial Arts Society, the International Folk Art Foundation, the Archdiocese of Santa Fe, and the School of American Research. The circumstances under which most of the collections were gathered are varied and reflect the characteristics of the ethnic art market in the Southwest during the past century.[2]

Since the arrival of the Santa Fe Railway in the 1880s, New Mexico has been an area in which "ethnic tourism" has strongly influenced the perception of and market for traditional arts.[3] In addition, a series of craft revivals beginning in the 1920s and encouraged primarily by Anglo-American artists and writers also influenced the styles and production of traditional arts from the northern part of the state.[4] During the 1930s, federal funds for traditional artists through Works Progress Administration (WPA) supported vocational schools further encouraged Hispanic craft production for outside markets and was another factor that altered the role of traditional artists in their communities.[5]

In many respects the collecting, encouragement, and marketing of folk art in New Mexico parallels the discovery of American folk art in general by galleries and museums in the 1920s and 1930s.[6] Although a few Hispanics aided the discovery, much of the early interest in the folk art was stimulated by the aesthetic tastes and preservationist views of outsiders.[7] Virginia Domínguez's comment on the amassing of "ethnological collections" in the late nineteenth and early twentieth centuries by museums and collectors also rings true for the collecting of Hispanic folk art in New Mexico: "everything about the collection itself—the way the objects were collected, why they were collected, and how and why they get displayed—points to us."[8] Perhaps in part because these collections were gathered largely under the impetus of outsiders, the exhibition *and* interpretation of New Mexican folk arts at MOIFA were of particular concern to members of the state's Hispanic community. In addition, the commercial importance of folk art in the state—and particularly in the northern counties where many Hispanic folk artists reside—also colors the views of the Hispanic community about the interpretation of their own folk art. In this context, it became important for the museum to define the significance of traditional arts in terms other than those of the commercial marketplace.

MOIFA is located in a region in which Hispanics have had a significant and continual presence for centuries.[9] Given the museum's proximity to the community from which much of the collections came, MOIFA recognized and dealt with several important challenges in the exhibition development process considered in this essay. The first challenge addressed the need for a permanent space in which to exhibit and recognize the Hispanic traditions of New Mexico. Second, the museum staff needed to provide an interpretive framework for the exhibit that was culturally sensitive and that would encompass the wide variety of objects and the long span of historical periods represented in MOIFA's New Mexican Hispanic collection. Finally, the museum recognized the importance of involving the local Hispanic population in the exhibition's planning and in the ongoing programs that accompany the long-term exhibition.

The development process for the "*Familia y Fe*" exhibition and related public programs involved over eighty project staff and outside consultants as well as numerous volunteers in a variety of tasks including extensive gallery renovations, research, field documentation, public programs, and the production of an interactive video disc program, a compact disc audio program, and a sixteen-page gallery guide. The planning phase of the exhibition process included architectural plans followed by building renovations that took place between 1985 and June 1988. The implementation phase of the project including production of the audio and video programs, the installation of the exhibition, and development of public programs began in July 1988 and concluded one year later. Due to the complexity of the exhibition development process, I concentrate in this essay principally on two interrelated aspects of developing folk art exhibitions that are well represented in the production of the Hispanic Heritage Wing. First, the exhibition illustrates many of the issues that arise in attempting to connect the past with the present in the interpretive components of folk art exhibitions.[10] Second, the development of the "*Familia y Fe*" exhibition demonstrates some of the challenges involved when a museum seeks input in the planning and implementation of an exhibit from members of the community whose culture is being presented.

The Project Team

The principal challenge in the early phases of the exhibition process required the museum staff to assemble a team capable of carrying out this ambitious project. The fund-raising effort for the exhibition (along with handling relations with the board of regents and the public) required much of Cerny's time and necessitated hiring an assistant director.[11] The latter position was filled by Stephen Becker and consisted of consulting with the curatorial staff in writing proposals and of tracking the numerous budgets and reports which the planning and implementation of the exhibition required. Donna Pierce, curator of Spanish Colonial Collections, and Helen Lucero, curator of New Mexican Hispanic Crafts and Textiles, served as codirectors at the beginning of the project. Pierce joined the MOIFA staff in 1983 as the assistant director, and Lucero assumed her curatorial position in 1984. Pierce, the principal author of the planning grants submitted to the National Endowment for the Arts (NEA) and the National Endowment for the Humanities (NEH) in June 1986, resigned from the museum in October 1987, near the end of the planning phase of the Hispanic Heritage Wing. William Wroth, her replacement, previously served as a planning consultant to MOIFA on the project. An ethnohistorian with extensive curatorial experience in Hispanic folk art at the Taylor Museum of the Colorado Springs Fine Arts Center, Wroth resides in Bloomington, Indiana.[12] During the implementation stage of the project, he was codirector of the Hispanic Heritage Wing project with Lucero. His work focused on developing the interpretive concepts and components of the exhibition and on writing the label texts and selecting most of the objects displayed in the Hispanic Heritage Wing. Lucero, although partly involved with these aspects of the exhibition, filled a number of nontraditional curatorial roles. A Hispanic and native of northern New Mexico, she dealt with local artists and community consultants, fielded numerous requests for media interviews about the project, and assisted the consultants who documented contemporary traditional artists for the audio and video programs produced for the exhibition. Robin Farwell Gavin began work at MOIFA as Pierce's assistant with the Spanish Colonial collections and was promoted to Pierce's curatorial position in March 1988. Her duties included assisting Wroth during the planning phase of the project. During the implementation phase of the exhibit, she coordinated the in-house aspects of the interactive video disc production with the outside consultants and helped compile the seven exhibit books used to track the objects selected for the exhibition. She also reviewed and edited all label text for the exhibit and video disc program. Rounding out the curatorial team were three curatorial assistants who worked exclusively on the Hispanic Heritage Wing project.

Four staff members outside of the curatorial department played key roles in the exhibit. Julie Bennett, the staff designer, worked from a general floor plan developed by the project architects and the outside design consultants and was responsible for the gallery installation and much of its New Mexican ambience. Claire Munzenrider, chief conservator of the Museum of New Mexico, directed a team of contract conservators who carried out a NEA-funded survey of three thousand Hispanic folk art objects at MOIFA and prepared the objects selected for the exhibition. Tom McCarthy, the museum's staff videographer, worked with the curatorial staff and Wilson Learning Corporation to produce the moving video materials for inclusion in the exhibit's interactive video disc program. Finally, Dana Everts, the New Mexico State Folk Arts Coordinator, developed the series of craft demonstrations, classes, and performances by Hispanic traditional artists and musicians which took place at the museum during the first year of the exhibition.

Exhibition Concept and Planning

In December 1985, MOIFA's curatorial and conservation staff began developing ideas for planning grant proposals for the Hispanic Heritage Wing. By April 1986, project codirector Pierce had contacted ten scholars and museum professionals from throughout the country concerning their willingness to serve as humanities consultants and received agreements from all of them to participate in the NEH planning grant for the project. (For a listing of all consultants identified in the NEH grant proposals, see the Institutional Profile.) To assist in the planning of the exhibition, MOIFA curators also organized two additional groups of consultants consisting mostly of Hispanic individuals residing in New Mexico. The two groups included twelve resource consultants who advised curators on specific exhibition topics related to their individual areas of scholarly expertise and fourteen community consultants—teachers, artists, and community organizers. Whereas the humanities consultants guided museum staff in the conceptual planning of the exhibit, the exhibit planners sought the advice of the resource and community consultants primarily on questions relating to issues of authenticity and cultural sensitivity. In June 1986, MOIFA submitted planning grant applications to NEA (Utilization of Museum Resources Program) and to NEH (Museums and Historical Organizations Program).

In the NEH planning grant proposal, the working title adopted for the exhibition was "New Spain, The Northern Frontier: Traditions and Art in New Mexico." In the proposal, Pierce explained that:

the exhibition will explore variations in the cultural atmosphere of the northern frontier created by changing political, social, and economic conditions. The exhibition will focus on both the Colonial period as well as contemporary Hispanic crafts, and strives to connect these traditions and explore the important decades of the 1920s and 1930s when survival and revival overlapped.[13]

In the initial plan, the exhibition would have consisted of two sections. The first would have been historical in organization and focused on the character of each of the past four centuries of New Mexican history. The second section was thematic and divided into the following categories: "Adaptation, Acculturation, and Accommodation," "Traditions through Time," Traditions through Space," and "Other American Frontiers." The latter section would have been a comparison of the impact of early Hispanic Catholic and Anglo-Saxon Protestant cultures on the settlement of their respective areas of what is now the United States. The ambitious and wide-ranging character of the early plan in many respects was an effort to present and interpret the depth and diversity of MOIFA's Hispanic collections and to relate the planned exhibition to the Columbian Quincentenary. The plan emphasized a view of traditional culture as a reflection of broad historical processes such as conquest, colonization, migration, immigration, and adaptation to the local environment.

The planning period that followed brought about substantial revisions in the concept of the exhibition. In early 1987, the MOIFA curatorial department embarked on a rigorous schedule of research and meetings with consultants hired under the NEA and NEH planning grants. Humanities scholars individually and in groups of three travelled to Santa Fe for one- to four-day meetings with the staff during the first eight months of the year. The administrative and curatorial staff also interviewed, selected, and met with consultants and in-house personnel about the interactive video disc, audio program, exhibition design, conservation, and public program aspects of the exhibition. In addition, the curatorial team visited numerous collections in Arizona, California, Colorado, New Mexico, Washington, D.C., Mexico City, and Puebla, Mexico, to research artifacts, photograph collections and to consult with curators and scholars. From the research and consultations, the staff developed a preliminary list of objects for the exhibit, located many historical photographs and other documentation, produced preliminary plans for the video disc, and refined the exhibition's original concept.

An early expression of the revised concept appeared in a memo dated 16 March 1987, from Wroth to Pierce and Lucero stating his preference for "the cohesiveness and stability of traditional Hispanic culture" as the focus of the exhibition in the following manner:

> With unity or cohesiveness as the organizing concept [of the exhibition], its different modalities, meanings and visual expressions can be developed. Religion is the most important aspect of this unity. In contrast to 50 or 100 religions in modern (and 19th century) America, traditional Hispanic culture had one, Catholicism, which organized all aspects of life. The social order, hierarchical and

structured, provided another source of unity, particularly at the community level. The family is a third source and expression of unity. The highly cohesive extended family contrasts sharply with the atomized American family of today.[14]

In a draft of the implementation grant to NEH prepared by Pierce in September 1987, the exhibition's title, "*Familia y Fe*," first appears along with seven proposed sections of the Hispanic Heritage Wing: "Introduction to Family and Faith/*Familia y Fe*," "Connections" [about Spanish Colonial influences], "Family Environment," "Faith," "Agents of Change and Revival," "Landscape and Climate," and "Changing Gallery." These proposed elements reflected the staff's first crystallization of the exhibition's major components. These elements would be elaborated (some considerably more than others) and adapted to the remodeled gallery spaces in the exhibition. Although these themes are in some respects similar to those expressed in the earlier plan, there is a greater emphasis on cultural *unity* in the final concept of the exhibit which emerged from the planning process and which was incorporated into the implementation grant sent to NEH at the end of 1987.

The differences between the two concepts of the exhibition are subtle but worth exploring because of the distinctive ways in which they portray folk art traditions as manifestations of Hispanic cultural continuity. In some respects— to draw an analogy from United States anthropological research—the two approaches may be compared with the explanations and emphases found respectively in the works of Franz Boas and Clyde Kluckhohn.[15] The earlier conception of the exhibition has similarities with Boas's concern with the historical forces shaping the formation of (in this case) material culture traditions, geographical distribution of cultural traits, and the effects of cultural contact. The latter conception of the exhibit associated with the title "*Familia y Fe*" places its emphasis on the selected elements of Hispanic culture which, as Kluckhohn suggested about myths and rituals, "are important agencies in the transmission of a culture. . . [that]. . . act as brakes upon the speed of culture change."[16] To be sure, the revised concept incorporated many of the cultural-historical approaches and the concerns with recent craft revivals of the earlier plan, but differences also are apparent in the final installation of the exhibit. For example, the title focuses attention on family life and Catholicism and in doing so lends a more thematic rather than chronological character to the exhibition's narrative and physical layout. In addition, when the exhibit's focus shifted to issues of family and Catholicism, concerns with conflict from within and with other groups were down played. The new emphasis also reflects the types of objects the staff selected for the exhibition and consequently the work of the conservators. The staff originally estimated using seventy polychromed *santos* (carved wooden saints) in the exhibit, but in the revised exhibit plan, the final number reached a total of 144 under Wroth's direction. The revision to the exhibit more than doubled the work that conservators had planned for these objects, which required complex and time-consuming conservation treatment.

The planning phase also required community input from a series of four planning workshops hosted by MOIFA and Mazrid Associates, the architectural consultants. MOIFA began community workshops in the fall of 1985, and they focused on the proposed exhibit's design, interpretive themes, modes of presentation, and public programs. The suggestions and concerns expressed by local citizens, many of whom were from the Hispanic community and included artists, community activists, scholars and political leaders, focused on three principal areas: (1) the need to portray the present vitality of Hispanic culture and not show it as a thing of the past, (2) the need to portray the objects in the

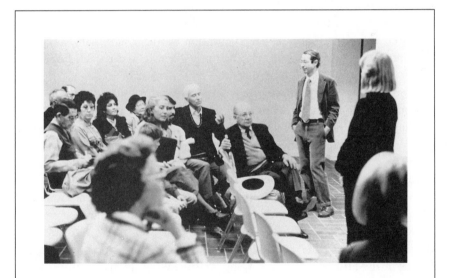

Project codirector William Wroth and MOIFA director Charlene Cerny address a meeting on 20 February 1988, for members of the New Mexican Hispanic community during the planning stage of the exhibition. At this meeting, community preferences for local and natural materials in the exhibit were voiced after seeing preliminary drawings by the design consultant.

Photo by Helen Lucero.
Courtesy Museum of International Folk Art.

exhibition in a respectful and dignified manner, and (3) the need to involve as many Hispanics as possible in the construction of the exhibition.

A meeting held in February 1988 at MOIFA sought to elicit the community's response to the nearly completed planning process. Approximately forty-five community members attended the meeting to hear presentations from the museum staff about the exhibition and to view the preliminary plans and schematic drawings produced by Rogow and Bernstein, the exhibition design consultants. Although MOIFA intended to use the design firm's plans primarily to convey the general layout and floor plan of the exhibit, the community responded principally to the appearance and style of the installation depicted in the consultant's drawings. As Cerny recalled, "It was a tough, tough meeting. What we were being told is . . . that [community members] didn't like the design." They objected, in part, to the design depicted in the consultant's illustrations as being, in Cerny's words, a modern "expo-ish" presentation. The rendering of the design ran counter to the community's preferences for local and natural materials in the exhibit's construction. At the time of the community meeting, the design consultant's work was somewhat more advanced that the curators' conceptualization of the gallery space, and thus, community members responded in actuality to a design that did not fully reflect the exhibit's eventual appearance. This situation changed after the curators completed their research and conferred with staff designer Bennett concerning ways to integrate community design suggestions in to exhibit.

During the implementation phase of the project, Bennett incorporated many of the community's concerns into the layout and appearance of the galleries. At the suggestion of the community advisors, the final design called for the following: the use of natural materials in the exhibit's construction, an architectural design that included exterior views and light, the incorporation of "intangible" cultural expression through the inclusion of an audio program with folklore and spoken recollections by Hispanic New Mexicans, a recognition of the present vitality of Hispanic culture through the inclusion of a changing gallery in the Hispanic Heritage Wing, and the covering of an existing open patio in the museum's main building to accommodate year-round demonstrations by traditional artists and performers.

Not all of the project's consultants were in agreement with the conceptual focus of the exhibition. Indeed some of the humanities and community consultants recommended topics that suggested conflicts and differences within the community, such as the distinctive roles of women and the place of New Mexican families who enjoyed an elite status through their ownership of large flocks of sheep. In addition, others mentioned the significance of the land and water (especially the *acequia* system of irrigation ditches) in New Mexican agricultural lifestyles—features that do not figure prominently in the exhibit. One humanities consultant expressed other concerns about the exhibition's emphasis in a memo to Pierce: "It seems to me that you need to be especially careful to range widely geographically in the state of NM. . . . Ideally, your clientele should include Hispanic peoples from throughout the state. The Hispanic heritage is not just the Rio Arriba in a V north of Santa Fe."[17] These criticisms suggest some of the limitations of the exhibition's conception and emphases. The consultant's comments also reveal the exhibit's tendency to interpret Hispanic culture from the perspective of the collection's strengths which closely parallel the emphasis on cultural unity developed in the project's planning. Thus, religious objects and family crafts are emphasized over, for example, occupational or ecological factors.

Exhibition Design and Installation

The Hispanic Heritage Wing incorporates four very different spaces into one exhibition: a courtyard entry or atrium of 1,136 square feet, which functions as an introductory area; a main gallery of 2,230 square feet which, contains the "*Familia y Fe*" exhibit; a changing gallery of 570 square feet, which primarily features traditional materials by contemporary crafts persons, and a glass-walled *mirador* (viewpoint) at one end of the atrium, which provides a view of the surrounding mountains and countryside.[18] MOIFA turned to Mazrid and Associates for the project's architectural renovations, completed in 1987.[19] Rogow and Bernstein, a Los Angeles design firm, developed a floor plan and schematic drawings of the exhibition that were submitted as a part of the project's NEH implementation grant proposal in late 1987. Codirector Wroth and designer Bennett developed most of the interpretive and design features in the introductory area and the main gallery, modifying to some extent the Rogow and Bernstein floor plan. Helen Lucero worked with the Hispanic artisans who produced doors, windows, and the title wall image for the exhibition, and she organized the opening exhibition for the changing gallery. Robin Farwell Gavin coordinated the production of the interactive video disc program in the gallery, a project which involved as much research and writing on the part of the curatorial staff as the exhibition itself. The curators frequently disagreed with the revisions that writers for the video consultants made in the program's script. The clashes—sometimes over cultural and historical accuracy and at other times over the style appropriate for a popular video presentation— greatly increased the time required to produce this element of the exhibit.

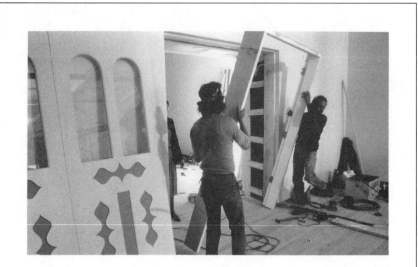

Installation in the Hispanic Heritage Wing of doors made by Aurelio Pacheco in the style of the carpenters of Penasco, New Mexico. Hispanic craftsmen were commissioned to produce doors, windows, and the title wall design using traditional designs and materials..

Construction on the exhibit began in February 1989, and object installation began in early June and was completed for the 7 July 1989 opening.

Community involvement, which began during the planning stage of the project, took different forms during installation of the exhibit. Consultants were brought in to advise staff members on the "period rooms." A local plasterer assisted the exhibition crew in finishing the gallery walls with the correct color and consistency of natural earth finishes such as *tierra blanca* and *tierra amarilla*. Hispanic artisans were commissioned for the doors and a window in the gallery. At a final community meeting held in May 1989, Cerny reported the specific ways in which community suggestions were incorporated during the implementation phase of the project. Reading from a list of twenty-four community suggestions made at the February 1988 community meeting mentioned above, she explained the steps taken to implement twelve of the

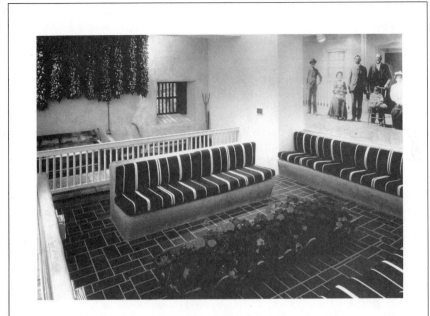

The introductory area or courtyard of the Hispanic Heritage Wing is lit by a large skylight and includes a photo mural of a Hispanic family from the village of Cordova, New Mexico, ca. 1910. Bancos or benches are covered with traditional weavings commissioned for the exhibit and provide a place for visitors to listen to the audio program.

Photo by Michel Monteaux.
Courtesy Museum of International Folk Art.

suggestions and the possibilities for addressing others in the future through public programs and possible additions to the wing.[20]

The Hispanic Heritage Wing

The high natural light levels from the atrium's skylight in the exhibit's introductory area presented a challenge for Wroth and Bennett. Natural light in the gallery was one of the requests made during the community meetings in the planning phase. Because of the high light levels, staff located many of the larger interpretive elements that do not incorporate objects in this area. The introductory area in the atrium, entered through a pair of unpainted hand-carved doors (one of four sets commissioned for the exhibit), has white walls and a slate floor and is the largest open area of the exhibit. The exhibition's logo at the entry is a life-sized color mural of the Holy Family adapted by Charles M. Carrillo from a painting by a nineteenth-century New Mexican *santero* (maker of saints' images). A series of four silk-screened maps show different periods of New Mexican history and the changing political boundaries and trade routes between Mexico and the United States. A life-sized photomural of three generations of a Hispanic family from the village of Córdova, New Mexico, in 1910, and a full-sized reconstruction of a *portal* (porch) of an adobe home cover two walls of this area. Nineteenth-century household and agricultural implements are displayed on the *portal.* The central and visually dominant elements of the introductory area include three *bancos* (couchlike benches covered with locally produced weavings) for visitors listening to the exhibit's audio program and an acrylic covered scale model of an 1840's New Mexican village plaza and church. The base of the scale model conceals the speakers and sound equipment for the audio program.

The visual impact of the interpretive elements in the sunlit atrium suggests the "sunshine and adobe" ambience for which New Mexico is well known, but designer Bennett has skillfully avoided the excesses associated with the recent infatuation with "Santa Fe Style."[21] The clustering of life-sized images, maps, and the audio program in the introductory area evokes the historical presence of Hispanic people in New Mexico's arid and often harsh environment. The audio program has excellent sound quality, but visitors can not make selections among the three-and-one-half hours of music, song, and narration, a limitation to its usefulness for learning and study.[22] Given the acoustics of the room, noise from large crowds sometimes overpowers the program. Rather than introducing the themes developed in the "*Familia y Fe*" exhibition, which follows in the main gallery, the introductory area suggests a historical and architectural context for what comes after it and provides important symbolic expression of Hispanic cultural and linguistic continuity and vitality through the audio program.

The main gallery's "*Familia y Fe*" exhibition is the core of the Hispanic Heritage Wing. It contains three distinctive display areas: a section depicting the role of the Catholic faith in the folk art of Hispanic New Mexico, an area devoted to artifacts and architecture relating to family economy and home life, and an "Agents of Change" area that interprets the effects of outside influences on Hispanic folk art production following the annexation and settlement of New Mexico by the United States in 1846. The transition from the brightness of the atrium to the dimly lit main gallery is marked by wood flooring and a distinctive mud wash on the wall dados suggesting local adobe architecture. Suspended from sections of the overhead lighting grid, *latilla*-style (poles used to form a ceiling) visually distinguish the different thematic subsections of the

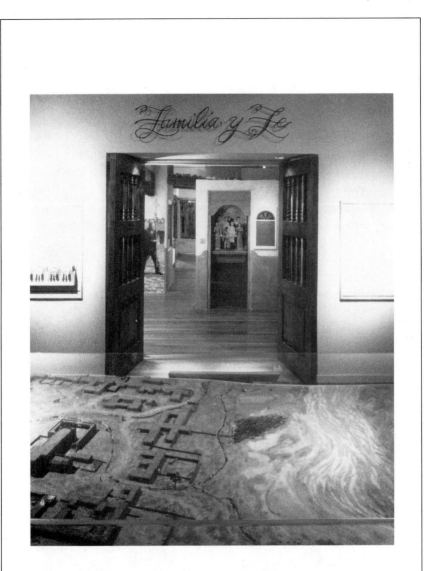

Model of an 1840's New Mexican village plaza and church in the courtyard faces the entry to the "Familia y Fe" section of the Hispanic Heritage Wing.

Photo by Michel Monteaux.
Courtesy Museum of International Folk Art.

gallery. About 90 percent or 324 of the 362 objects in the entire exhibit are concentrated in the main gallery—a space which constitutes only 55 percent of the square footage of the Hispanic Heritage Wing. All of the 56 historical photographs in the wing also appear in the main gallery. Thus, space was at a premium when designing this area of the exhibit, and the object density is much greater than in any other section of the Hispanic Heritage Wing.

A re-created village chapel interior sets the tone of the "Faith" section of the main gallery. The altar and religious objects displayed appear as they might have been used in the 1860s. Upon entering the chapel area, visitors stand on a mud floor and under a ceiling with traditional *viga* (pine log beams), *latilla*, and corbel construction.[23] The remainder of the "Faith" section portrays religion's influence on handmade objects from two standpoints. The first of these relates

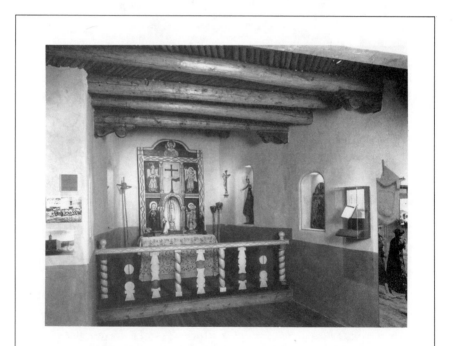

Re-created village chapel interior with alter as it would have appeared in the 1860s. Corbels for ceiling construction are from a local village church and required special installation techniques to protect them during construction of the exhibit.

Photo by Michel Monteaux.
Courtesy Museum of International Folk Art.

the central role of religious faith to individual, family, and community life through objects. For example, a *retablo* (religious painting) in a shepherd's leather bag eloquently conveys the importance of this "portable" religious image in its owner's life. Following this section of the exhibition is one that deals with the sources and analogues of New Mexican religious iconography. Here an art historical approach dominates. Groups of similar objects—mostly *santos* and *retablos*—are exhibited in cases and demonstrate stylistic similarities of these artifacts to other Hispanic and Catholic traditions. The stylistic innovations of eighteenth- and nineteenth-century New Mexican *santeros* are also illustrated.

All objects in the "Faith" section (except those in the chapel interior) are displayed in wall cases. Case linings of maroon ultrasuede and unobtrusive

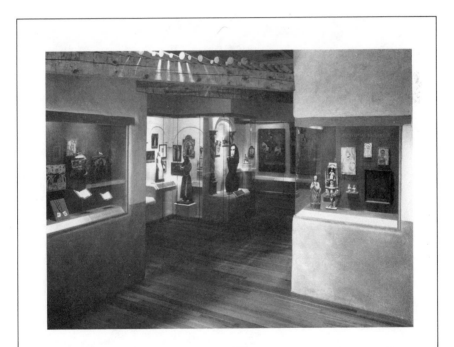

Interior of the "Faith" section of the main gallery with objects illustrating the role of religious folk art in the life of individuals. Overhead latilla-*style ceiling treatment visually indicates the transition to the next section of the exhibition.*

Photo by Michel Monteaux.
Courtesy Museum of International Folk Art.

object and text labels with lettering silk screened in black onto gold tone metal convey a display aesthetic of understated richness.

The second section of *"Familia y Fe"* stresses the continuity of craft traditions among Hispanic families. A genealogical chart of seven generations of weavers from two families in Chimayó, New Mexico, underscores the theme. An arrangement of textiles, a nineteenth-century loom, furniture, ironwork and tools, silver jewelry, and gold filigree dominate one side of the "Family" section. Opposite this display sits a reproduced domestic interior from the same period as the chapel in the "Faith" section. It is the largest and most elaborately interpreted element in the Hispanic Heritage Wing.

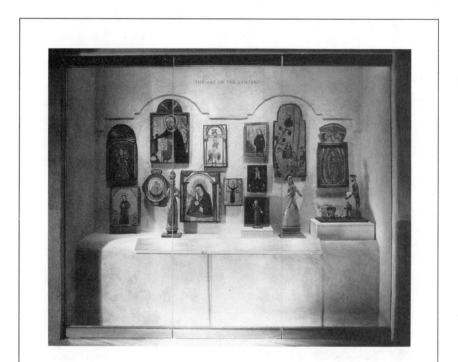

Bultos *and* retablos *illustrating the distinctive work of New Mexican* santeros *are exhibited behind heavy glass doors such as those used for department store entrances. These doors provided excellent access to the cases and eliminated the need for crawl spaces behind the case.*

An interactive video disc program enables viewers to inquire about how each class of objects featured in this "period room" is made and used and to learn more about an object's design history.[24] In addition to enabling the visitor to view 198 additional objects from the collections and 93 historical photos, the video program also includes footage of contemporary artists producing objects similar to those on display and a soundtrack with narrations available in English and Spanish. This program works exceptionally well in terms of informing visitors about the objects in the period room, and its clear and simple options also provide information appropriate to a variety of ages and levels of sophistication. The problems that I encountered with the system are related to

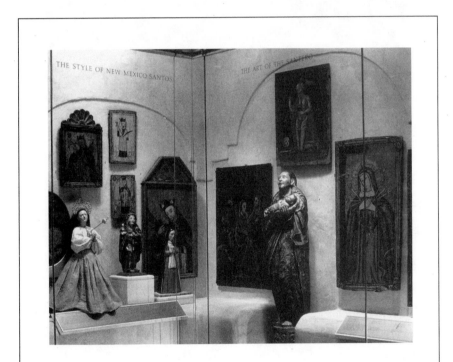

Groupings of santos *and* retablos *demonstrate stylistic similarities of New Mexican artifacts with similar objects from other Hispanic and Catholic traditions. Label placement at the bottom of the case is unobtrusive and encourages visitors to focus on visual and stylistic similarities of the objects.*

Photo by Michel Monteaux.
Courtesy Museum of International Folk Art.

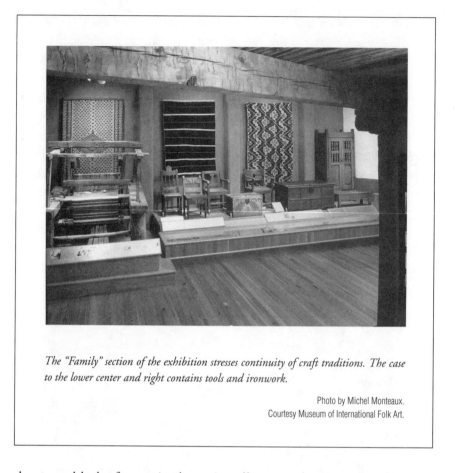

The "Family" section of the exhibition stresses continuity of craft traditions. The case to the lower center and right contains tools and ironwork.

Photo by Michel Monteaux.
Courtesy Museum of International Folk Art.

the general lack of space in the main gallery noted previously. The video program equipment sits near the entrance to the "Agents of Change" section of the main gallery—a transition area, occasionally congested with groups of visitors. There also is no seating for extended viewing of the program. Responses from users such as, "I'd still be there if they had chairs," paralleled my reaction.

Finally, the "Agents of Change" portion of the exhibit portrays the decline in religious art and textile production following New Mexico's conquest by the United States and the rise of tin work and the changes in architectural styles resulting from American influences in the nineteenth century. Also exhibited are traditional crafts such as textiles, furniture, and religious images that emerged from revivals of these traditions spurred by tourism and collectors during the 1920s and 1930s. The remainder of the exhibition consists of the

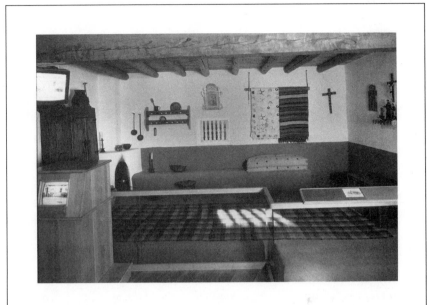

The interactive video system to the left allows visitors to inquire about the production, use, and history of each type of object displayed in this re-created 1860's domestic interior. English or Spanish text and audio may be selected by the user at any time during the program.

Photo by Michel Monteaux.
Courtesy Museum of International Folk Art.

mirador which contains a handful of agricultural implements and didactic text relating to the role of agriculture and the *acequia* system. The changing gallery opened with an exhibition of contemporary folk artists working in many of the traditions found in the main gallery.

Following the opening of the Hispanic Heritage Wing, "*Tradiciones Vivas*" ("Living Traditions"), a year-long series of demonstrations, workshops and performances, presented eight Hispanic crafts persons and seventy performers. The public programs and changing gallery are the most direct and ongoing links between the exhibit and the Hispanic community. For example, the woodworker who made one set of doors in the exhibit taught a woodcarving class, and performers heard on the audio program appeared for evening concerts. These programs and the changing exhibits frequently present other artists not represented in the exhibit whose works show the influences of the

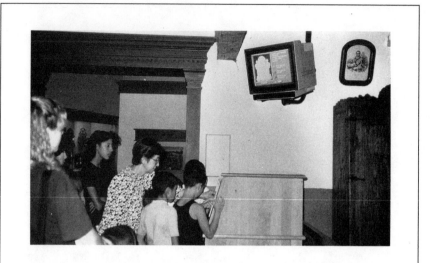

Project codirector Helen Lucero demonstrates the use of the interactive video disc to a youth group from Tierra Amarilla, New Mexico. Part of the community outreach program for the exhibition involved training local high school students to be docents for the Hispanic Heritage Wing.

Photo by Barbara Mauldin.
Courtesy Museum of International Folk Art.

commercial folk art market and new styles and media. Artists and performers representing the resurgence of Hispanic ethnic identity, which often reflects urban as well as rural or village influences, present additional programs.

The museum developed community outreach programs designed to increase Hispanic visitation during the exhibit's first year. MOIFA curators and staff made slide presentations after Sunday Mass at nine northern New Mexican village churches with the intent of connecting the architecture and folk art traditions of these communities to the Hispanic Heritage Wing in Santa Fe. To further encourage Hispanic visitation, presentations were followed by museum-sponsored bus trips from these villages to the exhibit and a training program for Spanish-speaking docents. The response to these outreach efforts was modest: 285 people attended the church presentations and only 142 individuals chose to take the free bus trip to the museum.[25] Nevertheless, over 75 percent of those on the bus tours were first-time visitors, and many returned with family and friends for repeat visits.

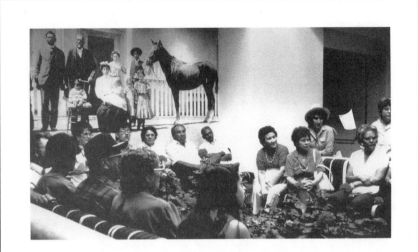

During the first year of the exhibit, a community outreach program brought groups from rural churches to the exhibit on buses chartered by the museum. In this photo members of the Chamita Church group listen to an orientation in the courtyard of the Hispanic Heritage Wing.

Photo by Helen Lucero.
Courtesy Museum of International Folk Art.

MOIFA curators also integrated an innovative cultural preservation effort into the Hispanic Heritage Wing's outreach programs. Aware that some Hispanic communities no longer know the history of their churches and that some individuals could not identify the many saints whose images were inside these structures, the museum's staff sought to share its knowledge of historically significant churches and religious objects. During the Sunday presentations in village churches, MOIFA curators provided information about the history of the church building and its associated *santos* and other religious objects. They also sought information about the local parish's material culture from the parishioners and compiled the information along with the results of their scholarly research relating to that particular church into illustrated binders. MOIFA curators deposited copies of these compilations with each of the nine churches that they visited. Local church members thereby gained access to the documentation needed for researching their own traditions and for conserving the adobe churches and folk art of their communities.

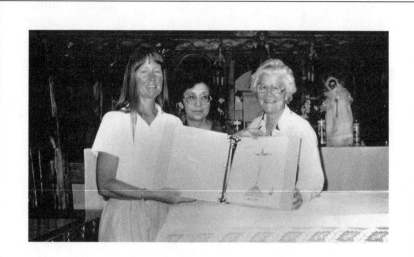

MOIFA curators Barbara Mauldin and Helen Lucero present Sister Ramona Johnson of Córdova, New Mexico, with a notebook of information about artifacts in that village's church. As a part of the museum's outreach program, many Northern New Mexican village churches were presented with similar notebooks based on the research done in preparation for the "Familia y Fe" exhibit.

Photo by Debbie Garcia-Ortéga.
Courtesy Museum of International Folk Art.

Reflections on the Exhibition Process

Compared to other exhibitions at MOIFA, "*Familia y Fe*" occupies a middle ground in terms of the museum's strategies for exhibiting folk art. A permanent exhibition, for example, of the Girard Foundation collection of folk art figures from around the world is displayed in visually exciting arrangements that reflect the artistic eye and tastes of Alexander Girard, the collector and donor. Elsewhere in the museum, a temporary exhibit entitled "Behind the Mask in Mexico" re-creates the social and cultural environments of six masked dance festivals through photomurals, costumed mannequins, and video programs. The exhibit creates a realistic stage set underscoring the masks' relationship to ceremonies in Mexico. Whereas the Girard exhibit immerses objects in the *collector's* imaginative context, the mask exhibition attempts to integrate objects, video, and sound into the home and performance contexts in which the objects were made and used in Mexico.

"*Familia y Fe*," of course, relates folk art objects to the cultural traditions and historical settings from which they came, but the exhibition's organization is thematic and based on conventional museum presentation modes. Objects are arranged (often in cases) with academic organizational schemes (e.g. art history, anthropology, geography). Period rooms and didactic elements such as maps and a scale model also are used. The audio program is not linked to specific displays of objects. As a result, the exhibit portrays a generalized cultural and historical context rather than re-creating the "natural contexts of everyday life" in which crafts and objects were made and used.[26]

To complement the interactive video program, the exhibit included a domestic period room larger than probably existed during the historical era MOIFA portrays. In this instance, the video program required the clustering of examples of architectural features, *bultos* (carved figures of saints) and *retablos*, *colcha* (wool embroidery), furniture, straw applique, tin work, weaving, and ironwork into one room. Determining the content, size, and configuration of the room was further complicated by the lack of precise historical data on home interiors of this period. Consultations with community members to help determine the attributes of the room often yielded conflicting information. In an attempt to resolve these various complications, the exhibit included more furniture and objects than some of the curators felt would have actually been in a single room during this time. Wealthier families would have had these items in two rooms, and poorer families would have had one room homes with fewer objects. Gary Kulik's observation that early American period rooms, the first use of this display strategy in history museums, "were almost always overfurnished by colonial standards" seems to apply also to this modern counterpart at MOIFA.[27] In this instance, however, the concentration of items in the period room was determined mostly by the video program rather than by curatorial tastes.

The "Agents of Change" portion of the gallery was reduced in size during the exhibition development process in order to accommodate the period room. With the reduction of space, many of the important issues about culture contact and exchange and the cross fertilization and "revivals" of craft traditions are only suggested. While "Agents of Change" enables "*Familia y Fe*" to avoid the pitfall of portraying folk art as products of a stereotypically isolated community, the gallery also raises questions about these issues. One such question is implied in the title "Agents of Change." Some visitors may interpret this section as conveying the notion that before American annexation in 1846, social change in this region was insignificant, or perhaps that change can only be measured by the influence of outside (i.e. non-

Hispanic) factors. This notion of social change as coming later and only from "outside" forces is at odds with other interpretations presented in the Hispanic Heritage Wing. For example, maps in two galleries suggest exploration, trade, and pilgrimage routes prior to 1800 that brought "outside" influences and change. The juxtaposition of Pueblo Indian, Saltillo (Mexican), and New Mexican textiles on the same wall in "*Familia y Fe*" indicates that cross fertilization or borrowing of material cultural features among Indians, Spanish, Mexicans, and Anglo-Americans has a long history. Why is continuity emphasized in some parts of the exhibit while this area stresses change?

Curatorial Voices in the Exhibition

During the implementation phase of the project, Wroth became the senior staff person who cleared almost all aspects of the exhibit. His leadership role along with that of Cerny's was crucial to the successful completion of the exhibit. Strong leadership and a commitment to the goals of the project helped solidify a curatorial and design staff with little previous experience in mounting large permanent exhibitions. As an out-of-state resident, Wroth began his work on the implementation phase of the project by spending several months in Santa Fe during the summer of 1988 selecting objects, researching and writing label and text copy, and consulting with the curatorial staff. He returned to the city several times for brief stays during the planning and implementation phases of the exhibit's development. As a guest curator, however, he was frequently out of town and not available to provide the immediate feedback that some of the curatorial staff desired during the installation of the exhibit.

Wroth's position as an outsider and respected curator enabled him to successfully navigate some of the conflicts that arose during the project's implementation phase. For example, the IFAF board of trustees purchased an expensive straw inlaid black cross from a local traditional artist, and some members of the board felt strongly that the piece should be used as the exhibit's logo and title wall image. Wroth and Cerny thought otherwise. As an alternative, Wroth proposed using an enlarged image of the Holy Family, an image that could be painted in color by a contemporary local artist in the style of a nineteenth-century master *santero*. His suggestion helped resolve the conflict and offered something to all parties involved: the board got an appealing logo, and their cross was included elsewhere in the exhibit; curators got their way and resolved a sensitive conflict with trustees; and another local Hispanic artist's work was commissioned expressly for the exhibition. As an outsider, Wroth understood that the successful guest curator must in some instances orchestrate the conflicting wishes of clients.

Project codirector Helen Lucero was the only Hispanic involved in a curatorial position in the production of the Hispanic Heritage Wing.[28] During the exhibition's development, she was acutely aware of her visible role at MOIFA:

> As a Hispanic curator, I . . . find myself in the unenviable position of having to balance my professionalism with my ethnicity. Hispanics come to me as one of them. This means that quite often they do not think it is necessary to make appointments. They also expect me to take their side and understand the difficulties [that] they experience in gaining access to museums. Ideally, they would like me to buy their art work on the spot. When I explain the involved museum procedure by which works are acquired, I share in their disappointment.[29]

As a curator who deals with materials from her own heritage, she often was asked to provide "Hispanic" input for the project, and she was frequently called upon to meet with the media. As the sole Hispanic curator, she found herself in the uncomfortable position of being a spokesperson for an entire ethnic group. While recognizing the importance of her role as "conscience" (to use her word) of the exhibit, she also was aware of the special responsibilities which she bore. "I am a curator in the midst of a living culture," she says. "What I curate," according to her, "is subject to immediate judgment [from the Hispanic community]."[30]

The Hispanic Heritage Wing presents several curatorial voices. One stresses historical connections and continuities in New Mexican folk art with Hispanic and Catholic traditions from outside of the region. This voice is found in the maps and art historical approaches of parts of the exhibit as well as in the visual unity and dominance of *santos* and *retablos* in the "Faith" section of the main gallery. The second curatorial voice speaks to the role of New Mexico as the specific historical setting in which a particular group of Hispanics have created their life style. This voice is discernible visually and audibly in the village model and audio program in the atrium. It is also communicated through the clustering of New Mexican family crafts along one wall of the main gallery and in the "Agents of Change" section. These two voices reflect the two conceptual approaches noted earlier which crystallized during the planning phase of the project. One attribute they share is that they both speak primarily in the past tense. In "*Familia y Fe*," there is a strong *visual* message that Hispanic traditional culture in New Mexico is rural and village based. The dominant interpretive elements—the chapel, domestic interior, and the village model—all reflect these emphases. The curatorial voices in "*Familia y Fe*" also portray New Mexican Hispanic life with a pronounced emphasis on the conservative and conventional aspects of Hispanic culture and Catholicism, and with a strong orientation toward the northern part of the state. Although these thematic and temporal emphases in the exhibition *are* a reflection of the strengths of the MOIFA collection and of New Mexican folklore research in general, they are also conscious curatorial decisions, communicating to the public a particular image of Hispanics in New Mexico.[31] The long-standing and volatile issues of ownership and control of land and water and such potentially controversial subjects as relations between Hispanics and American Indians or the Penitente Brotherhood do not appear in any depth in the exhibition.[32] Urban, industrial life appears only subtly in the Hispanic Heritage Wing in, for example, scenes of craftsmen using power tools in the video program and in the final section of the audio program.

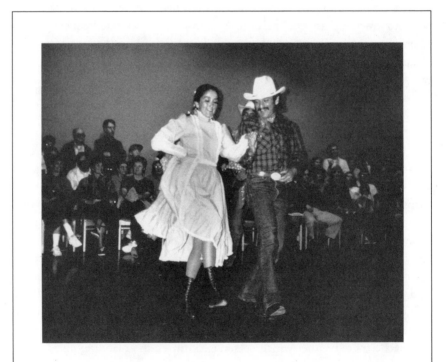

Baile Folklorico del Norte performs in the auditorium for Cinco de Mayo, 1990, as part of "Tradiciones Vivas," a year-long series of demonstrations, workshops, and performances marking the opening of the Hispanic Heritage Wing.

Photo by Dana Everts.
Courtesy Museum of International Folk Art.

Museum staff members contend that as an initial effort at presenting Hispanic culture in a permanent exhibition, the *"Familia y Fe"* concept is justified in its emphasis. As Cerny explained, MOIFA "didn't take a bold approach, we took a pretty conservative approach which I think was appropriate for the first such exhibit." "One of the main thrusts [of the *"Familia y Fe"* exhibit]," noted Cerny, "is that we have this fabulous [Spanish] Colonial collection" and by focusing on contemporary popular culture, "we would have alienated some of the very people we are trying to satisfy." In addition to the exhibit's conceptual underpinnings, the size of the collection and the limited space available for displaying objects (because of the high light levels of the atrium) also may have encouraged the exhibit planners to opt for a view of Hispanic life that stresses unity. Similar thinking accounts for the didactic elements that were object rich, such as the chapel, domestic interior, and the video program. Also perhaps due to the lack of space, the actual representations of people in the object rich main gallery are limited to the video program and historical photographs. No mannequins appear in the domestic interior or elsewhere in the exhibit. The contemporary presence of Hispanics and their material culture traditions today appear principally in the changing gallery separated from the rest of the exhibit's interpretive framework. Contemporary issues also are presented in the audio program and through public programs—elements located outside of the main gallery.

Museum staff made a conscious effort to include the audience—or at least the Hispanic audience—in the exhibit's development. In this regard, the development of Hispanic Heritage Wing exemplifies the "contested terrain" that Steven D. Lavine believes museums have become in recent years as historically excluded groups demand a say in the way in which their heritage is presented.[33] Contestation, in this exhibit, took several forms including the manner of exhibiting objects, the interpretations presented, and the inclusion of Hispanics in the production of the exhibit. The conflicts that arose during the process were usually contained within the parameters set by the institution, however. With the exception of one public clash over the museum's decision to exclude a potentially controversial poem from the audio program, most of the differences with the community took place at meetings called by MOIFA.[34] Although Lucero was the sole Hispanic in a decision-making role on the staff, others from the Hispanic community were involved in a variety of capacities including roles as trustees, staff, consultants, and artists. In this respect, MOIFA both differs from and is similar to other institutions presenting the folk art of their surrounding community. Interest in New Mexican folk traditions by insiders and outsiders has created a somewhat unique blend of scholarship, an active folk art market, and a long-standing but still limited Hispanic involvement in local museums. On the other hand, the New Mexican situation is similar to other parts of the world in which ethnic and tourist arts are a dominant image of the region and folk art is an important commodity. In this context the Hispanic Heritage Wing functions primarily as a counterbalance to commercialization, but due to the economic importance of traditional crafts to the Hispanic community, the exhibition also participates in the commercial valuation of them. By commissioning and exhibiting the works of New Mexican Hispanic artists, the museum enhances the reputations of these artists and thereby adds to the demand for and value of their works in local galleries and in the annual Spanish Market in Santa Fe.

The interpretive and physical separation between the main gallery's emphasis on the past and the recognition of the present in the changing gallery, public programs, and the audio and video programs of the exhibit may be more striking to outsiders than to members of the Hispanic community. The Hispanic Heritage Wing is of great value as a symbolic means of recognizing the Hispanic community's present cultural life as well as its past. Insiders may perceive *santos* carved by a member of a well-known family as symbolizing both past and present efforts to maintain Hispanic cultural identity in New Mexico.[35] At the opening ceremony for the exhibition, a traditional *entriega* composed and recited for the occasion said in part:

En este día provechoso	On this propitious day
con los poderes conscientes,	by the powers that be,
entregamos este museo	we deliver this museum
a su dueño que es la gente.	to its owner, the people.
El museo es la casa	The museum is the home
que nos brindó el estado	the state has given us
para guardar el tesoro	to guard the treasure
que nos enseña del pasado.	that teaches us the past.[36]

The combination of the contemporary act of taking control of the portrayal of one's heritage with sentiments of reverence for the past expressed in these verses suggests the dual influence of the community on the exhibition. On the one hand, the exhibit is a "sacred space" that respectfully and conservatively exhibits the past according to the community's wishes. The valuation of these objects in terms of the community's collective heritage is stressed in this space over that of the present Hispanic folk art market. On the other hand, present-day Hispanic presence is acknowledged separately in the exhibition's layout and programs, and these arenas give voice to the conflict and diversity of views from within the community. Thus, the community's influence exerted restraints on the exhibition process and provided some of its greatest strengths in terms of connecting past and present.

Institutional Profile

Name: Museum of International Folk Art
Location: 706 Camino Lejo, Santa Fe, New Mexico 87501
Size of institution: 75,000 square feet; 120,000 objects
Date of founding: 1953
Number of professional staff: 11

Exhibition Data

Name of exhibition: Hispanic Heritage Wing, "*Familia y Fe*"
Dates of exhibition: 7 July 1989, permanent exhibition
Cost: Approximately $1.2 million
Names and titles of exhibition personnel: Charlene Cerny, Director; Stephen Becker, Assistant Director; Helen Lucero, Curator, New Mexican Hispanic Crafts and Textiles and Project Codirector; Donna Pierce, Curator, Spanish Colonial Collections and Project Codirector (Resigned in October 1987); William Wroth, Guest Curator and Project Codirector; Robin Farwell Gavin, Assistant Curator, Spanish Colonial Collections, and after March 1988, Curator, Spanish Colonial Collections; Andrea Gillespie, Assistant Curator, New Mexican Hispanic Crafts and Textiles; Barbara Mauldin, Assistant Curator, Spanish Colonial Collections; Joan Tafoya, Curatorial Assistant; Julie Bennett, Exhibition Designer; Dana Everts, Public Programs; Tom McCarthy, Film and Video Programs, Museum of New Mexico; Claire Munzenrider, Chief Conservator, Museum of New Mexico; Ian Rosenkrantz, Lighting Designer.
Date of original conception: 1985
Duration of exhibition development process: four years
Sources of funding: National Endowment for the Arts, National Endowment for the Humanities, the New Mexico State Legislature, International Folk Art Foundation, Brown Foundation, Inc., Nonesuch Foundation, L.J. Skaggs and Mary C. Skaggs Foundation, Mountain Bell, PNM Foundation, Inc., Spanish Colonial Arts Society, Hearst Foundation, John Ben Snow Memorial Trust, Gannett Foundation, Binney Foundation, and the Van Vleet Foundation.

Humanities consultants: Richard Ahlborn, Barbara Anderson, Charles Briggs, Adrian Bustamante, John L. Kessell, Yvonne Lange, Marc Simmons, Margaret Vázquez-Geffroy, Marta Weigle.

Resource consultants: Miguel Celorio Blasco, Charles M. Carrillo, Fray Angélico Chávez, Tobias Durán, Reyes Jaramillo, Christine Mather, Ward Alan Minge, Rowena Rivera, Alan Vedder, Elisa Vargas Lugo.

Community consultants: Josefita Córdova, Reynalda Ortíz Dinkel, Edward Gonzales, Margaret Gutiérrez, Arturo Jaramillo, Félix López, Mela Ortíz y Piño de Martín, Pedro Ribera-Ortega, Max Roybal, Pedro Tafoya, Anita Gonzales Thomas, Jacobo Trujillo, Horacio Valdez, Maria Vergara-Wilson.

Design consultants: Dennis Kaysing and Associates (model builders), Mazria and Associates (architectural design), Rogow and Bernstein (exhibition layout and floor plan).

Interactive videodisc program consultants: Wilson Learning Corporation (producers of the video program), Concentrics Inc. (software engineering), Marni Sandweiss, (planning consultant).

Compact audio disc program consultants: Enrique Lamadrid, Jack Loeffler.

Number of objects exhibited: 362

Related programming:

Publications:

Familia y fe. Sixteen-page, illustrated, color gallery guide available free of charge in English and Spanish versions at the entrance to the Main Gallery. (A scholarly publication for the exhibition is planned for 1992, but is not available at the time of this writing.)

Media:

"*Familia*" Interactive video disc program for the main gallery featuring approximately 83 minutes of video programming including 23 minutes of rolling video, 93 historic photographs and 198 object photographs and bilingual narration keyed to the objects in one of the exhibit's period rooms.

Los tesoros del espiritu: familia y fe/ Treasures of the Spirit: Family and Faith (A Portrait in Sound of Hispanic New Mexico). Three compact disc recordings in a boxed set with twenty-four pages of program notes. (This set makes available for sale to the public the entire recorded sound program heard in the atrium of the Hispanic Heritage Wing.)

Other programs:

"La música de los viejitos," a folk festival featuring traditional New Mexican musicians held at the time of the exhibit's opening.

"Tradiciones vivas," a series of twenty-four workshops, demonstrations, and performances in conjunction with the exhibition held at the museum between July 1989 and June 1990.

Traveling Outreach Program consisting of curators visiting thirteen New Mexican communities, giving slide presentations on the background of local churches of historical significance, and providing buses for community members to travel to see the Hispanic Heritage Wing. This program also included training of high school students as docents and brought over 150 Hispanics to the exhibit between October 1989 and October 1990.

Notes

The interviews that I conducted in preparation for writing this essay are listed below. Audio cassette copies of those interviews which were tape recorded at MOIFA are deposited with that institution's library. *Tape-recorded interviews:* Stephen Becker, 4 April 1990; Julie Bennett, 2 April 1990; Charlene Cerny, 4 April 1990; Dana Everts, 4 April 1990; Robin Farwell Gavin and Helen Lucero, 2 April 1990; Robin Farwell Gavin, Helen Lucero, and Barbara Mauldin, 3 April 1990; Barbara Mauldin, 3 April 1990; Claire Munzenrider, 3 April 1990. *Additional interviews:* Helen Lucero, Albuquerque, New Mexico, 11 March 1991; Donna Pierce, telephone conversation, 22 March 1991; Marta Weigle, Santa Fe, New Mexico, 5 April 1990; William Wroth, Bloomington, Indiana, 23 March 1990.

1. In this essay, I use the term *Hispanic* to refer to New Mexicans of Spanish or Mexican descent. It is the name that the MOIFA staff selected as most appropriate for use in the exhibition. Ethnic labels are a matter of self ascription, and for that reason no one term will be universally acceptable for all members of a group. Readers should note that many Hispanic individuals in the state may refer to themselves as *Mexicanos*, Mexican-Americans, Chicanos, or Spanish-americans. Some scholars have adopted the term *Hispano,* to refer to members of this group and their culture. See, for example, Charles L. Briggs, *The Wood Carvers of Cordova, New Mexico: Social Dimensions of an Artistic "Revival"* (Knoxville: University of Tennessee Press, 1980); and Suzanne Forest, *The Preservation of the Village: New Mexico's Hispanics and the New Deal* (Albuquerque: University of New Mexico Press, 1989).

2. For an overview of this story, see Edwin L. Wade, "The Ethnic Art Market in the American Southwest, 1889–1980," in *Objects and Others: Essays on Museum and Material Culture* ed. George W. Stocking, Jr. Vol. 2 of *History of Anthropology*, (Madison: University of Wisconsin Press, 1985), 167–91.

3. For an account of the relationship of tourism to traditional culture in New Mexico, see Marta Weigle, "From Desert to Disney World: The Santa Fe Railway and the Fred Harvey Company Display the Indian Southwest," *Journal of Anthropological Research* 45 (Spring 1989): 115–37. The concept of *ethnic tourism* is defined and elaborated in Valene L. Smith, "Introduction," in *Hosts and Guests: The Anthropology of Tourism*, ed. Valene L. Smith, 2d ed. (Philadelphia: University of Pennsylvania Press, 1989), 1–17 and by Nelson H. H. Graburn, "Tourism: The Sacred Journey" in the same volume, 21–36.

4. See, for example, Sylvia Rodríguez, "Art, Tourism, and Race Relations in Taos: Toward a Sociology of the Art Colony," *Journal of Anthropological Research* 45 (Spring 1989): 77–99; and Marta Weigle, "The First Twenty-five Years of the Spanish Colonial Arts Society," in *Hispanic Arts and Ethnohistory in the Southwest: New Papers in Honor of E. Boyd*, ed. Marta Weigle, with Claudia Larcombe and Samuel Larcombe (Santa Fe: Ancient City Press; Albuquerque: University of New Mexico Press, 1983), 184–86.

5. Forest, *The Preservation of the Village*; and Lorin W. Brown with Charles L. Briggs and Marta Weigle, *Hispano Folklife of New Mexico: The Lorin W. Brown Federal Writers' Project Manuscripts* (Albuquerque: University of New Mexico, 1978).

6. Barbara Kirshenblatt-Gimblett, "Mistaken Dichotomies," *Journal of American Folklore* 101 (April–June 1988): 146.

7. Most of the folklorists of Hispanic descent working in the state concentrated on oral traditions rather than material cultural studies of Hispanic folklife. For an overview of their work see Marjorie F. Tully and Juan B. Rael, comps. *An Annotated Bibliography of Spanish Folklore in New Mexico and Southern Colorado*, The University of New Mexico Publications in Language and Literature, 3 (Albuquerque: University of New Mexico Press, 1950); and Marta Weigle and Peter White, *The Lore of New Mexico* (Albuquerque: University of New Mexico Press, 1988), 441–44.

8. "The Marketing of Heritage," *American Ethnologist* 13 (August 1986): 554.

9. In the 1980 census, 36.6 percent of New Mexico's population was listed as Hispanic with eight out of thirty-two counties having a population of over 50 percent Spanish speaking. These statistics are cited in Maria Barrera, *Beyond Aztlan: Ethnic Automomy in Comparative Perspective* (Notre Dame, Indiana: University of Notre Dame Press, 1988), 166.

10. On this subject, see Willard B. Moore, "Connecting the Past with the Present: Reflections upon Interpretation in Folklife Museums," in *Folklife and Museums: Selected Readings*, ed. Patricia Hall and Charlie Seemann (Nashville: American Association for State and Local history, 1987), 51–58.

11. MOIFA organized an Honorary Board and Steering Committee of fifty-four individuals to assist with fund raising for the Hispanic Heritage Wing. This group included dignitaries, politicians, media personalities, and prominent individuals from New Mexico including numerous members of the Hispanic community.

12. Wroth's publications include *Hispanic Crafts of the Southwest* (Colorado Springs, Colorado: Taylor Museum of the Colorado Springs Fine Arts Center, 1977); *Christian Images in Hispanic New Mexico: The Taylor Museum Collection of Santos* (Colorado Springs, Colorado: Taylor Museum of the Colorado Springs Fine Arts Center, 1982); and *Images of Penance, Images of Mercy: Southwestern Santos in the Late Nineteenth Century* (Norman: University of Oklahoma Press, 1991).

13. "Planning for Inaugural Interpretive Exhibition in the Hispanic Heritage Wing (Columbian Centenary Project)," grant proposal to the National Endowment for the Humanities, 12 June 1986.

14. William Wroth to Donna Pierce and Helen Lucero, memorandum, 16 March 1987. Museum of International Folk Art, Santa Fe, New Mexico.

15. For the perspectives of these two scholars see Franz Boas, "The Growth of Indian Mythologies," in *Studies on Mythology*, ed. Robert A. Georges (Homewood, Illinois: The Dorsey Press, 1968), 15–26; and Clyde Kluckhohn, "Myths and Rituals: A General Theory," 137–67 in the same volume.

16. Ibid., 152.

17. Marta Weigle to Donna Pierce, memorandum, 27 February 1987, Museum of International Folk Art, Santa Fe, New Mexico.

18. Figures for the square footage of each gallery are based on numbers provided in "Background Memorandum: The Hispanic Heritage Wing at the Museum of International Folk Art: a sixteen-page document provided by Media Works of Albuquerque, New Mexico, for the Museum of New Mexico Public Information Office. The document was distributed to the medial prior to the opening of the exhibition.

19. The total cost of the renovations was $600,000. Half of this sum was provided by the New Mexico Legislature and the remainder was raised by MOIFA's Hispanic Heritage Wing Steering Committee from private and public funds. The architectural design fee was $30,670, which was provided by IFAF.

20. In a memorandum entitled "Summary of Community Consultants' Meeting for HHW [Hispanic Heritage Wing]" to Charlene Cerny 25 February 1988, Helen Lucero summarized twenty-four comments and suggestions made by individuals attending the Community Consultants's meeting for the Hispanic Heritage Wing, 20 February 1988. Below is a verbatim excerpt from Lucero's memo that lists the ideas put forth at the meeting. The items marked with an asterisk were the ones that Cerny reported to those in attendance at the May 1989 meeting as having been incorporated into the exhibition.

Attendees' comments and suggestions

*1. Round corners so they will be more in keeping with NM adobe architecture.

2. Soften the edges on the capitals of the two columns in the patio.

*3. Install adobe bancos in the patio or mirador.

*4. Finish the walls with structo-lite to suggest adobe walls.

5. Incorporate water (a fountain?) in the center of the patio.

*6. Include flowers (especially geraniums) in the patio.

7. Include herbs in the patio area that provide smell.

8. Install a manta ceiling in the 1860's period room.

*9. Install an adobe floor in the chapel. Slate floor criticized as wrong.

10. Install a well in the center of the patio.

*11. Address "foodways" in the permanent exhibit.

*12. Consider including old photographs of people in found frames.

*13. In map section, show the Eastern U.S. in relation to the Southwest to provide a larger frame of reference.

*14. Incorporate vigas and latillas into the exhibit.

15. Repaint the outside of the roof to cut down the glare.

*16. Exhibit the saints in a contextual framework, not in rows.

17. Commission Frederico Vigil to make a mural to go over the map area in patio.

18. Purchase "La Comadre," sculpture from Joseph Chavez of Albuquerque to install in the patio or outside the museum to call attention to Hispanic women's contribution.

19. Place more emphasis on the role "la tierra" [the land] played in Hispanic life; land should be given a role equivalent to family and faith.

*20. Address the non-tangible Hispanic values such as respect, honor, continuity, etc.

*21. Mention the male and female roles in all aspects of Hispanic society throughout the exhibit, e.g. role of abuelitas, sacristanas, curanderas, and as the nucleus of families.

22. Mention the role of the families who owned large flocks of sheep. These families were often the patrones, alcaldes of different ordinarios, head of partido systems, and the merchants who traded with Durango, Parral and Chihuahua. As wealthy families, they were often the ones who sent their sons away to study for the priesthood in St. Louis or in Mexico. They were also sought out as padrinos or compadres within their immediate and surrounding communities.

23. Stress the great importance of water and the acequia system and water rights in the lives of hispanics.

24. Address the issue of social customs and manners.

21. The Hispanic heritage Wing was awarded a 1989 Casebook Award for exhibit design by *Print Magazine.*

22. It should be noted that the audio program is available for sale in the museum shop as a set of three compact discs with program notes for those who wish to listen to the program for private study and enjoyment.

23. During the planning of the exhibition, MOIFA had the good fortune to acquire the corbels used in the chapel re-creation from a recently demolished church. They were purchased with funds from IFAF after obtaining approval of the village for their use in the exhibition. One complication was the question of whether or not these items were objects to be accessioned or simply building materials for the exhibit. The corbels were eventually accessioned, and special precautions had to be taken not to harm them when they were installed in the exhibit.

24. For more details on this system and its operation, see Helen R. Lucero, "Touching the Hispanic Spirit: An Audio Program and an Interactive Videodisc System Augment the Exhibitions in the Hispanic Heritage Wing," *El Palacio* 95:1 (Fall/Winter 1989): 57–60; and Rorick Sellers, "CD-ROM Bilingual Assistance for Interactive Multi-Media System," *CD-ROM EndUser* (August 1989): 21–22.

25. These attendance figures are from Helen Lucero, "Traveling Outreach Programs: Re-examining and Rethinking the Traditional," (Paper delivered at the Western Museums Conference Annual Meeting), San Jose, California, 26 October 1990.

26. Robert Baron, "Folklife and the American Museum," in *Folklife and Museums,* 16.

27. "Designing the Past: History-Museum Exhibitions from Peale to the Present," in *History Museums in the United States: A Critical Assessment.* ed. Warren Leon and Roy Rosenzweig (Urbana: University of Illinois Press, 1989), 15.

28. Hispanics are represented on the board of trustees of the International Folk Art Foundation and on the board of regents of the Museum of New Mexico.

29. "Challenges of Being a Minority (Hispanic) in a Culturally Diverse Community" (Paper delivered at "The Challenge of Curating Contemporary Art in a Culturally Diverse Community" conference), Museum of Fine Arts, Santa Fe, New Mexico, 30 June 1990, 2.

30. Ibid., 3.

31. For an overview of New Mexican Hispanic folklore scholarship see Aurelio M. Espinosa, *The Folklore of Spain in the American Southwest: Traditional Spanish Folk Literature in Northern New Mexico and Southern Colorado* (Norman: University of Oklahoma Press, 1985) and Marta Weigle and Peter White, "Selected Resources for New Mexican Folklore: Pioneer New Mexico Folklorists," in *The Lore of New Mexico* (Albuquerque: University of New Mexico Press, 1988), 435–45.

32. The relationship of land and water issues to Hispanic ethnic identity are analyzed in Sylvia Rodríguez, "Land, Water, and Ethnic Identity in Taos," in *Land, Water, and Culture: New Perspectives on Hispanic Land Grants* ed. Charles L. Briggs and John R. Van Ness (Albuquerque: University of New Mexico Press, 1987), 313–403. For other recent scholarship dealing with the role of conflict in the history of the New Mexican Hispanic community, see Rodolfo Acuña, *Occupied America: A History of Chicanos*, 2d ed. (New York: Harper and Row, 1981); John R. Chavez, *The Lost Land: The Chicano Image of the Southwest* (Albuquerque: University of New Mexico Press, 1984); Sarah Deutsch, *No Separate Refuge: Culture, Class, and Gender on an Anglo-Hispanic Frontier in the American Southwest, 1880–1940* (New York: Oxford University Press, 1987); Robert Rosenbaum, *Mexicano Resistance in the Southwest: "The Sacred Right of Self Preservation"* (Austin: University of Texas Press, 1981); and Frances Leon Swadesh, *Los Primeros Pobladores: Hispanic Americans on the Ute Frontier* (Notre Dame, Indiana: University of Notre Dame Press, 1974.)

33. "Museums and Multiculturalism: Who Is in Control?" *Museum News* 68:2 (March/April 1989): 37.

34. David Steinberg, "Albuquerque Poet, Folk Museum Disagree Over Censorship Claim," *Albuquerque Journal*, 14 June 1989, 1 and 3. This controversy revolved around poet E. A. "Tony" Mares's contention that MOIFA had removed his poem entitled "Once A Man Knew His Name" from the exhibition's audio program. Museum officials contended that it was removed from the program because of its length and because the poem was a twentieth-century interpretation of Spanish-Indian relations and therefore was inappropriate in a section of the program that featured readings of seventeenth-century chronicles of the period. Other reasons given for its exclusion were that it was an "oversimplification" of Spanish and Indian relations following the Pueblo Revolt of 1692. In the above article, Mares contended, "It was a rather high-handed exercise of

authority. . . . As far as I am concerned, it was an act of censorship and I don't want to see censorship applied to any work of art."

35. For a detailed analysis of the evolving historical role of santos in maintaining Hispanic identity, see Briggs, *The Wood Carvers of Córdova, New Mexico.*

36. Excerpted from "*Entriega del Museo*" ("Delivery of the Museum") composed by Enrique Lamadrid and recited during the inauguration ceremonies for the Hispanic Heritage Wing, 8 July 1989. The English translation is by the composer.

"FOLKS ROOTS, NEW ROOTS: FOLKLORE IN AMERICAN LIFE"

Serious Intentions, Popular Presentations

Mary Ellen Hayward

Planned originally to celebrate the centennial of the American Folklore Society in 1988, the Museum of Our National Heritage's traveling exhibition "Folk Roots, New Roots: Folklore in American Life" has commanded national, scholarly attention for its attempt to blend the often-warring disciplines of history and folklore. Created by a project team led by cultural historians (then Assistant Director for Museum Programs Barbara Franco and Jane S. Becker, a doctoral candidate in American studies at Boston University) but relying heavily on the input of some of the most respected folklorists in the country, the exhibit began life as a history of the discipline of folklore as it had evolved over the past one hundred years. Conflicts over definitions emerged early: just who were "the folk" at any given time; and, among those who studied them, who were the true folklorists and who were popularizers, social workers, or worst of all, amateurs.

In an attempt to resolve these dilemmas and to create an exhibition that might have more popular appeal, the project team, after the initial planning period, turned the original exhibit script upside down. What had been the dominant theme—the history of the academic practice of folklore—now became a subtheme. The general cultural background of folklore studies in America moved to the exhibit's forefront, and the show focused instead on how changing images and perceptions of "the folk" have affected popular culture and our concepts of national identity. In the development process, an exhibit that began in the discipline of folklore opened its arms to not only academic historians but also gurus of popular culture. Negotiating the shoals between academic communities that strain for definitions and jealously guard territory cannot have been easy. That the project team made the attempt speaks to its credit and intellectual determination. The resulting exhibit, unfortunately, suffered from the strains, disappointing many of its folklorists audience and confusing nonspecialists and the general public. The high level of intellectual content developed for the initial exhibit concept was abandoned in the attempt to popularize the subject. Sure-fire attention-getters like advertising art and 1950's cowboy memorabilia replaced a solid explication of themes.

The exhibit, as conceived by designer Michael Sand, with its interactive stations, audio components, and large-scale "environments," apparently proved appealing to general museum audiences. But, I still have to wonder, what did visitors actually learn about the meaning of folklore, the history of folklore studies, or even the expressed exhibit theme, the popularization of "the folk"? The story of "Folk Roots, New Roots" is a story of very serious intentions but

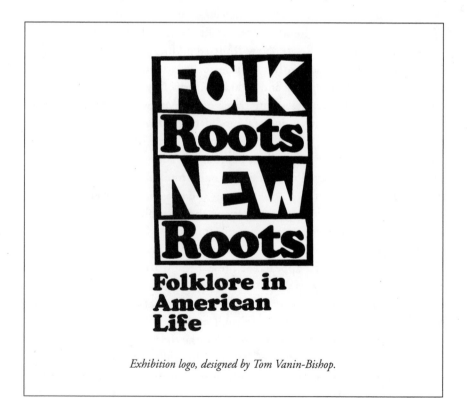

Exhibition logo, designed by Tom Vanin-Bishop.

ultimately of lost opportunities. How those opportunities may have been lost is the subject of this essay.

The Institution and the Exhibit

Opened in 1975 as a history museum devoted to changing exhibits on all aspects of the American past, the Museum of Our National Heritage in Lexington, Massachusetts, has an impressive record of successfully presenting interdisciplinary exhibits to a general public audience. Although founded and sponsored by the Scottish Rite Masons and dedicated to collecting and interpreting materials of fraternal organizations, the museum has a much broader mission. The museum regards itself as an important catalyst in the public's understanding of history and devotes attention to exhibitions and public programs that (1) introduce the public to history and explore historical themes through related disciplines; (2) make primary sources, artifacts, and current scholarship available to the general public; (3) provide visitors with the skills needed to interpret primary materials; and (4) translate the knowledge of specialists and scholars into formats that appeal to a wide audience.

From the museum's inception the institution has specialized in collaborative exhibits, bringing together scholars, community representatives, and collections from both public and private sources to create research-based exhibits that make a solid scholarly contribution and that have popular appeal. A recent example of such an exhibition is "Unearthing New England's Past: The Ceramic Evidence," which focused on the discipline of historical archaeology and which combined the expertise and approaches of ceramic experts, archaeologists, and social historians. "Paul Revere: The Man behind the Myth" (opened at the museum in 1989) employed a variety of primary research tactics to bring to life the complex man who was Paul Revere.

Many of the museum's collaborations are with other New England institutions. Harvard University's Peabody Museum of Archaeology and Ethnology, the Shelburne Museum, and the Society for the Preservation of New England Antiquities make use of the museum's exhibition facilities on a regular basis. Other exhibits showcase private collections interpreted for the public by guest curators and scholars. Many of the collaborative exhibits travel to participating institutions and, farther afield, to related museums that express interest.

"Folk Roots, New Roots," clearly followed the past and present philosophy and the exhibit history of the Museum of Our National Heritage. The exhibit was initially planned in response to a community need: a way of celebrating the one hundredth anniversary of the founding, in Cambridge, Massachusetts, of the American Folklore Society and providing an exhibit experience for AFS members during their annual meeting in Boston in the fall of 1988. The exhibit brought together scholars from several different disciplines; it made their knowledge available to the public in an attractive, often interactive, and clearly self-consciously popularizing manner. Almost all of the objects on exhibit were borrowed from other institutions and private collectors, and the exhibit was designed to travel to three other sites. Although not a collaborative exhibit in the sense of an interaction among two or more different institutions, "Folk Roots, New Roots" represented a collaboration among scholars, resource specialists, and the design team.

"Folk Roots, New Roots" opened at the Museum of Our National Heritage in October 1988, after a development period of more than two years. Major implementation funding ($235,449) came from the National Endowment for the Humanities; initial planning funds ($11,900) came from the Massachusetts Council on the Arts and Humanities. Michael Sand, Inc., of Boston served as the designer. As opened in Lexington, the exhibit occupied some 3,600 square feet of space. It first moved to the McKissick Museum at the University of South Carolina in Columbia for a three-month stay from August to November 1989. In April 1990, it reopened at the Strong Museum in Rochester, New York, for another three-month venue before traveling on to the Oakland Museum in California for an August to November 1990 showing.

The exhibit features seven thematic units that are essentially chronological, depicting how Americans have perceived, interacted with, and popularized "the folk" from the 1880s to the present. There is an introductory audio-visual presentation (a multiprojector slide show) and an interactive computer station at the exhibit's conclusion. Motion activated audio units and button operated headsets dispersed throughout the exhibit present the music that is such a crucial element of the story line. The publication accompanying the exhibit contains a series of essays that more-or-less relate to the various exhibit units; it is in no sense an exhibit catalog, although it does provide illustrations of some of the more interesting images used in the exhibit.

A three-projector slide show serves to introduce the visitor to the discipline of folklore as it is practiced today. Using members of Folklorists in New England (FINE) as subjects, Michael Sand and Paul Lenart, the project's recording engineer, created a lively six-minute aural and visual introduction to just what folklorists do today. The FINE members talk about their discipline— what they study and how they study it—as images of folklore subjects, their craft work, and skills flash by. The underlying, oft-repeated message is that we all have folk roots and that we are all part of the continuum of folklore studies.

Moving into the exhibit proper, we are greeted with large, stylized graphic figures representing the seven thematic units, placed above the show's title and two large-type introductory labels. The figures appear also on a small hand-out that serves as an exhibit guide by asking specific questions of the visitor for each unit. A figure introduces each of the thematic sections in the exhibit itself. The "folk" chosen for the symbolic characters are, in order of appearance an Indian, a Southern mountain woman, a Ukrainian-American woman in traditional dress, a rural fiddle player, a cowboy, a hippie with guitar, and an Asian-American father and child. As conceptualized and designed by Sand's graphic designer Tom Vanin-Bishop, the characters' somewhat whimsical appearances reinforce the "popularizing of the folk" theme of the show. In like manner Vanin-Bishop's design of the "Folk Roots, New Roots" logo with its bold characters expressively evokes the common man aspects of "the folk".

The text of the introductory label identifies the intellectual and educational goals of the exhibit.

> Many of the images and customs we identify with being American are associated with folklore—the songs that we sing, the crafts we admire, the images that sell our products, even our clothing and lifestyles.
>
> 100 years ago the American Folklore Society was formed by individuals interested in collecting and studying American folklore. Throughout the past century, as the academic discipline of folklore has expanded, other aspects of folk culture have been popularized and incorporated into mainstream culture through the media, the arts, and advertising.
>
> This exhibition reflects the ways in which Americans have understood their relationship to traditional folk culture and how these interpretations have contributed to changing concepts of community and national identity.

The exhibit guide reflects the same ideas in slightly different form and adds the important concept of relating folklore to our own lives.

> Boy Scouts singing cowboy songs round the campfire. Buffalo Bill's Wild West Show. The Marlboro Man. Long-haired college kids singing Delta Blues. The WPA. *The Whole Earth Catalog.* Ethnic heritage days. Local oral history projects. What do these all have in common?
>
> Throughout the past century, many of the images and traditions connected with America and being American have been associated with ideas about "the folk." This exhibition examines Americans' relationships to "the folk" and how folklore has been popularized and incorporated into mainstream culture.

This exhibit guide provides some questions for you and your family to think about and discuss as you go through the exhibit. Use them to help you discover the role of folklore in your own lives and the life of the nation.

The first exhibit unit, "Romantic Visions," focuses on native Americans—their study by early folklorists and ethnographers, their popularization and marketing by such early media savants as Buffalo Bill and Fred Harvey, and their appearance in mythic and symbolic form in advertising art, household objects, and popular music. The music track pairs an 1895 field recording of an Indian song with an early twentieth-century popular "Indian" song, "Red Wing." A period setting represents the array of Southwest Indian wares sold in Fred Harvey's Alvarado Hotel store in 1905, as a scrim imprinted with an image of the exterior of the Albuquerque hotel hangs in front of a life-sized photo

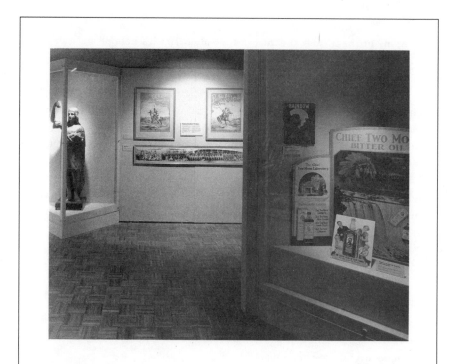

The "Romantic Visions" section features advertising art and Buffalo Bill.

Photo by John Miller.

blowup of the inside shelves stocked with baskets, pottery, jewelry, and textiles. A case displaying such objects adjoins.

"Social and Aesthetic Reform" treats the period of the early 1900s when settlement house workers and reformers took interest in the plight of the folk (synonymous at the time with rural Appalachian whites and, to a lesser degree, rural Southern blacks). Folklorists collected mountain ballads, and reformers established "settlement schools" to encourage the continuance of local traditions and to market folk produced craft items like baskets, quilts, and woodcarvings. The focal point of the unit is a life-sized reconstruction of a Southern mountain cabin facade with a cutout photo blowup of ballad collector Cecil Sharp on the porch and a local woman in the doorway. Exhibited objects include several large groupings of baskets and some woodcarvings made at two of the Appalachian settlement schools and a group made more recently in the folk tradition of a rural black South Carolina community. The motion activated music track

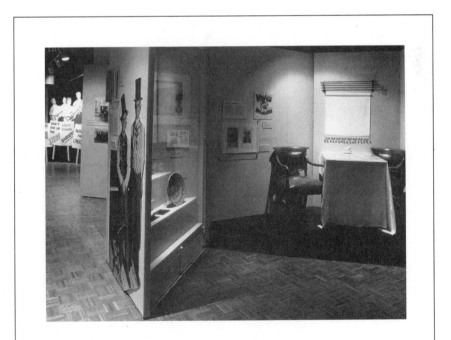

In "Romantic Visions," Santa Fe Railroad setting appears on the right, and Fred Harvey store artifacts are displayed in the case to left.

Photo by John Miller.

combines two ballads collected by Francis Child with a 1929 commercial recording of a mountain song.

"Cultural Nationalism" refers to many Americans's growing interest in their preindustrial past, as exemplified by Henry Ford's collecting activities and creation of Greenfield Village in the 1920s and a new scholarly and popular interest in folk art. The period also saw an emerging interest in Old World folk traditions, brought to public attention by the "Homelands" exhibitions beginning in 1916. The highlight of the unit is a re-creation of one of the period settings (a Polish "white room") and an ethnic artifact exhibit from a 1930's Homeland Exhibition at the New Jersey State Museum. Recordings from Henry Ford's Old Time Dance Orchestra augment displays of a dulcimer used in the orchestra and photo blowups of Ford and the winners of his fiddling contests. Classic examples of the folk art collected in this era—an Edward Hicks's *Peaceable Kingdom*, a Schimmel eagle, a weather vane—set off a painting showing early collector and folk art promoter Robert

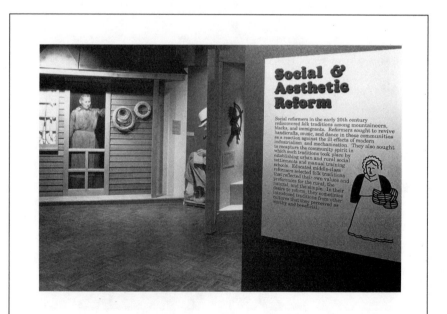

"Social and Aesthetic Reform" includes the Southern mountain cabin porch-front. An example of a section logo designed by Vanin-Bishop appears on the right.

Photo by John Miller.

Laurent's living room arrayed with more of the same. A case devoted to Robert Winslow Gordon and the Archive of American Folk Song features a headset offering two traditional songs recorded by Gordon in the early 1930s for the Library of Congress.

New Deal programs and their focus on "The Common Man" form the next unit. A life-sized photo blowup of a guitar-playing "Okie" set behind a clothesline strung with laundry provides the introduction to an array of photographs of the rural poor captured by Farm Securities Administration photographers like Walker Evans and Dorothea Lange. The Federal Artists Project's Index of American Design—represented in the exhibit by many examples of the artists' work—recorded some twenty-two thousand examples of pre-twentieth-century traditional design. Professional folklorists toured the South, collecting and recording folk songs for the Library of Congress and the Works Progress Administration, as represented in recordings of Mississippi fiddling and the music of Leadbelly (discovered by John Lomax). As part of the

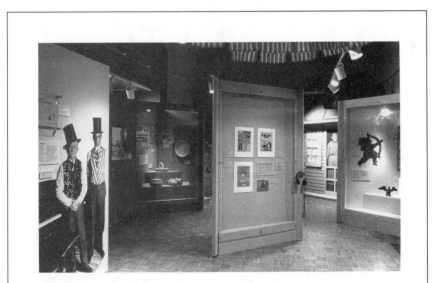

"Cultural Nationalism" displays Henry Ford, folk art, and Archive of American Folk Song sheet music and headset recordings. To the rear, cases hold South Carolina and Appalachian baskets in the "Social and Aesthetic Reform."

Photo by John Miller.

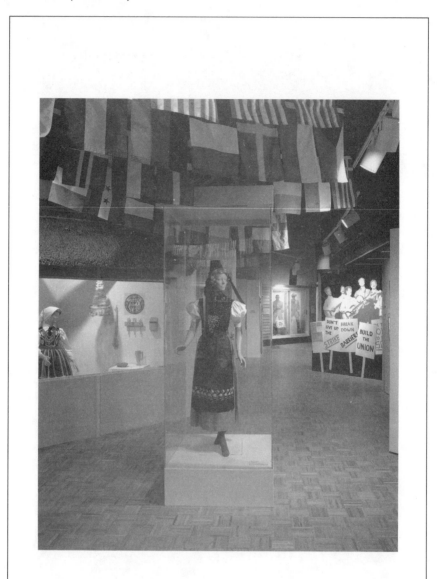

"Cultural Nationalism" includes a Polish "white room" re-creation modeled after the 1930's Homelands Exhibition at the New Jersey State Museum.

Photo by John Miller.

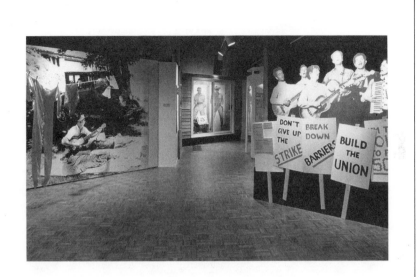

In the "Common Man" section, the Almanac Singers appear on the right.

Photo by John Miller.

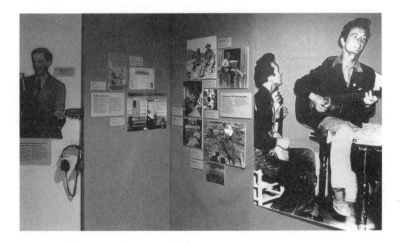

The "Common Man" includes Pete Seeger and Woody Guthrie and Standard Oil photographs. To the left, Alan Lomax with headset recordings from CBS's American School of the Air are included in the "Consumerism and Mass Media" section.

Photo by John Miller.

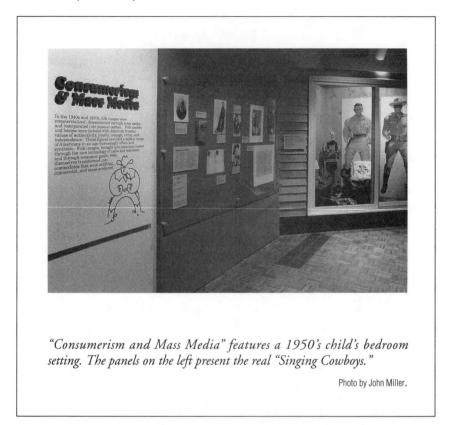

"Consumerism and Mass Media" features a 1950's child's bedroom setting. The panels on the left present the real "Singing Cowboys."

Photo by John Miller.

country's reaction to the depression, labor leaders and members of the American left turned to folk songs for inspiration. Woody Guthrie, Pete Seeger, and their group, the Almanac Singers, collected and performed traditional music of the common man for political purposes. The focal point of this unit is a re-created stage on which stands a life-sized photo blowup of the Almanac Singers. The accompanying motion activated music track features four of their prounion songs.

The 1940s and 1950s saw a mass communications boom that capitalized on popular images of "the folk." "Consumerism and Mass Media" focuses on America's obsession with cowboy culture—as exemplified by popular radio, movie, and television personalities—interpreted in the exhibit through a re-creation of a 1950's child's bedroom, complete with Hopalong Cassidy, the Lone Ranger and Tonto, and Roy Rogers lunch boxes, posters, guns, toys, and every other imaginable type of memorabilia. The audio track provides examples of real singing cowboys of the 1920s and self-created versions like Gene Autry

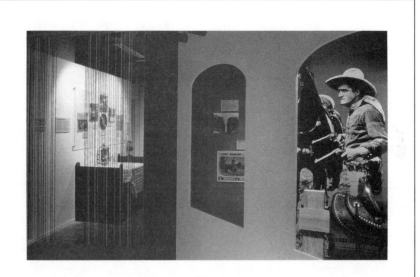

"Consumerism and Mass Media" includes Tom Mix, Gene Autry, and Gene Autry's saddle in a western adobe setting. The 1960's glass beads lead to diner, folk revival albums, and headset recordings of the "Grassroots and the Folk Revival" section.

Photo by John Miller.

in the 1930s. Period photographs of some of the singing cowboys, examples of cowboy sheet music, and cowboy songs as collected by John Lomax are contrasted with a large case exhibit on the romantic cowboy, as exemplified by Tom Mix and especially Gene Autry. Further exploring the role of the media in popularizing folk culture is a small section devoted to Alan Lomax and his CBS radio program, begun in 1940, the "American School of the Air." A motion activated recording of a 1941 broadcast provides an example of the way in which Lomax introduced folk songs and the stories behind them to the American public.

In the 1960s and 1970s, youth turned to the grass roots and a new appraisal of the folk in its attempt to create a counterculture. "Grass Roots and the Folk Revival" revolves around a re-created hippie sitting room with batik floor cushions, a spool table, beaded and woven wall hangings, and activist posters. Such representative artifacts of the period as handwoven and embroidered clothing and handmade jewelry share case space with album covers of music by

Dylan, Baez, and Peter, Paul, and Mary. An audio track presents their protest songs, continuing in the tradition of Guthrie and Seeger. A section on the earlier folk music revival presents selections from Burl Ives, the Weavers, Harry Belafonte, the Kingston Trio, and the New Lost City Ramblers emerging from a motion activated track set next to a re-created diner table and jukebox. A large photograph of the Freedom Singers at the Newport Folk Festival in 1963 accompanied by an audio track of their version of "We Shall Overcome" and a display of one of the first Freedom Quilts convey the folk music revival's role in the civil rights movement. A final panel focusing on our new-found concern with the environment makes a nice concluding touch by featuring the well-known 1972 advertisement, "Pollution—It's A Crying Shame," showing an Indian with tears running down his cheeks.

The final unit, "Community Roots," returns to the present and the theme of "Doing Folklore." A recent project conducted by the Rhode Island Black Heritage Society to record and interpret the musical traditions of two Rhode Island black churches is presented in both photographic and audio form. An oversized, wall mounted "family photo album" shows how we are all involved in creating our own family folk traditions.

A special segment titled "Doing Folklore" clearly articulates the definition of "folklore" presumed by the exhibit's creators.

> Folklore is the knowledge and skills that are passed from one person to another in informal ways. Families, in particular, communicate how they think and feel about themselves through folklore expressed in stories, songs, customs, celebrations, photographs, and other traditions. Folklore helps families identify themselves and connect their present with the past.

The visitor is then encouraged to "share his family traditions and be a folklorist" by answering specific questions on printed cards set out in racks. The questions ask whether there is a special naming tradition or nickname in the visitor's family, what holidays are most important to the family and whether any special traditions are used to celebrate them, what games the family plays, and what recipes have been passed down in the family and by what means. Cards filled out by exhibition visitors are posted so that subsequent visitors can learn about others' family traditions.

The conclusion of "Folk Roots, New Roots" draws on new technology to engage the visitor in doing folklore. A computer program created by Michael Sand and based on the 1982 Women's Quilt Project of the Cambridge Oral History Center uses a touch activated screen to lead the visitor through a series of questions relating to the quilt and its makers. Produced by twenty-four

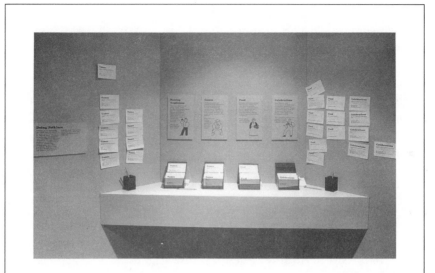

In "Doing Folklore," talk-back cards ask questions about naming traditions, games, foods, and celebrations.

Photo by John Miller.

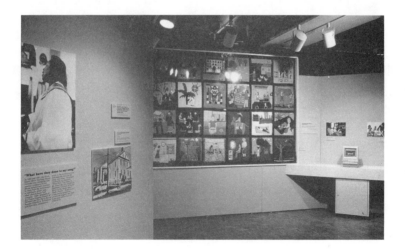

"Doing Folklore" features the Women's Quilt Project of the Cambridge Oral History Center with a touch activated computer terminal.

Photo by John Miller.

different hands ranging in age from eight to eighty and representing seventeen different cultural heritages, the displayed quilt is re-created in graphic form on the screen. The visitor chooses a patch that he or she wants to know more about and then asks a variety of folklore related questions, leading to information on the creator's age, her cultural background, the story of the patch, and other information. As stated in the label, the goals of the Oral History Center and of the quilt project directly relate to the exhibition's own definition of folklore: "The center's goals are to help people find the sources of strength in their own traditional cultures and help people of different backgrounds see what they have in common in order to strengthen community and bridge generational, ethnic, and class differences."

It should be clear from this description of "Folk Roots, New Roots" that threads of the history of the academic discipline of folklore are mixed in with an examination of the larger cultural picture, as well as with material exploring the process of folklore today. It is interesting to consider the relative importance of these different threads as one moves through the exhibit. On what themes have the exhibit creators lavished the most attention, either in the design, or in scholarship? How is the visitor aided in perceiving the intellectual content of the exhibit? What, in fact, does the visitor end up thinking the exhibit is about?

It is on this point that the exhibit has encountered some problems. Planned to celebrate the centennial of the AFS and opened in time to host folklorists from all over the country, the exhibit often failed to engage this particular audience. Those with whom I spoke, as well as the folklorists who reviewed the exhibit in national journals, did not grasp the "real" subject of the exhibit. They thought it was about folklore, and, being about folklore, was confusing and uneven in its treatment of the subject.

Many members of the general public had trouble identifying the subject of the exhibit as well. Those visitors I encountered seemed to enjoy it and to engage in the participatory activities, listened to the music, and spent a lot of time with the more recent material with which they were familiar. But the museum education staff member in charge of training the docents at one of the traveling sites confessed confusion and no clear understanding of the "story line." A curatorial staff member at another site found the introductory placement of the slide show confusing, since it didn't seem to have any clear relationship to the exhibit proper.

How did these confusions arise? How did the folklore elements get lost in an exhibit subtitled, "Folklore in American Life"? How did the dominant theme become instead American popular culture and its use of "folk" images?

The Development Process

The story begins in the spring of 1986 when Barbara Franco and Millie Rahn, the museum's public relations director, took Dillon Bustin, Massachusetts's newly appointed state folklorist, to lunch to discuss the idea of a centennial exhibit. All seemed enthusiastic about the project, and Rahn, a member of FINE, brought in other members of the organization to take the concept further. These included: Anthony Barrand, a professor at Boston University; Hugh Flick, assistant professor of folklore at Harvard and president of FINE; Jeanne Guillemin, associate professor of sociology, Boston College and a trustee at the American Folklife Center, Library of Congress; and Robert St. George, assistant professor of American studies at Boston University. St. George suggested hiring one of his graduate students, Jane Becker, to do initial research and to write a grant application to the Massachusetts Council on the Arts and Humanities for exhibit planning funds. Becker, a student of cultural history, with interest in the early twentieth century, had chosen as a dissertation subject the Boston settlement houses. She had previously worked on the well-received "The Art That Is Life: The Arts and Crafts Movement in America, 1875–1920" at the Boston Museum of Fine Arts.

At this time, the project team began to operate. Becker, reporting to Franco, tackled the preliminary content and object research. Rahn, Laura Roberts, of the museum's education staff, Jacquelyn Oak, registrar, and Addis Osborne, exhibit designer, joined weekly brainstorming sessions. Members of FINE offered their expertise on the history of the AFS and on particular folklorists and regularly critiqued versions of the grant proposal.

As submitted to the Massachusetts council in August 1986, the proposal, asking for a planning grant "to develop a major exhibition on folklore in America," read in part as follows (this from Director Clement M. Silvestro's cover letter):

> To my knowledge the concept is unique. Presenting the historical trends associated with the study of folklore in America in a visual context has never been done. The subject itself is timely because more than ever, Americans are anxious to learn about their roots and their heritage. Folklore is an important segment of this knowledge. Further, the subject will enable general audiences to become aware of, and more appreciative of the pluralistic character of this nation; and to learn that the folk tradition has persisted throughout our history, and is an important aspect of the American character.
>
> We are also pleased that this project will enable the Museum of Our National Heritage to continue our well-established practice of cooperating with outside

specialists and scholars, by bringing their knowledge and expertise to the attention of general audiences in exhibitions and special programs.

You may know that the exhibition is timed to coincide with the 100th anniversary of the American Folklore Society. The Society will hold its centennial meeting in Cambridge, in October, 1988. Massachusetts has been an important center for the study of folklore so it is quite appropriate to have folklore specialists from across the nation meet here.

The exhibit would "examine the relationship between folklore and culture, exploring the historical trends in the study of folklore in America and the ways in which these trends reflect or influence other cultural development." The exhibit would also look at "the popularization of folklore and the phenomenon of folk revival in social and cultural context." The proposal clearly states the three interpretive goals of the exhibition: (1) to explore the historical trends in folklore as a discipline, (2) to explore the ways in which these trends have responded to and interacted with other cultural developments, and (3) to explore the ways in which folklorists' work has been popularized and incorporated into mainstream culture. In good material culture studies fashion the grant application went on to say that the exhibit would convey that "like history, the collection, presentation and interpretation of folklore is a cultural and social product of the particular time, place and culture in which it is collected and interpreted."

To carry out these goals the exhibit would have an initial section introducing the principal players in the study of folklore: "the folk," or tradition bearers; the folklorists/collectors and interpreters; and the revivalists and popularizers. Key concepts and terms such as "folk" and "folklore" would be defined. The main body of the exhibit was to be organized chronologically and thematically with a special case study in each unit that would explicate major trends.

As in the final exhibit, seven chronological units spanned the period from the 1880s to the present, though they had not yet attained their eventual names. Each unit contained six content areas:

A) The case study
B) The context (related developments that occur in the wider culture and the relationship of general cultural and social trends to developments in folklore study
C) The folk (who was considered "the folk" in this period? What were the collecting interests?)
D) Folklorists and collectors
E) Revivalists and popularizers

F) Uses and applications

This scenario translated into the first exhibit unit (later to become "Romantic Visions") in the following manner:

A. Case study
  1. Native Americans
B. Context
  1. Search for distinctly American culture and interest in antiquities and preservation
  2. English model or "popular antiquities"
C. The Folk
  1. Native Americans
  2. Southern Negroes
  3. Anglo-Americans with "surviving" traditions from England
  4. French Canadians
  Collecting interests:
  1. Oral traditions
  2. Customs
D. Folklorists and collectors
  1. Examples: William Wells Newell, Francis James Child, Fletcher Bassett, Horace Scudder
  2. Anthropological and literary schools
  3. Bureau of American Ethnology
E. Revivalists and popularizers
  1. Literature: Nathaniel Hawthorne, Mark Twain
F. Uses and applications
  1. Federal government and Bureau of Ethnology

The initial approach to the exhibit was grounded clearly in the academic discipline of folklore and reflected strong input from the folklorists involved with the planning effort. Issues and questions pertained almost exclusively to the field of folklore studies: What is folklore/folklife and how have perceptions of this changed? What kind of work does the folklorist do? What is the role of the folk revival? What is the impact of technology on collecting? How and why is folklore maintained? What is the relationship of folklore to history, anthropology, literature, and sociology?

The rest of the outline applies the six content areas to each of the remaining units. Many individual folklorists are named, "the folk" are defined for each unit, collecting interests, uses and applications are discussed, and the context is explored historically. Almost all of this material was lost as the exhibit later underwent transformation. What consistently remained from this first outline, however, were the topics in "Revivalists and Popularizers" and the subjects of the "Case Studies." Interestingly, missing from the first outline is any mention of the cowboy as a focus of media interest and mention of the political use of folk music in the 1930s and 1940s—both of which received much attention in the exhibit's installation.

What happened? When the museum submitted the initial proposal, two categories of outside consultants had been identified, but the exact persons had not yet been chosen. Because of the dual nature of the exhibit's goals, the project team sought both a folklorist and a cultural historian, hoping that either Roger Abrahams, chairman of the AFS committee for the centennial, or Simon Bronner could be engaged as folklore consultant. Cultural historians under consideration included Jackson Lears, Alan Trachtenberg, and David Whisnant.

When the planning proposal received funding in November 1986, Lears and Abrahams became the key consultants, and there is little doubt that their ideas affected the shape of the final product. Lears, professor of history at Rutgers, specializes in studying the effects of advertising and consumerism on American culture in the post–Civil War period and earlier had published on the topic of antimodernism and its cultural effects in the period 1880–1920. Lears's interests are clearly reflected in the exhibit's implementation grant and final script. Abrahams, a past president of the AFS and professor of folklore and folklife at the University of Pennsylvania, is an acknowledged dean of the profession. His presence on the project lent credibility and presumably stifled argument. As Becker suggested, "If Roger said it was okay, who would dare complain?"

Real work started in January 1987. Becker returned to begin writing the NEH implementation grant, due in June. Sometime soon after she and Franco began seriously talking about changing the premise of the exhibit. After months of dealing with professional folklorists, wrangling over just who qualified as a folklorist in any given period and whether or not folk revivalists had any place in the story, Becker broached the idea that perhaps emphasis should be switched from the folklorists themselves to the general public and their reaction to folklore. Rather than carefully presenting the opinions of folklorists on folklore, it suddenly seemed much more interesting to explore what other people thought of as folklore and folk traditions. Franco enthusiastically embraced a conceptual change, feeling that the new emphasis would be much more appealing to the public *and* more important from a cultural history perspective. The exhibit could then explore broader themes, such as how folklore was used by political activists, the federal government, and special interest groups like advertisers and promoters to shape concepts of American identity.

The exhibit planners would use the basic exhibit outline developed under the planning grant, but would de-emphasize themes relating to the history of the discipline of folklore and bring to the fore the previous subtext—the cultural background of folklore studies in America. In the process the folklorists slated to be profiled disappeared (with a few exceptions), to be replaced by the revivalists and popularizers—Buffalo Bill, Henry Ford, Burl Ives, and others. The intellectual underpinnings moved closer and closer to those associated with popular culture studies.

From this point Becker assumed the lead role in undertaking research, meeting with consultants, preparing exhibit scripts, and locating objects. In April she traveled to Philadelphia for a joint meeting with Abrahams and Lears to discuss the new exhibit themes and content and to work on refining the script. After the meeting she continued to draw on their expertise by telephone and letter, relying on Abrahams for reading suggestions in the history of folklore and on Lears for reviewing the cultural context interpretations she was developing. Her research was synthetic—putting together work previously done on many different topics by many different, recent authors, most of whom were in some way involved with the project. The research involved not only a great deal of reading but also much time spent on the telephone, running ideas and interpretations by scholars and checking on specific information for label copy, object identification, and printed materials.

With the new broader cultural emphasis, five content experts joined the project, their expertise falling into the chronological categories outlined in the exhibit script. Each would also write an essay for the planned catalog. Rayna Green, director of the American Indian Program, National Museum of American History and a member of the Cherokee Nation of Oklahoma, contributed her special knowledge about the way Indians have been studied, romanticized, and mythologized to the first exhibit unit. A past president of the AFS, her approach is decidedly cultural and historical. Eugene W. Metcalf, Jr., Miami University, and Claudine Weatherford, University of Maryland, were tapped for their past work on folk art collecting. Alan Jabbour, director of the American Folklife Center at the Library of Congress and a specialist in American fiddle styles, served as resource person for the early musical content of the exhibit. Robert Cantwell, of Georgetown University and the Office of Folklife Programs, Smithsonian Institution, provided expertise on the music of the folk revival.

Although Addis Osborne, museum staff exhibit designer, had planned to work on the exhibit, his retirement led to the hiring of Michael Sand, Inc., of Boston for work on the projected final exhibit. Coming in during the implementation grant-writing stage, Sand joined the project team for conceptual discussions and prepared a schematic layout for the grant proposal. His ideas proved critical to the final form the exhibit would take, both physically and intellectually.

The designer of the original Boston Children's Museum, Sand believed in interactive devices and state-of-the-art technologies. Still concerned about the possibly "pedantic" nature of the exhibit topic, Franco wanted a designer who could give the subject matter "a playful aspect." Sand, having created exhibits—most recently at the National Museum of the Boy Scouts of America in Murray, Kentucky—that featured innovative questioning techniques and a nontraditional approach to didactic material, seemed to fit the bill. Once the project received NEH funding and Sand joined the team, he ably served the function Franco envisioned. She believed that the best exhibits are those in which concerns for content and design are pulling equally against each other, and she relied on Sand to make dramatic suggestions to add life to a content heavy, intellectualized script. At times his suggestions seemed too radical, and Franco, acting as referee, threw her weight on the side of the content. When content needed paring back to meet the goal of appealing to a popular audience, Franco pushed towards lighter solutions. She played a similar, intermediary role with the label copy. As primary researcher and the team member in closest contact with the array of consultants, Becker pulled for content in the label writing; Franco, representing the interests of the visitor, worked for succinctness.

Although the shift in the exhibit's focus from the discipline of folklore to Americans's adoption of folk images was clearly Franco and Becker's idea, Sand's approach to the script as designer quickly confirmed the change. He suggested interviewing living folklorists for the introductory media presentation, whereas the show proposed in the implementation grant involved an equal treatment of past folklorists. In like manner his concept for the concluding interactive computer program and talk-back cards proved much less didactic about the processes of "Doing Folklore" than the grant script had called for.

It was Sand who suggested the concept of period settings, or "environments," as the focal point for each unit. Eliciting ideas from the project team as to what was the most "symbolic moment" to be represented in each unit, Sand created three-dimensional groupings that would engage the visitor's interest and help "lead him through" an exhibit that otherwise relied on much flat material. Each of the settings chosen is an example of the popularization or commercialization of "the folk" and strongly reinforces the new direction of the story line. In a corollary effort to add life to flat material, Sand created smaller-scale contextual devices, such as a re-creation of a train dining car to display

Indian-motif Harvey hotel menus and playing cards and a diner table with jukebox to augment a collection of folk revival album covers.

Sand's approach to exhibiting the many black-and-white photographs had a similar goal of adding life and engaging scale to the design. If areas of the developing exhibit script seemed object poor, they were not photograph poor. Both at the turn of the century and in the 1930s, documentary photographers recorded rural peoples. The problem for the exhibit team was how to translate these compelling images into compelling artifacts. Sand's solution became the life-sized photo blowup—sometimes a part of the created "environment," sometimes accompanying cased objects. Once brought face to face with a photographic image, the visitor might then turn to the displays of small-scale photo reproductions on adjoining walls.

The exhibit had always been planned to travel, thereby affecting the design from the beginning. Once the environments had been incorporated into the design, Sand worked out a system of modular cases and panels that would fit the designated space at the museum but that could also be easily broken down and packed for shipment. Firm member Alan Ransenberg created the final layouts and was responsible for all design detailing. Objects were arranged in multishelved, internally lit, triangular cases. Fabric covered and color keyed, four-by-eight-foot wall panels displayed framed material, photo blowups, small-scale photo reproductions, a variety of flat material—sheet music, album covers, printed ephemera—arranged behind acrylic panels, and the object labels. Photo reproductions and labels attached to the panels with velcro.

Unfortunately, the size, complexity, and sheer number of objects in the original installation did not travel very well. At the Strong Museum in Rochester, key interpretive elements (the environments for the "Social and Aesthetic Reform" and the "Common Man" sections) had to be left out entirely because of a lack of space. In like manner the fabric covered wall panels were not used as background because the museum's design team found them difficult to fit into the available exhibit space. (Sand's standardized panel design was altered by the exhibit builders at Lexington to maximize the use of their gallery space; as a result it lost its planned modular aspect.) The walls and risers sent to create a four-hundred-square-foot theater also could not be used at the Strong Museum, where the introductory slide show was installed in its large auditorium.

The first venue, the McKissick Museum in Columbia, South Carolina, had equal difficulty using the large wall panels, and staff members had to redesign the exhibit to fit their own spaces. They were able, however, to retain all of the environments and managed to squeeze a thirty-six-hundred-square-foot exhibit into a twenty-four-hundred-square-foot space by mounting the introductory

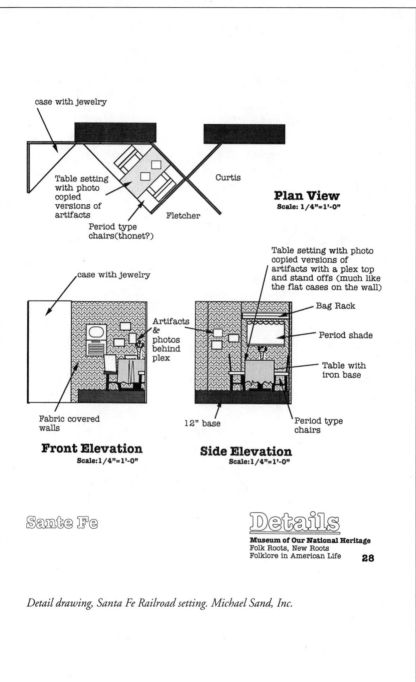

Detail drawing, Santa Fe Railroad setting. Michael Sand, Inc.

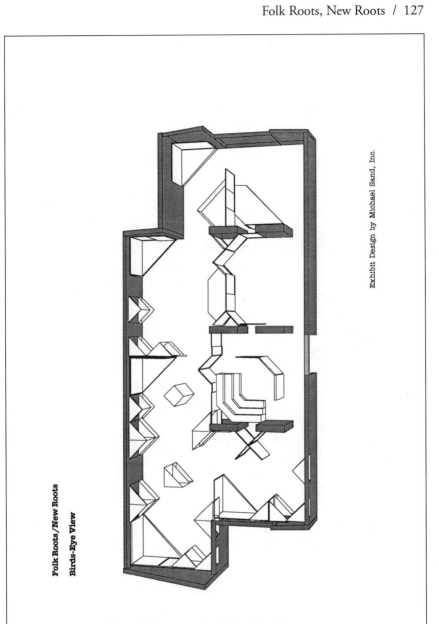

Folk Roots/New Roots
Birds-Eye View

Exhibit Design by Michael Sand, Inc.

Bird's eye view of the exhibition modules. Michael Sand, Inc.

audio-visual component in a separate gallery. Both installations lacked major artifacts such as the cigar store Indian and most examples of folk art that did not travel with the show.

At Oakland, exhibit space was not a problem. In fact, as part of the museum's general commitment to provide a California component to the traveling show it hosts, "Folk Roots, New Roots" was expanded by some 400 objects to occupy a 7,000-square-foot space. Ironically, however, because the gallery was so much larger than the one at Lexington, and because so many more objects had to be fitted into cases, the museum's installation team also did not use the panels or cases sent with the show. All of Sand's environments, however, survived intact.

Difficulties encountered with off-site installation might have been avoided, according to Sand, if the project budget had allowed for predesign site surveys at the other locations. He also suggested that the integrity of content and design of traveling exhibits could be ensured if project budgets allowed for the designer's help in installation at other venues.

For a traveling exhibit that comprised twenty-five large crates and over three-hundred objects, an introductory audio-visual unit, and a concluding computer unit, not to mention sixteen music installations, the design and fabrication proved generally successful, however, if difficult to move and set up. At the McKissick Museum, for example, it took a staff of ten individuals three weeks to install. A detailed set of slides showing each exhibit component, a workbook showing floor diagrams of the Lexington installation with color-coded object identifications, and a detailed object list greatly aided off-site installation. The McKissick Museum's addition of crate packing lists helped clarify the tremendous volume of objects for the Strong Museum's staff. To the credit of Lenart, the project's recording engineer, the audio equipment held up quite well. The interactive computer station proved equally trouble free.

One of the most interesting aspects of "Folk Roots, New Roots" is the large role that music plays, both in terms of objects exhibited and in terms of the general story line. Considering that the collecting and recording of music is a major aspect of the history of folklore studies in America and that the popularization of folk music is probably the single most obvious way that forms of traditional culture have entered our own lives, it is entirely appropriate that music—in both aural and visual forms—assumes such a large percentage of the exhibit's content.

The motion activated music tracks were Sand's idea, implemented by project sound engineer and jazz musician Lenart. Although discussion took place regarding whether ambient sound or earphones were the optimal method of presenting music, Sand felt strongly that visitors should activate elements of

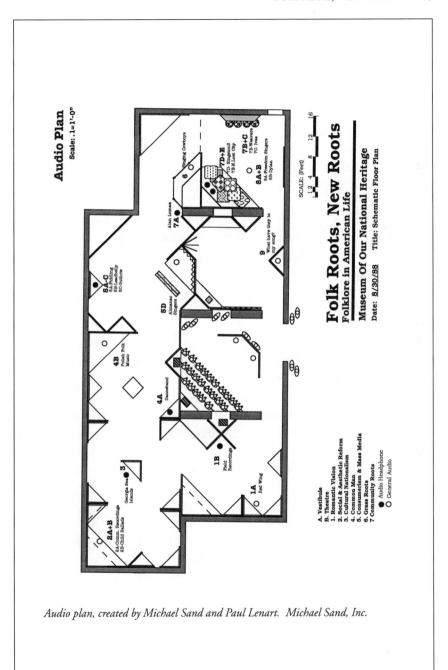

Audio plan, created by Michael Sand and Paul Lenart. Michael Sand, Inc.

the exhibit as they walked through. As designer, his goal was to create a "succession of experiences" timed "like a musical score." He and Lenart laid out the sound in script form, with separate sound zones, as one would a story board for a film. The pieces that project team members felt were a must for all visitors to hear were recorded for the motion activated devices; because there was so much music, however, headsets were also used for selections deemed of more limited interest.

The successful collection and presentation of music is arguably one of the exhibit's strongest features. It is also an area of investigation that nicely unites the academic and popular threads of the first and second exhibit concepts. In all but the last two exhibit units, "original" music collected or recorded by academic folklorists shares space with popular or revival versions. In some cases, pieces are combined on the motion activated tapes; more often the folklorists' recordings are made available through headsets, and the popular versions sing out as you walk by. In like manner, displays of published songs collected by folklorists coexist with popular album covers and sheet music, and photo blowups of traditional music makers match those of the revivalists and popularizers.

Since the exhibit concept did not evolve from a discrete collection or known body of objects, exhibit planners spent much time locating objects that could illustrate major themes. As with the environments selected, the objects chosen represented the popularization, revival, or commercialization of folk images, traditions, and products. Few exhibited objects related to the work of academic folklorists, just as there remain few photographic images of the folklorists at work.

To identify objects and photographs Becker spent substantial time on the road, examining collections at the Smithsonian Institution, the Campbell Folk School in North Carolina, and the Hindman Settlement School in Berea, Kentucky, the Library of Congress, Hull House, and the Rhode Island Black Heritage Society. An equal or greater amount of time was spent on the telephone, trying to find categories of objects that seemed particularly elusive— record album covers and posters of the mid-twentieth century and printed ephemera in general.

Music collection proved equally challenging. Working with Sam Brylawski in the Recorded Sound Division of the Library of Congress, Becker searched through catalogs, listened to tapes, and identified those selections which would record the best. Later music pieces came from records that had been commercially available and were now accessible through Library of Congress tapes or records. Recording of folk revival music came from local folk song collectors. Consultants Rayna Green and Alan Jabbour pointed the way to pieces they considered important.

The balance between academic folklore and popular culture fares somewhat better in the exhibit catalog than in the exhibit itself. Jabbour's introduction attempts to define folklore and to describe the work of folklorists over the last one hundred years, noting where the academic discipline and popular culture interests have been in accord or in conflict. Abrahams contributes a piece examining William Wells Newell, one of the founders of the American Folklore Society, and the first interests of folklorists in late nineteenth-century America. In Becker's overview essay, she identifies the major folklorists working in each era and explores the larger cultural context of changing interests in "the folk." This essay, in fact, closely matches in content the exhibit script (and sample text labels) submitted with the NEH implementation grant; a comparison of it and the final exhibit content speaks clearly of the influence of Sand and Franco in pulling the exhibit into the popular arena.

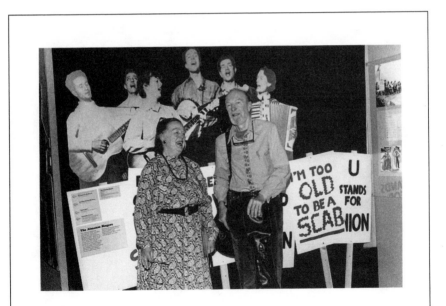

Pete Seeger and Bess Hawes pose in front of their photographs after Seeger's concert at the Museum of Our National Heritage.

Photo by Julie O'Neil.

The remainder of the essays, contributed by project consultants, decidedly fall on the popular culture studies side of the historical fence. Green polemicizes on Americans's predilection for "playing Indian"; Lears discusses the use of images of "the folk" in American advertising, 1880–1940; Eugene Metcalf, Jr. and Claudine Weatherford look at the reasons for early twentieth-century interest in folk art; and Robert Cantwell explains the cultural meaning of the folk music revival.

In sum, both exhibit and catalog ended up being much more about popular culture than about folklore. But whatever the balance, one essential element seems to me to be lacking. The events described in the exhibit units and in the catalog essays took place within the general context of American history but it is that context that is sorely missing. The fact that early folklorists became interested in the American Indian for their own specific reasons is presented with little relationship to the idea that Americans and Europeans have always been fascinated with the Indian as noble savage and as a rapidly disappearing survivor of a particular culture. Americans romanticized the West long before 1888, Buffalo Bill, Fred Harvey, or the Lone Ranger. Americans looked to their

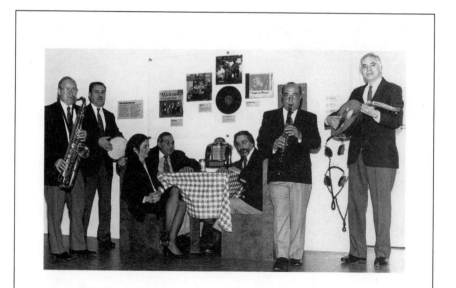

A traditional Armenian band, part of the public programming series created to enhance "Folk Roots, New Roots," enjoys the 1950's diner setting.

Photo by Julie O'Neil.

colonial past several generations before the period identified in the exhibit unit "Cultural Nationalism," and for many of the same reasons, a concept that is a key element in understanding American culture. WPA photographers were sent out to document poverty, not quaintness or folk traditions; FSA workers were there to help the poor, not study them. In some cases, the interests of folklorists coincided with those of particular segments of the culture at large, and it is those cases that the exhibit documents. But to suggest a casual relationship ultimately misleads. Examples of the popularization of "the folk" illuminate but make little sense outside of the historical context. And because this context is missing, it is very difficult for the visitor to fully appreciate the complex interpretations offered.

Adding to the confusion regarding what the exhibit was about, the extensive public programming offered by the Museum of Our National Heritage in conjunction with the exhibit focused almost exclusively on the theme of "Doing Folklore." Martha Norkunas, a folklorist-in-residence, worked with the education department both before the exhibit opened and during its run, offering teachers' workshops on community folklore and spending time in selected schools conducting similar programs. Other major events, organized by Rahn of public relations, included a well-attended concert with Pete Seeger, a film series looking at stereotypical images of the folk as portrayed by Hollywood, a series of concerts offering traditional ethnic music, and programs at Christmas focusing on family folklore and holiday traditions. The culminating event occurred just before the exhibit ended its run—a one-day folk heritage festival featuring ethnic and traditional foods, crafts, music performances, and a continuously running tape of the Seeger concert. According to Rahn, the programming aimed toward both an adult and children's audience with about equal attention given to music and oral traditions.

Likewise at the McKissick Museum, a wide range of public programs, developed by two folklorists on the staff, distinctly and successfully focused on themes of "Doing Folklore." At Oakland, folklorists-in-residence created school programs on the techniques of folklore collecting and on family traditions. A wide range of public programming began with a folk festival celebrating California folk traditions followed by: "Sundays with Folklorists" talking to visitors in the exhibit about collecting family stories; a "Celebration of the American Cowboy" day; a lecture by Rayna Green; and a concert by the folk revival group, the New Lost City Ramblers.

An interesting aspect of the Oakland stay was its purposeful timing to coincide with the 1990 annual meeting of the American Folklore Society. Just as "Folk Roots, New Roots" opened to mark the centennial of the AFS, it reopened two years later playing to the same audience, with special programming and concerts to enhance the members' stay in Oakland.

The folklore related public programs proved quite popular and in all of the locations attracted interested audiences to the museums. Both in Lexington and on the road, the most appealing aspects of the exhibit turned out to be the interactive "Doing Folklore" sections—the introductory slide show, the talk-back cards, and the Cambridge Community quilt computer program—and those elements of the exhibit that featured artifacts of popular culture with which we are all familiar, artifacts relating to cowboys, Indians, hippies, and folk music performers. The exhibit team engaged the public in the latter sections by displaying nostalgic items, things that many of us remember or once possessed. There is, in fact, less emphasis in these sections on content, on cultural background, or the relevant work of folklorists than in earlier portions of the exhibit. And that academic thread seems to have had little meaning for audiences exclaiming over cowboy lunch boxes or rattling 1960's glass curtain beads.

The project team is to be commended for the level of public interest in the "Doing Folklore" sections. Why was the visitor willing to fill out (often quite extensively) the five talk-back cards, positioned at the end of an exhibit that really had little to do with the questions asked on the cards? Is it because other peoples' completed cards were prominently posted and acted as incentives to subsequent visitors to make sure that the important things in *their* lives received equal attention?

I have to conclude that "Folk Roots, New Roots" worked when the subject matter touched our own lives—through memories and experiences of the artifacts exhibited or through direct engagement via specific questioning in the talk-back cards and computer program. Could the original exhibit concept have been made equally engaging? Could the serious cultural history interpretations of the second script have been successfully communicated via the exhibition medium without relying on catalog essays for explication? And if so, would the public have found them equally as compelling as the mid-twentieth-century materials to which they seemed so drawn?

Can we only personalize and create engaging exhibits by reaching towards the sphere of popular culture? Is popular culture, in fact, our only common intellectual ground today, the arena in which the general public, scholars, and museum professionals all at least possess shared experiences? And if this is true, then how do we solve the dilemma of exhibiting a past that audiences cannot collectively share or remember?

The successful aspects of "Folk Roots, New Roots" suggest a possible answer. By reaching out to museum visitors and asking them to think about their individuality (in this case, their folk traditions), particularly as they may relate to those of other museum goers, visitors are engaged on so personal a level that their museum experiences immediately become meaningful. If this sense of relationship and comparison with others can be achieved with individuals of the past—by sharing their concerns, experiences, traditions, and material culture—then visitors should be able to be led back in time in a way that *will* prove engaging and popular. If successfully achieved, this connection will give visitors a special relationship with the past that will lead to intimacy and, ultimately, understanding.

Institutional Profile

Name: Museum of Our National Heritage
Location: 33 Marrett Road, Lexington, Massachusetts 02173
Size: 83,164 square feet
Date of founding: opened 1975

Exhibition Data

Name of exhibition: "Folk Roots, New Roots: Folklore in American Life"
Dates and venues: Museum of Our National Heritage, Lexington, Massachusetts, October 1988–June 1989; McKissick Museum, Columbia, South Carolina, August 1989–November 1989; Strong Museum, Rochester, New York, March 1990–July 1990; Oakland Museum, Oakland, California, August–November 1990
Size of exhibition: 3,000 square feet
Cost: $396,752 (including salaries)
Names and titles of exhibition personnel: Barbara Franco, Assistant Director for Museum Programs; Jane Becker, Project Coordinator; Laura Roberts, Education Director; Jacquelyn Oak, Register; Millie Rahn, Public Relations.
Date of original conception: Spring, 1986
Duration of exhibition development process: Spring 1986-October 1988
Sources of funding: Museum of Our National Heritage, National Endowment for the Humanities, Massachusetts Council on the Arts and Humanities
Consultants:
Content consultants during planning: Dillon Bustin, Anthony Barrand, Hugh Flick, Jeanne Guillemin, Robert St. George.
Content consultants during implementation: Roger Abrahams, Jackson Lears, Rayna Green, Eugene W. Metcalf, Jr., Claudine Weatherford, Alan Jabbour, Robert Cantwell.
Design consultants: Michael Sand, Inc.

Number of objects exhibited: 350

Related Programming: At the Museum of Our American Heritage, a wide
assortment of public programs on family and holiday folklore were led by
folklorist-in-residence, Martha Norkunas. A film series entitled "Folk on
Film" showed how folk and traditional cultures have been used in popular
media. Norkunas also held teacher workshops on how to integrate folklore
into school curriculum that resulted in class projects of memory boxes that
were presented and displayed at the museum. A concert with Pete Seeger was
one of a number of performances. A folk festival on the museum grounds
brought together traditional foods, crafts, music, and dance representing
ethnic groups in the Boston area.

Professional journal reviews:

Michael Ann Williams, "Folk Roots, New Roots: Folklore in American Life
Journal of American History 76 (December 1989): 861-67.

Charles F. Mc Govern, "Real People and the True Folk," *American Quarterly* 42
(September 1990): 478-97.

Ray Allen, "Folk Roots, New Roots: Folklore in American Life, *Journal of
American Folklore,* 104 (Summer 1991): 348-51.

"FIT FOR AMERICA"
How Fit for Visitors?

Lizabeth Cohen

I n almost every way, the exhibition "Fit for America: Health, Fitness, Sport, and American Society, 1830–1940," is a museum success story. It opened in April 1986 at the Strong Museum in Rochester, New York, after a three-year development period about as smooth as they come. Historian and Deputy Director for Interpretation Harvey Green had actually thought about the idea of doing a show on the history of Americans's obsession with fitness and health soon after he had arrived to work with the Margaret Woodbury Strong collection a decade earlier. Within a year of the opening of a permanent museum building in 1982, Green had submitted a planning grant to the National Endowment for the Humanities. Already, however, Green and other staff members had become deeply involved in researching and collecting for what they called "the physical culture show." By the time the NEH planning grant period began in January 1984, a team of committed museum professionals at the Strong were doing all the right things: undertaking original research in documentary and artifactual sources; mining the rich Strong collections as well as using their generous acquisitions budget to acquire artifacts of popular health and sport; collaborating as a historian, curator, educator, and designer to develop the first truly "team" product in the museum's history; consulting with experts in sports and medical history from the academic world; and most importantly, creating an exhibit around a topic of undeniable public interest.

By the winter of 1985, "Fit for America" had gathered great momentum. The museum had received an implementation grant of $125,000 from NEH to help produce the show, and Green had a book manuscript almost ready for submission to Pantheon Books. This semischolarly division of Random House had agreed to publish a serious but popular book based on Green's ground-breaking research to serve as a catalog for exhibit visitors as well as to reach beyond them. Already museum officials has made arrangements for the show to travel to other museums for at least two years after its year-long run at the Rochester institution. When the exhibition finally opened in April 1986, almost a decade after Green's initial brainstorm and three-and-one-half years after real work had begun, two public events celebrated how well the popular and scholarly had been brought together in "Fit for America": a well-attended community "Dance to Fitness" and a weekend symposium featuring major scholars in the field, whose papers would later be published in a volume entitled *Fitness in American Culture: Images of Health, Sport, and the Body, 1830–1940.* A more perfect conception, gestation and birth of a history museum exhibition were hardly imaginable.[1]

I took all this knowledge of the exhibition's history with me as I traveled to Seattle's Museum of History and Industry (MOHI) to see the traveling version of "Fit for America" in late April 1990. (The exhibit's tour had been extended until April 1992.) I had already talked at great length with Green, now a professor of history at Northeastern University in Boston, and with staff members at the Strong Museum. I had also heard from other museum professionals and historians that "Fit for America" was a model interpretive exhibition. To say the least, I was curious to see the show with my own eyes and, to the best I could, through the eyes of visitors. In many ways that I will detail, "Fit for America" was indeed an extraordinary exhibition. It brought out of closets and attics forgotten objects documenting how Americans had tried for more than a century to perfect their bodies, and it made exciting new connections between seemingly unrelated aspects of material culture such as vacuum cleaners, Grape Nuts cereal, Walter Camp exercise records and craftsman-style furniture.

But in one very important way, it was less successful. I could not ignore, and I would be remiss not to discuss, that despite the subject of fitness and health, in which everyone agrees museum visitors have great interest, this exhibition—at least in its traveling format—did not capture the public's imagination. I watched people in the galleries. I talked to docents and educators who complained of their difficulty teaching with the exhibition. I observed my own reactions. This essay is an effort to understand how "Fit for America" could break ground in the professional history museum world, yet be less appreciated by the general public. About this paradox, at least, the exhibition has much to teach us.

In analyzing what went right and what went wrong, my attention focused first on the development process. Here so many history exhibitions go awry. Objects get lost in the documentary evidence, visitors' needs are rarely considered, and designers enter too late in the process. What I discovered is that "Fit for America" represented a model collaboration among historian, curator, educator, and designer—the kind that many museums desire, even boast of, but that rarely happens.

Although Green had initiated the exhibition concept, early on he had drawn curator Patricia Tice into the project, requesting that she collect objects that might someday have a place in an exhibit on physical culture. Home

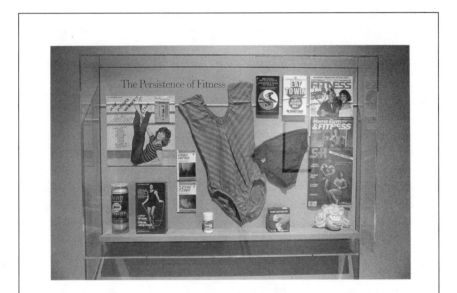

Visitors to "Fit for America" were not sure if the exhibition's message stressed change or continuity. Installations at the Strong Museum and the Museum of History and Industry (MOHI) in Seattle both ended with this case demonstrating that popular obsession about fitness persists today. The exhibit, however, in featuring the quirkiness of nineteenth-century inventions and reforms, seemed to emphasize difference over similarity. This lack of clarity about how and why concern about health and fitness changed over time detracted from the exhibition's impact.

Courtesy Howard Giske, Museum of History and Industry.

gymnasiums, folding bathtubs, electric belts and brushes, and "Indian Clubs" were on the museum's wish list long before the exhibit was on its schedule. Before joining the Strong Museum's staff in 1976, Green had studied American cultural history at Rutgers with Warren Susman, and then, receiving his Ph.D. in the worst years of the academic job crisis, had attended the Cooperstown Graduate Program in History Museum Studies for a year. He thus came to museums more object literate than the typical historian. Tice had arrived at the Strong in 1980 with a masters in museum studies from the University of Michigan and three years of experience at the Edison Institute of the Henry Ford Museum. Sound in her curatorial training, Tice also had a broad conceptual orientation to her work. Green and Tice were well suited to each other and to the Strong. The museum, built from the eclectic collection of toys (particularly dolls), household accessories, advertising artifacts, and paper ephemera amassed by Rochester heiress Margaret Strong over her lifetime, required and attracted unconventional professionals not content with narrow definitions of curatorial fields. This was particularly true in the exciting early years when the staff set about to turn cabinet upon cabinet of curiosities into a social and cultural history museum devoted to interpreting the impact of industrialization on daily life in the nineteenth and early twentieth centuries. Green and Tice, despite different trainings, were closer to each other intellectually than most historians and curators. The result, clearly evident in "Fit for America," was a mutual sensitivity to ideas and objects rare in history museum collaboration.[2]

Joining Green and Tice on the exhibition team by the NEH planning period in 1984 was an educator, Dorothy Ebersole, and a designer, Pamela Myers. Ebersole had been at the Strong for several years, but Myers had just come from the North Carolina Museum of Art with many new ideas for changing what she viewed as the restrictive, mazelike design of typical history exhibitions, including many at the Strong Museum. According to Green, although historians and curators had been collaborating on exhibitions at the museum from the start, their interaction was not well structured, and designers and educators had been left out of the early planning stages. "Fit for America" became, then, the first major exhibition at the institution to be developed by a collaborative team of historian, curator, designer, and educator. By the time the Strong Museum received NEH funding for implementation, it was operating with a structure, carefully spelled out in a written document, that gave each team member specific duties but also required that all major decisions be made by the entire team.

From what I have reconstructed of the development of "Fit for America," the team approach worked in this exhibition. Its creation seemed surprisingly free of the usual tensions among educators and curators, curators and historians, historians and designers. In interviews, team participants had only the most respectful things to say about each other. And most significantly, the Strong now handles all exhibitions with teams, although the process has become somewhat less democratic than it was in these initial years. In the most recent version of the policy, the Vice President for Interpretation has authority over team participants and responsibility for enforcing all schedules and budgets. It seems that teams lacking the good chemistry of Green, Tice, Ebersole, and Myers had gotten bogged down. Nonetheless, "Fit for America" left a legacy of integrating historical and artifactual research and educational and design considerations early in the exhibition process.[3]

Another unique aspect of the creation of "Fit for America" that I felt warranted investigation was the simultaneous production of a book and an exhibition. How, I wondered, did the two genres relate to each other, and might I find here an explanation for the exhibit's mixed success? The book *Fit for America: Health, Fitness, Sport, and American Society* grew out of several existing commitments of the museum's staff. First, staff members had decided that rather than publish traditional catalogs to accompany exhibitions, they preferred serious, well-illustrated books written and marketed for a popular audience. Such books would do more justice to the depth of research and conceptual innovation that went into Strong shows and would reach out further to historians and the general public alike. Two similar books written for Strong exhibitions, Green's *Light of the Home* and Susan Williams's *Savory Suppers and Fashionable Feasts: Dining in Victorian America*, had already been published.

The staff also established that book manuscripts, based on primary research into documentary and artifactual evidence, would serve as what the Strong referred to as "narratives" for exhibitions. The Strong Museum's commitment to interpretive history exhibits had created an environment where exhibits were recognized to have arguments, much like books. Requiring an extensive text for a major exhibition, therefore, served to encourage in-depth historical analysis before objects were assembled. Exhibition narratives were expected, in the language of the Strong Museum's "Procedure for Exhibition Development," to "delineate the content of the exhibition, carefully utilizing the collections as evidence." Those who read the narrative were expected to pay "close attention to the relationship of the artifactual materials to the written argument."[4] Green's book manuscript became the analytical and artifactual bible for "Fit for America." All that followed—wall labels, classroom lessons, gallery guides—would derive from it.

However, in one crucial way—in the organization of the book and the exhibit—the two genres differed. Why they did resulted directly from the input of the team. Green had organized the book chronologically, with eleven chapters divided into three major parts. Part I, "Millennial Dreams and Physical Realities, 1830–1860," focused on how religious enthusiasm and concern for the fate of the republic after the deaths of the founding fathers provided the impetus to reform human beings and their life styles. In the antebellum period, lay health reformers challenged Americans's bad habits as well as the authority and practices of the medical profession and urged new diets, temperance, and cures through water, magnetism, electricity, and exercise. Part II, "The Price of Civilization, 1860–1890," examined how after the Civil War the new maladies of a more urbanized middle class along with new technologies and new theories about disease stimulated a renewed drive for health. The sanitation movement, wilderness cures, mineral waters, patent medicines, athletics, and vegetarianism, it was thought, promised to put an end to everything from consumption to "neurasthenia, the new American nervousness." Part III, "Regeneration, 1890–1940," explored how a profound sense of cultural pessimism had set in among many of the nation's middle class and elite that impelled them to develop new standards for the human body. Sports, the "strenuous life," body building, bicycling, breakfast cereals, and boy scouting were only a few of the ways in which Americans developed a new kind of "physical culture," one they hoped would prove native-born Americans superior to the eastern and southern Europeans rapidly invading "their" land. At the heart of all three parts—despite their different chronological settings—were lively descriptions of various strategies promoted and undertaken to achieve bodily perfection.

When Tice, Ebersole, and Myers sat down with Green to transform his book into an exhibition, they rejected the chronological structure as too complex and repetitious. A thematic approach rather than repeated treatments of diet, sports and fitness, cleanliness, and home medical remedies within each chronological period seemed more powerful to them. Green, committed to the team process and convinced by the others' arguments, consented. The exhibition "Fit for America" was divided into five thematic sections: health and medicine; diet reform to cure "dyspepsia"; cleanliness, physical exercise, and electricity as remedies for "neurasthenia"; and nostalgia for the past as cultural regeneration.

It is likely that Tice and Ebersole, who were the major proponents of a thematic reorganization, were right. Although a treasury of little-known forms of popular culture, Green's book was repetitious in ways that would have been particularly confusing to the fast-moving museum visitor. But the root of the problem was not repetition. Rather, Green's narrative lent itself so easily to thematic restructuring because it had never developed a convincing historical argument about how and why change took place in American attitudes toward health and fitness over these one hundred years. Instead, the eleven chapters focused on various reform schemes roughly situated in historical eras demarcated by the three parts of the book. In the absence of an overarching argument that inextricably tied health fads and phobias to historical time, little was lost in the shift from what was ostensibly a diachronic approach to a synchronic one. In fact, the five new themes had enough historical grounding—with the first focused on the antebellum era and the last on the turn of the century—that despite its thematic structure, the exhibit hardly seemed less chronological than the book.

Nonetheless, neither visitors to "Fit for America" nor readers of the book received a satisfactory historical understanding of how American ideals of health and physical form altered over time, nor what the larger meaning of that change was. The problem can be traced back to early drafts of the book. On 18 December 1984, before the NEH implementation period began, Green's editor at Pantheon Books, Wendy Wolf, wrote him a seven-page, single-spaced response to the first draft of the book. Although greatly appreciative of his research feat, she called throughout for placing the story of health and fitness in larger historical context.

> I think we can well afford to point to various agonies and ecstasies, booms and busts, changes in administrations, presidential candidacies, etc.—the concern for the well being of the body physical as an embodiment of the body politic can't take place without much, much more direct discussion or at least allusion to other indices of the American self-image.[5]

A letter from consultant Donald Mrozek six months later continued to push for a more historical analysis. Although he too felt it was a fascinating and insightful manuscript, he warned:

> The area in which I think the manuscript is weakest is in tying its several sections together. I think the epilogue may go farther toward providing an interpretive construct than any other one part; but it would seem that the assertion of diversity and eclecticism as a continuing theme ought to come early, and early, receive a great deal of elaboration. . . . You may also get some criticism on the extent to which you explain *why* certain emphases in fads and exercise systems and so forth appear, as distinct from detailing their characteristics and discussing how they were advanced. All fads were not created equal, and there was more to the success or failure of one of them than the forcefulness of the persons advocating them.[6]

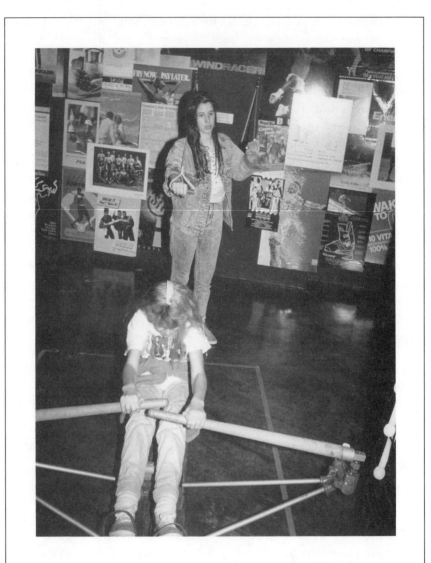

Here high school visitors use exercise equipment in the introductory gallery developed at MOHI in Seattle. The introductory gallery—filled with posters, clothing, equipment, videos, computer programs, and other paraphernalia documenting contemporary obsessions with health and fitness—oriented the exhibition's interpretation toward continuity rather than change, which museum staff hoped would make it more accessible to the public.

Courtesy Howard Giske, Museum of History and Industry.

What Wolf and Mrozek identified as flaws in the book persisted as problems in the exhibition. The lack of a clear historical argument meant that health fanaticism was never sufficiently related to the larger cultural context nor were causality and agency satisfactorily identified in changes that took place over time. As a consequence, people who encountered the exhibition were never sure if the exhibit's message stressed change or continuity, nor whether it told a story of reformer ideals or American realities. Confusion over all these issues interfered with visitors' receptivity to the exhibition.

Green was not unaware of these issues, but he held out different expectations. When I asked Green for a statement of his argument, he suggested it had to do with the secularization of concerns about staying healthy. Most importantly, however, he wanted to convey that Americans's concern for the health of the body was not new, that it was the product of our distinctive culture, and that it involved a whole series of strategies with diverse motives. "What does it all mean? We left that to the public," he acknowledged. He felt that a more precise argument, connections to the larger cultural context, and a more developed causality could not be developed in the exhibition format.

As for the relationship between reformers and the larger public, Wolf had also raised the problem in her December 1984 memo on the book. "My underlying reaction to the work as a whole is that you've made your case well for the ideal—the reformers' urges, impulses, attitudes, and actions. What comes through less clearly is what reality looked like." A combination of the difficulty of locating sources on the reception of reformer schemes and Green's own conviction that the plethora of artifacts and material he had found indicated well enough that the public had responded enthusiastically led him to do little more with this issue.[7] "Fit for America" remained a book and an exhibition that made claims about American habits while mostly documenting reformers' theories and inventions.

One could argue that Green was right that there are limits to what can be accomplished in an exhibition built around material culture and that demands for greater analytical complexity come more from the academic historian than the typical museum visitor. I would agree if these ambiguities did not prove so problematic to "Fit for America"'s audiences. When, for example, education staff in Seattle took a close look at the book, exhibit script, and gallery guide in the months before "Fit for America" arrived, it realized that the public would be confused about "what to make of all this stuff."

Recognizing some of the concerns discussed above, museum educators at Seattle made two strategic decisions. First, they decided to stress continuity over change. After all, they had sought the exhibition for the spring and summer of 1990 to complement Seattle's hosting of the Goodwill Games. They thus developed an introductory gallery preceding the canned show in which they amassed exercise equipment, videos, and clothing, nutrition computer programs, and other paraphernalia demonstrating contemporary obsessions with health and fitness. And they organized public and school tours around this same message, equipping docents with University of Washington Huskies's gym bags filled with modern-day artifacts closely resembling the historical ones in the exhibit cases. Visitors on tours passed around Comet cleaner containers, deodorant soap, water filters, and the like. "Fit for America," in Seattle at least, became a way of saying, "See, nothing is new under the sun." Here, comparisons between the present and the past, involving three major themes—cleanliness, diet, and exercise—helped provide a larger cultural context for the historical artifacts. The remedy was superficial, however. The Huskies's bags were only present when docents were in the gallery. Staff concluded that juxtapositions of contemporary and historical artifacts within the exhibit would have sustained this line of interpretation more effectively. Comparison with the

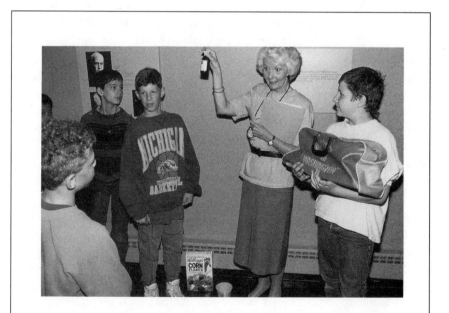

Docents leading school groups through "Fit for America" at Seattle's MOHI carried University of Washington Huskies's bags equipped with modern-day equivalents of the artifacts on display.

Courtesy Howard Giske, Museum of History and Industry.

present also peaked visitors' curiosity about the scientific validity of the fitness theories and inventions of the past featured in the exhibition. Seattle staff wished "Fit for America" had helped them better to assess this aspect of continuity and change as well.[8]

The second strategy Seattle educators and docents adopted was aimed at overcoming what they felt was a serious lack of evidence about how ordinary people responded to these health and fitness schemes. On tours, docents focused instead on the reformers portrayed in the exhibition, such as Horace Fletcher, Catherine Beecher, Bernarr MacFadden, Sylvester Graham, and John Harvey Kellogg. At least, they felt, they were putting people, not just things, at the heart of an exhibition promising to interpret habits and attitudes. Although this approach helped, docents remained frustrated that they could not respond to audience inquiries about the popularity of these reforms. That so many of the reformers mentioned in the exhibition were only superficially introduced, and that they were overwhelmingly male, also caused problems.

What can we learn from these observations about the book and the exhibition? First of all, it should be clear that conceptual problems in an exhibition like "Fit for America" generally can be traced back to the original document, whether it be book, catalog, script, or narrative. It is crucial, therefore, that analytical weaknesses identified there—in this case, context, argument, causality, and agency—be addressed. Second, museum exhibit developers often assume, and sometimes even lament, that visitors are more interested in the artifacts than the argument. They portray the public as attracted to curiosities rather than curious about larger meanings. The case of "Fit for America" demonstrates that although visitors may be drawn to unusual objects, they still look for context and argument. The latter are not abstractions unnecessary in public history; they are the required foundation for all interpretive exhibitions. Finally, visitors need to identify with people in the past in order to connect to an exhibit. In museum shows, much like in a novel or a movie, they search for protagonists to associate with the material culture on display. Exhibition developers should do whatever they can to clearly link objects to actors, whether they be "all Americans" or a narrower, more researchable group like health reformers.

The other major factor contributing to the paradox of the exhibit's success—that it has earned more acclaim among professionals than the public—was its design. I should begin by acknowledging that "Fit for America" raised a complex design challenge. The exhibition's subject was an abstraction—ideals of good health and physical fitness—and the artifacts available for display were hundreds of small things such as medicine bottles, product containers, advertisements, cabinet photographs, and patented inventions. Larger items such as bicycles, furniture, bathtubs, and scouting costumes were exhibited at the Strong Museum's installation but could not travel. Hence, as much as possible of the casework and graphics had to be designed for both home and the road, with the knowledge that the show would be contracted in size and even more exclusively made up of small things when it traveled. This was the design problem. The solution arrived at by designer Myers reflected these constraints as well as her own inclinations.

As mentioned, Myers arrived at the Strong with experience in designing art museum exhibits and with a desire to break out of the exhibit formulas so common in history museum exhibitions. "I had not dealt with as large a number of objects in a single gallery before, nor with as great a variety of objects. There was also certainly more text than I had been accustomed to," Myers recalled in reflecting back on her initial reaction to "Fit for America." Much of Myers's design solution worked. She correctly recognized that visitors did not have to follow a linear path, that if the five thematic sections were clearly identified through color, lighting, and labeling people could make their own choices about where to go once in a particular area. She selected handsome soft tones of grey, mauve, blue, and peach and used windows and vistas to draw visitors forward without subjecting them to a serpentine route.[9] Also, a number of simple interactive devices scattered throughout the exhibition—tape measures hanging next to full-sized photographic enlargements of "ideal physiques" from the early twentieth century and talk-back boards where visitors filled out and posted questionnaire cards about foods they thought were good and bad for them, exercise they enjoyed doing, and contemporary health—allowed the public to compare themselves to people in the past.

What I feel worked less well, and contributed to "Fit for America"'s interpretive problems of denying the larger historical context and removing objects from the lives and experiences of real people, was the way the artifacts were presented. Small objects were carefully arranged in cases with painted wooden bases and acrylic bonnets. Larger items such as furnishings, bathtubs, rugs, and brooms were dramatically placed on platforms or hung on walls. The result was that quite ordinary things were aestheticized. Cereal boxes and medicine tins were arranged in cases as if they were precious jewelry to be admired. Vacuum cleaners and commodes displayed on strategically placed platforms became high art. Any intrusion of labeling was held to a minimum. The three levels of labels that the Strong uses—primary for major themes and sections, secondary for subthemes and groups of artifacts, and tertiary to describe single objects—all were done in a smaller type size and with less color contrast than I would have liked. Myers had turned a social history exhibition into an art show. Why other members of the "Fit for America" team went along is not clear.

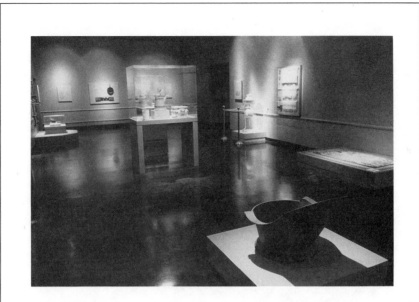

The designer of "Fit for America" brought many art museum techniques to her exhibition plan. She tried to highlight the objects, minimize the presence of text, and give visitors freedom of movement within particular sections of the exhibit. Color, lighting, and vistas functioned to draw visitors forward through the show.

Courtesy Howard Giske, Museum of History and Industry.

My guess is that, to their credit, they were design conscious as historian, curator, and educator and that they were searching for alternatives to the busy design in which the artifact is often lost amid collages of words, objects, and photographic blowups. In retreating from that sometimes overpowering design solution, however, the team failed to come up with a way of visually linking the artifacts to the exhibition's larger ideas. Artifacts selected for their historical significance appeared to the public as rare aesthetic treasures out of context. While some museum professionals and visitors were surely impressed with the elegance of "Fit for America"'s design, others I spoke with felt that its discordance with the subject matter detracted from the exhibition's power.

Seattle museum staff complained about several other aspects of the design that bear mentioning. Cases in "Fit for America" are thirty-nine inches, too high for many children and people in wheelchairs to view. Print on primary and secondary labels would have benefited from a larger point size and greater color

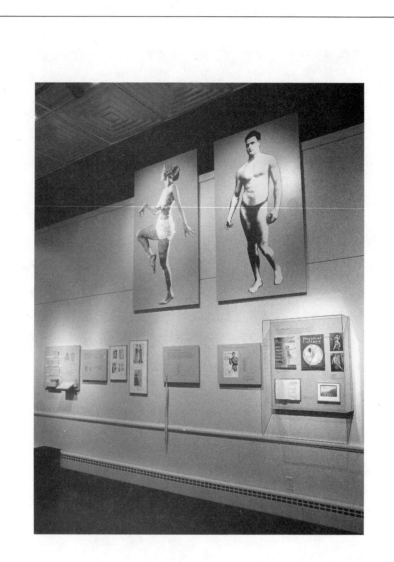

"How do you measure up?" asks the panel below the life-sized photographic enlargements of what were considered ideal physiques a century ago. A simple tape measure hanging on the panel allowed visitors to participate without requiring complicated equipment vulnerable to frequent breakdown.

Courtesy Howard Giske, Museum of History and Industry.

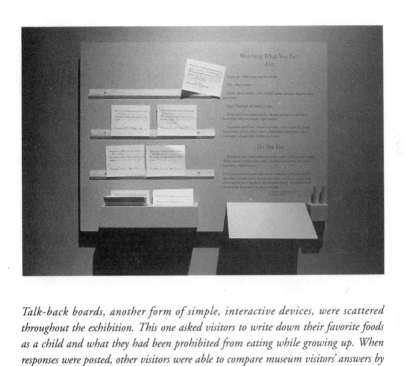

Talk-back boards, another form of simple, interactive devices, were scattered throughout the exhibition. This one asked visitors to write down their favorite foods as a child and what they had been prohibited from eating while growing up. When responses were posted, other visitors were able to compare museum visitors' answers by generation as well as contrast them to the advice of Dr. Joseph Edwards in his 1894 book, Hygiene.

Courtesy Howard Giske, Museum of History and Industry.

contrast to make the exhibit's interpretive organization more apparent to visitors. Labels inside cases were laid flat, not angled, and were printed in a point size and typeface that made them difficult for anyone with imperfect vision to read. To be fair, in the five years since "Fit for America" was designed, museums have become more sensitive to the diverse needs of visitors. The Strong Museum now uses larger point sizes and bolder typefaces for labels. Designers there make greater use of big headlines in primary and secondary labels and tilt tertiary labels in cases. Cases have been dropped from a height of thirty-nine inches to thirty-four to thirty-six inches. Thus, many of the technical problems in the design of "Fit for America" are fortunately part of the Strong Museum's past. In fact, during my visit there I was impressed with the sensitivity to visitors' needs articulated by design staff.[10]

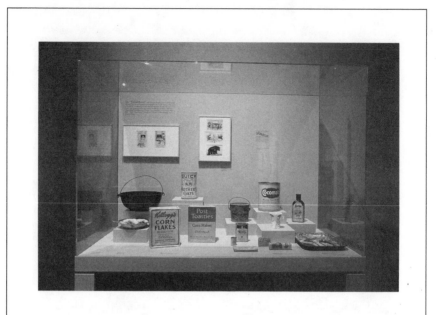

Ordinary things like cereal boxes, food tins, and iron pots were carefully arranged in cases as if they were precious objects. With labeling kept to a minimum and no social context provided, this material culture of everyday life was aesthetized as fine art.

Courtesy Howard Giske, Museum of History and Industry.

The last aspect of "Fit for America" that I will discuss concerns its existence as a traveling exhibition, which played a role in the exhibition's uneven success. On the one hand, the professional interest in "Fit for America" that has kept it on the road for five years is impressive. Rarely do history museum exhibits as topical and artifact rich as this one become available. More common are shows from organizations like the Smithsonian Institution Traveling Exhibition Service made up primarily of graphic material mounted on two-dimensional panels. Recipients of "Fit for America" indeed received an impressive package: a huge exhibition, twenty-five free copies of the Pantheon book, twenty-five-hundred gallery guides, educational materials, and a video for gallery use. Museum professionals understandably were excited that an exhibition this comprehensive could be secured as a canned show.

On the other hand, visitors like myself who saw only the traveling version of "Fit for America" missed many of the most powerful artifacts that had graced the Rochester installation, such as the female bicycling costumes and the

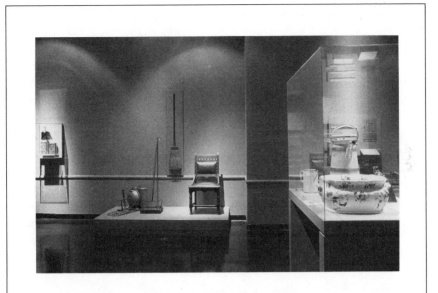

Objects as down-to-earth as a carpet sweeper and a broom became part of elaborate collages that decontextualized the material culture presented. Seeing such artifacts presented in this way made it difficult to understand them as evidence of health reformers' obsession with germ carrying dust.

Courtesy Howard Giske, Museum of History and Industry.

innovative plumbing devices of the late nineteenth century, all deemed too fragile to travel. For us, the artifacts turned out to be less diverse and visually impressive than for those who saw the exhibit at the Strong Museum. This helps to explain some of the public's reticence observed by Seattle staff. Although the "Fit for America" team in Rochester intended to suggest to receiving venues the kinds of local objects they might substitute for objects not sent with the show, Seattle museum staffers claimed they never received such a list, and by the time they unpacked and mounted the show, it was too late to add them.

This kind of miscommunication characterized other aspects of the relationship between the Strong Museum and the Seattle Museum of History and Industry. For obvious reasons, "Fit for America" was not an easy show to travel. Hundreds of small objects had to be packed, unpacked, inspected, installed, and disassembled, while acrylic cases were subjected to stress and scratches. The Strong Museum tried to anticipate problems recipient museums might have unpacking and installing the show and sent blueprints of the Rochester installation and a detailed handbook along to help. Despite these aids, the designer and registrar in Seattle had numerous complaints. They claimed the artifacts were not well packed; they never received an official objects list, making unpacking very difficult; the crate contents did not relate well to the exhibit cases; the photographs in the handbook detailing the way the cases should look did not show all angles, so it was hard to figure out where everything went; the blueprint was faded and very hard to read; the touch-up paint was dried up, and there were no color specifications for the case and label panels so that wall colors could be coordinated; and so forth.

It is hard for me to sort out responsibility. There was inexperience on both ends. This was one of first shows the Strong Museum staff traveled, and given its complexity and size, more experience probably would have helped the exhibit producers develop a simpler, clearer system. Nonetheless, whenever the Seattle designer, Bruce Christofferson, or registrar, Martha Fulton, made

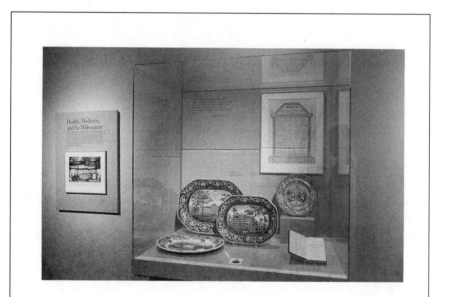

The staff of MOHI in Seattle complained that Strong Museum cases at a height of thirty-nine inches were difficult for children and people in wheelchairs to see into. Labels in cases were also flat, not tilted, and in a point size and typeface that further hindered people's access to them.

Courtesy Howard Giske, Museum of History and Industry.

inquiries or brought problems to Strong Museum exhibits coordinator Fred Shroyer, they found him helpful and accommodating. On the MOHI side, Christofferson is an imaginative designer with expertise in sound who had not had long experience designing exhibitions and particularly handling traveling shows. His inexperience likely contributed as well to the difficulties Seattle encountered installing "Fit for America."

I have concluded that problems are probably inevitable when shows as large and complex as "Fit for America" travel. Museums at both the sending and receiving ends should, therefore, do everything possible to anticipate the snags and their resolutions. I would recommend sending the designer from the recipient institution to visit a previous locale or, if that is not possible, requesting that the earlier venue videotape its installation for future reference. Staff at sending institutions should try to overcome the human propensity to fall into an "out of sight, out of mind" mentality, and should seek reports on how well their exhibition is traveling, making adjustments in handbooks,

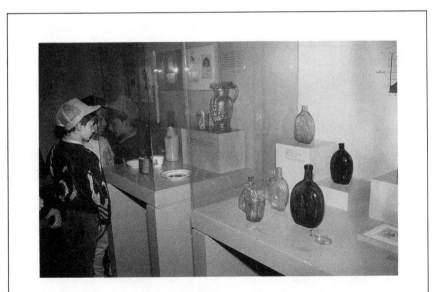

The wall label to the left marked the exhibition's first section, "Health, Medicine, and the Millennium." Its small size and graphic subtlety made the thematic organization of "Fit for America" less significant for visitors than it might otherwise have been.

Courtesy Howard Giske, Museum of History and Industry.

packing approaches, and installation instructions as needed. Staying in contact with the exhibit as it travels could lead to more substantive coordination as well. For example, the Strong might have kept track of the visitor talk-back responses generated as "Fit for America" made its way around the country and might have analyzed regional diversities to be shared subsequently with its own members as well as new publics that attended the exhibition.[11]

In conclusion, I would like to take stock of what this examination of "Fit for America" has revealed about the exhibition's fitness for visitors. On the positive side, it has offered the public access to previously unknown or underappreciated material culture and insight into the way Americans have tried to perfect their bodies through diet, exercise, home medical remedies, and cleanliness schemes for more than a century. Green and Tice discovered as much as they did, it might be argued, because of the model mix of documentary and artifactual research they undertook. Moreover, although visitors may have been unaware of it, the team approach to creating the exhibition offered them an integrated experience where artifacts, major labels, gallery guides, educational materials, media, and special programs all reinforced the same interpretive message. They certainly would have noticed had that not been the case.

Less successful, as I have already discussed, was the exhibition's effort to explain the larger historical meaning of the health and fitness artifacts

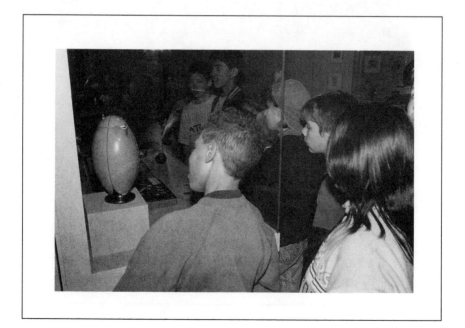

assembled. This difficulty emerged first in the book manuscript, persisted in the exhibit script, and was reinforced through the design. Specifically, problems with argument, context, causality, and agency created too large a gap between the conceptual ambitions of the exhibition and the way the public encountered the artifacts burdened with telling that story.

How are we to explain the paradox I identified earlier between the way museum professionals and visitors responded to "Fit for America?" Why were the former more likely to find the exhibition satisfying than the latter? I have concluded that "Fit for America" is a show that pleases the connoisseur of artifacts of popular culture more than visitors interested in learning about the

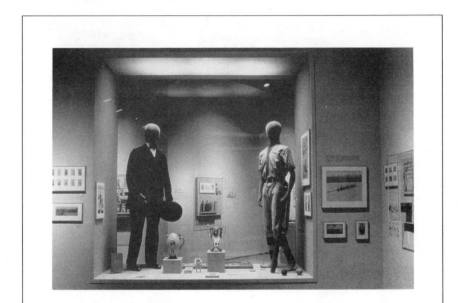

Children examine a glazed earthenware pitcher shaped like a football exhibited in the traveling version of "Fit for America." The same pitcher appears as it was displayed in the exhibit's installation at the Strong Museum alongside several large and dramatic artifacts such as costumes which were unable to travel with the show. The absence of many of the Strong Museum's most powerful artifacts in the traveling version of "Fit for America" made it harder for museum visitors to put objects in context, to understand this pitcher, for example, as evidence of native white efforts at the turn of the century to emphasize manliness through exercise and sports.

Photo, left, courtesy Howard Giske, Museum of History and Industry.
Photo, right, courtesy the Strong Museum.

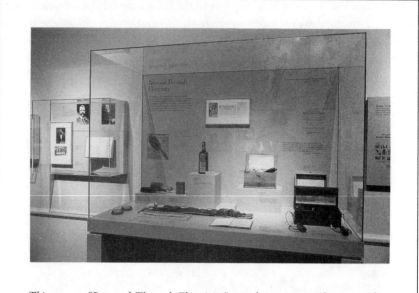

This case on "Renewal Through Electricity" raised questions without providing answers for visitors about how devices designed to shock the body actually worked and whether there was any scientific validity to their operation.

Courtesy Howard Giske, Museum of History and Industry.

history of ordinary people's concerns about health and fitness. Ironically, Green and his team started out with just that goal of bringing a historical dimension to the public's growing obsession with eating the "right" foods, exercising the "right" amount, and treating their ills with the "right" remedies at home. But over time the team became caught up in a fetishism about the artifacts. In the end, objects became significant beyond the stories they had been selected to tell of the real people who had made, purchased, and used them.

"Fit for America"'s creators, whether they realized it or not, were deconstructing the "text" of the history of Americans's pursuit of fitness, while the public was still in search of more straightforward explanations of what these objects had meant to those who used them and how and why changes in those attitudes took place. As the installation decontextualized the material culture on display and the exhibit's interpretation avoided speculating about causality, visitors would have been happier with period settings and efforts to explain change. Diary entries describing rest cures and home remedies, a reconstructed turn-of-the-century home library filled with exercise equipment to show the middle-class man's new commitment to "the strenuous life," comparative data on water purity and filter devices between 1840 and 1940—this is the kind of contextualization I suspect visitors would have liked. Much of it, particularly period settings, museum professionals might dismiss as hokey, inelegant, and unknowable. Perhaps. But to the extent that we can learn and speculate about context, causality, and agency, we have to decide whose needs our exhibitions should meet—the profession's or the public's. If we are not careful, we may run the danger of talking only to ourselves.

This book addresses the issue of how the exhibition development process shapes the final product visitors experience in the museum. It is imperative, then, that in closing I consider what my assessment of "Fit for America" can contribute to that larger concern. I would argue that the team approach pioneered in this exhibition was both its strength and its weakness and that to the extent that any exhibition process can be a model, it will emerge from further perfecting the ideal interaction among curator, historian, designer, and educator. The Strong Museum took an important step with "Fit for America" toward transcending the balkanization that has plagued much exhibition development. Early collaboration between historian and curator avoided the "book on the wall" syndrome. Involving the educator and the designer from the start prevented the misfit that often exists among object and interpretation, concept and design.

Nonetheless, the three areas that I have criticized—limitations in the historical analysis, a design that denied context, and inadequate concern for the visitors' total experience—can also be traced back to the team approach in the following way. Ironically, the admirable desire of the Strong Museum staff to make the team experiment work smoothly may have undermined the checks and balances that usually result from more contentious interaction among individuals representing different interests. Of course, it is hard to know if historian Green might have fought harder to present a more fully developed historical story if he had faced a curator who cared only about objects. Or if designer Myers might have designed a show that put artifacts more in context had other team members questioned her art museum approach. Or if educator Ebersole might have demanded more for the average visitor had she been less integrated into exhibition development. Certainly, I am not advocating a return to the days when historical interpretation, object integrity, and visitor satisfaction were always in conflict. But because it is so clear that in museum exhibition development, product cannot be separated from process, I am convinced that many of the strengths and weaknesses in "Fit for America" can be traced back to its creation. As history museum professionals work to perfect the exhibits they present to the public, they also need to strive toward establishing a development process that ensures staff cooperation as well as creative conflict, diverse input as well as interpretive brilliance.

Author's note: I would like to thank Paula Shields for accompanying me on my first visit to "Fit for America" at the Museum of History and Industry in Seattle and for sharing her insights with me. I am also indebted to the present and former staff members of the Strong Museum and the Museum of History and Industry in Seattle who assisted me in so many ways.

Institutional Profile

Name: Strong Museum
Location: One Manhattan Square, Rochester, New York 14607
Size of Institution: 160,000 square feet
Date of Founding: charter secured 1968; museum opened 1982
Number of Professional Staff: 33

Exhibition Data

Name of exhibition: "Fit for America: Health, Fitness, Sport and American Society, 1830–1940"
Dates and venues: Strong Museum, April 1986–March 1987; Hudson River Museum, Yonkers, New York, April–July 1987; Museum of Our National Heritage, Lexington, Massachusetts, September 1987–March 1988; Buffalo and Erie County Historical Society, New York, May–August 1988; Kansas City Museum, October 1988–May 1989; Oakland Museum, California, August–January 1989; Museum of Science and Industry, Seattle, March–October 1990; Henry Ford Museum and Greenfield Village, Dearborn, Michigan, November 1990–September 1991; Ohio Historical Society, Columbus, October 1991–April 1992.
Size of Exhibition: 4,500 sq. ft. at the Strong Museum; 3,500–4,000 sq. ft., traveling (though could be more if museum embellished)
Cost: exhibition development at Strong: $ 294,046 (including salaries); rental fee for traveling show, $5,000 per three-month period, plus shipping
Names and titles of exhibition personnel: Harvey Green, Historian; Patricia Tice, Curator; Dorothy Ebersole, Educator; Pamela Myers, Designer; Kathryn Grover, Editor; Richard Sherin, Conservator, Fred Shroyer, Traveling Exhibition Coordinator.
Date of original conception: 1977–1978
Duration of exhibition development process: 1983–1986
Sources of funding: Strong Museum, National Endowment for the Humanities

Consultants:
Content: Neil Harris, Michael Harris, Edward Atwater, Donald R. Mrozek.
Design: Kevan Moss
Number of objects exhibited: approximately 600 at the Strong Museum; 431 in traveling version
Related programming:
  Publications: Harvey Green, *Fit for America: Health, Fitness, Sport and American Society* (New York: Pantheon Books, 1986; paperback edition Baltimore: Johns Hopkins Press, 1988); Kathryn Grover, ed. *Fitness in American Culture: Images of Health, Sport, and the Body, 1830–1940* (Amherst: University of Massachusetts Press and Rochester: The Margaret Woodbury Strong Museum, 1989); Gallery Guide: "Fit for America: Health, Fitness, Sport and American Society, 1830–1940."
  Media: video of 1920's and 1930's sporting events traveled with show
  Gallery talks: Noon-time gallery talk by Harvey Green in museum's "Summertime Gallery Talks" series; prearranged school visits
  Other: two-day symposium at Strong Museum; public programs including "Box Office Heroes: American Athletes on Film," "Summertime Sports Saturdays"—three, day-long programs where visitors learned about and played tennis and lawn games, baseball, and Highland Games by traditional rules; "Dance to Fitness" open to public; summer games programs for children; classroom lessons coordinated with museum visits; other programs developed at host museums as exhibition traveled.
Professional journal reviews:
  Roberta J. Park, "Fit for American: Health, Fitness, Sport, and American Society, 1830–1940," *Journal of American History* 77 (June 1990): 261–66.

Notes

1. Harvey Green, *Fit for America: Health, Fitness, Sport, and American Society* (Baltimore: Johns Hopkins University Press, 1988; originally published New York: Pantheon Books, 1986); Kathryn Grover, ed. *Fitness in American Culture: Images of Health, Sport, and the Body, 1830–1940* (Amherst: University of Massachusetts Press and Rochester: The Margaret Woodbury Strong Museum, 1989). My understanding of the history of the "Fit for America" exhibition comes from interviews with Scott Eberle, Harvey Green, Kathryn Grover, Marie Hewett, Fred Shroyer, and Patricia Tice; "'Steam to the Machine,' The Making of Fit for America," *The Strong Annual* 1 (1987): 4–11; and Harvey Green's files which he generously lent me.

2. For a helpful review of the Strong Museum's history as well as a critique of its strengths and weaknesses as a museum, see Warren Leon, "The Margaret Woodbury

Strong Museum: A Review," *American Quarterly* 41 (September 1989): 526–42. A survey of the Strong Museum collections can be found in William C. Ketchem, Jr., *The Collections of the Margaret Woodbury Strong Museum,* (Rochester: Strong Museum, 1982).

3. For the latest statement of the team approach, see "Strong Museum Procedure for Exhibition Development," available from the museum. I reconstructed the historical background on the team approach from my interview with Harvey Green, 14 April 1990, New Ipswich, New Hampshire, and from "Steam to the Machine," *Strong Annual.* Specific team member responsibilities include the following, in addition to everyone's participation in brainstorming, research, script, and design development, and fund raising. Educators are considered the "representative of the audience" and are expected to pay special attention to strategies of interpretation. They also take charge of preliminary, formative, and summative evaluations, develop school lessons and other public programs, and work closely with public affairs personnel to handle market surveys and promotion strategies. Curators work with the historian and their collections staff to acquire items when necessary and to draw up object lists, and they coordinate conservation needs with the conservator. In some cases, they may write the exhibition script. Designers develop the exhibition design and supervise its planning, construction, and installation. Historians perform historical research and analysis and usually generate the narrative essays, exhibition scripts, and other necessary documents related to the exhibition. They work closely with the curator on the objects list. Any team member may initiate an exhibition.

4. "Strong Museum Procedure for Exhibition Development," 8.

5. Wendy Wolf to Harvey Green, 18 December 1984, letter in possession of Harvey Green.

6. Donald J. Mrozek to Harvey Green, 21 July 1985, letter in possession of Harvey Green.

7. Harvey Green, interview, 14 April 1990; Wendy Wolf to Harvey Green.

8. Information about "Fit for America" at the Museum of History and Industry in Seattle comes from interviews with staff members and docents, 30 April–1 May 1990, in Seattle, and on 12 April 1990, 16 April 1990, and 7 January 1991 by phone. These individuals included: Carl Lind, director; Sheryl Stiefel, chief curator; Bruce Christofferson, designer; Martha Fulton, registrar; Kathy Henwood, educator; Linda Macri, educator; Suzanne Johnson, public relations; Teresa Tillson and Mary Anne Barron, development and marketing; and several docents and museum visitors who wished to remain anonymous.

9. For Pamela Myers's comment on the design, see "Steam to the Machine," *Strong Annual,* 9–10.

10. Bruce Christofferson, phone interview with author, 16 April 1990, and Seattle, Washington, 1 May 1990. Fred Shroyer and Kevin Murphy, interviews with author, Rochester, New York, 24 April 1990.

11. Problems encountered by the Seattle Museum of History and Industry were detailed to me interviews with Martha Fulton and Bruce Christofferson.

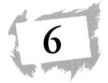

6

"MINOR LEAGUE, MAJOR DREAM"
Keeping Your Eye on the Idea

Tom McKay

Analogies and metaphors about lines surround and intersect the planning process for "Minor League, Major Dream," an exhibition at the Stearns County Historical Society on the twenty-six year history of the St. Cloud Rox, a member of professional baseball's Class C Northern League. When speaking of exhibitions, Kevin Britz, deputy director of the society, likens the planning process to playing jazz, "laying down a bass line and then improvising from there." Baseball, the subject of the exhibition, creates a game of endlessly varied action within a formal framework of predetermined points and lines.

Exhibitions also have lines that form boundaries and lines that define direction. Just as the chalk lines laid down for baseball form a playing field, the intellectual lines established by an exhibition topic form a field of inquiry. Within the boundaries of the topic, an exhibition's planners define the direction of thought by the lines of interpretation they choose to follow. Like the action in baseball or the progressions in jazz, movement along any line in exhibition planning leads to new sets of connections, a nearly infinite universe of intersections and directions for creative action.

Between the foul lines of a baseball field, a ball never travels a straight line but traces instead the arcs and parabolas determined by the forces of a natural world. Within the boundaries of an exhibition topic, the human forces traced by historians often appear in arcs, ellipses, and circles rather than direct lines of reason leading to action. The exhibition planners who must interpret these ever-bending paths of history work in museums that vary as widely as baseball's sandlots do from the major league's stadiums and that employ approaches to exhibitions as diverse as the individualistic styles of jazz musicians. Defining boundaries, choosing paths to follow, and recognizing points at which to diverge form much of the art of exhibition development.

The Exhibition

While St. Cloud, Minnesota, is not a major-league-sized city, it can point with pride to its cultural institutions. Among those institutions, St. Cloud State University claims the most outside notice, but the Stearns County Historical Society has established an important role in the cultural life of the area. The society occupies an attractive twenty-three-thousand-square-foot museum built in 1983. The museum stands on the edge of St. Cloud looking out over a small prairie park. On this fringe of the community, the steady pace of strip development common to small cities brings motels, shopping plazas, restaurants, and an ever-increasing number of their customers into the museum's proximity each year. The museum's St. Cloud location places it where the majority of the county's residents live even though most of the county extends physically to the west.

"Minor League, Major Dream" presents the twenty-six year history of the St. Cloud Rox and the team's participation in the Northern League during the years from 1946 through 1971. This Class C minor league had teams in Minnesota, Wisconsin, the Dakotas, and Canada; but only St. Cloud and Aberdeen, South Dakota, held franchises throughout the entire twenty-six years of the league's operation following World War II. As "Minor League, Major Dream" examines the history of the Rox, the exhibition focuses on the human side of baseball expressed in the community's devotion to the team and the lingering memories of the Rox players.

The exhibition consists of five sections. It devotes the first two sections to the community's involvement with the team. Two sections about player life and highlights of play in the Northern League follow. The exhibition concludes with a section describing the end of the Rox but also honoring the players who achieved the dream of making the major leagues. Upright four-by-seven-foot panels weave along the exterior of the exhibit area to define spaces and create the sections of the exhibition. In the center of the exhibit area, narrow panels arranged in a circular shape form a "shrine" exhibiting the official team photographs for each year and championship pennants won by the team during its history. In each section the exhibition uses red panels with blue highlights, the original team colors of the Rox.

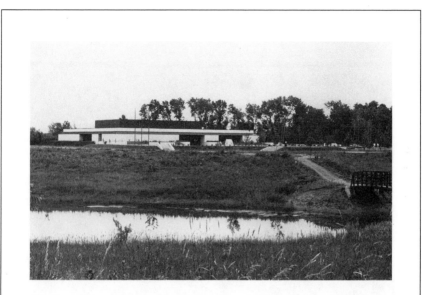

The Stearns County Historical Society stands on the edge of St. Cloud overlooking a small prairie park.

Courtesy Stearns County Historical Society.

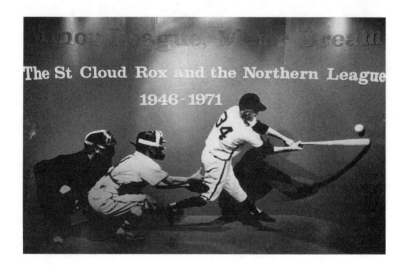

The opening panel of "Minor League, Major Dream" scores a hit.

Courtesy StearnsCounty Historical Society.

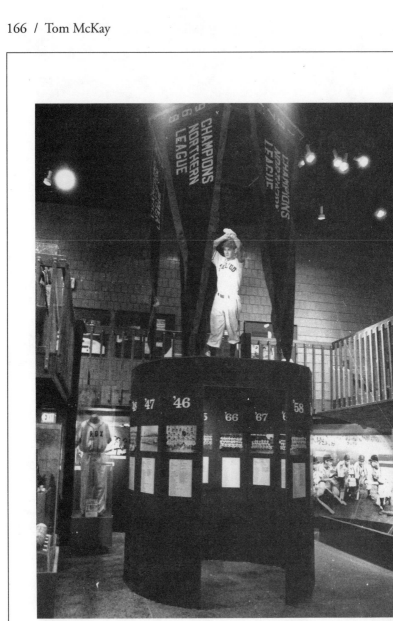

A "shrine" featuring team photographs and pennants creates a focal point in the exhibition.

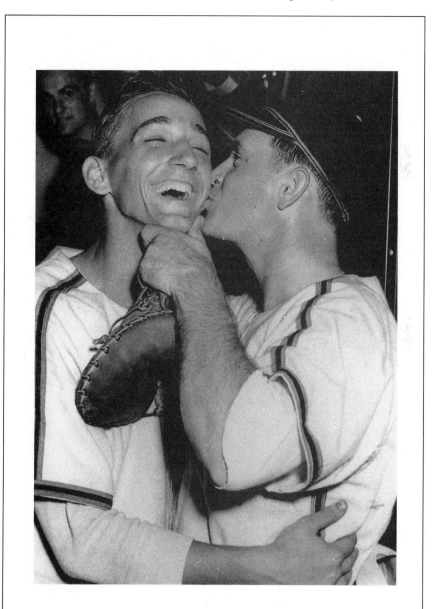

"Four Base Smack" pictures Rox players celebrating a game-winning home run in 1950.

Courtesy Stearns County Historical Society.

The nickname Rox symbolizes the conjunction of community pride and the national sports industry that took control of minor league baseball after World War II. Spelled in the style of the many baseball teams using Sox in their nicknames, the Rox made reference to the granite quarries that formed a major St. Cloud industry. The exhibition begins its story with the local efforts to attract a franchise, the naming of the team, and, most important in the community's memory, the construction of a stadium. Despite postwar shortages, the team's organizers managed to have a temporary park constructed for the 1946 season and a first class minor league stadium completed just two years later. Volunteerism and communitywide cooperation played vital roles in the success of both construction projects. Through the combination of photographs and team documents, the exhibition chronicles well the story of the community spirit invested in Municipal Stadium. Upon its completion, locker rooms and covered grandstands made the permanent home of the Rox

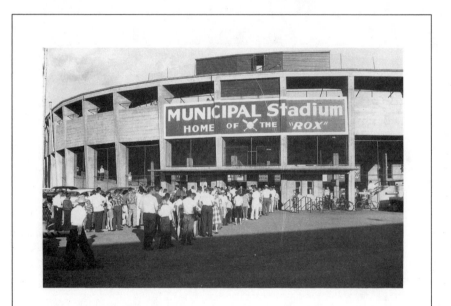

Municipal Stadium, home of the Rox, was a first-class, minor league ball park and a symbol of community pride.

Courtesy Stearns County Historical Society.

not just a ball field but a stadium. The efforts of volunteers and local businesses made it not just a stadium but a symbol of community pride.

Photographs and team documents play the major role in communicating content throughout the exhibition. These parts of the historical record, by their existence, speak of the community's love affair with the Rox. Most of the pictures came from a larger collection of newspaper photographs. The number and content of the images used in the exhibition leave little doubt that the *St. Cloud Times* lavished attention on the Rox. The franchise's last business manager preserved the team documents that appear in the exhibition. His custodianship of the records was a seventeen-year labor of love.

The second section of "Minor League, Major Dream" presents the continuing community support for the baseball team. Images of Rox fans and the volunteers who took tickets, worked concessions, and tended the field fill this section of the exhibition. Dominating this entire area, and spilling over into most of the exhibition with sound, is a re-created radio broadcast of a Rox

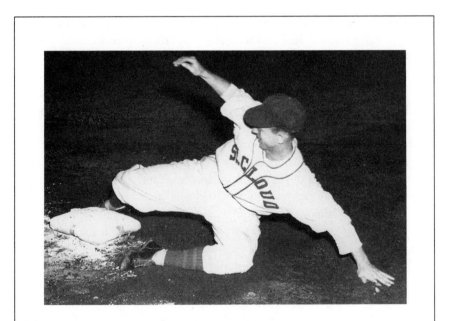

Action photos fill the third and forth sections of the exhibition.

Courtesy Stearns County Historical Society.

game.[1] A retired broadcaster who re-created Rox road games in the 1950s prepared this new recording especially for the exhibition.

Two sections of the exhibition shift the spotlight primarily to the players. A welcome addition to the anticipated baseball bats, action photos, and uniforms is material taken from a *Minneapolis Tribune* article about the Rox and the lonely life on the road in the minor leagues. Images of stark hotel rooms, pictures of cheap lunch counters, and comments about long bus rides show the minor league reality that players faced while clinging to their major league dreams. The exhibition also takes the visitor onto the field for some St. Cloud Rox lore. Photographs and recollections of ball players recount the pennant drive of 1958, the incredible triple play in the 1946 Northern League all-star game, and a near riot by fans in Fargo.

The exhibition draws liberally on oral history, which project interns collected from players, fans, bat boys, and others who followed the Rox. Through its focus on the specific story of the Rox, the exhibition capitalizes on one of the real strengths of local history museums—the ability to use specific information to make general points. The exhibition makes reference not merely to long bus trips but to "the 255-mile bus ride from St. Cloud" to Sioux Falls. In "Minor League, Major Dream" ball players are real people with real names, not the anonymous practitioners of the national pastime who might populate a more general exhibition about baseball in a national or regional museum. The exhibition also mirrors minor league playing days as the names of all-time greats Lou Brock, Gaylord Perry, and Hank Aaron share the spotlight with local heroes Willie Reigstad, Bob Pelz, and Micky McNeeley. Some of the most interesting information comes from the memories of John Sworski, the 1958 Rox bat boy. Using these memories in conjunction with a photograph, the exhibition team fabricated a replica of a dugout at Municipal Stadium. The re-created dugout serves as an interesting punctuation mark between the sections on player life and Rox lore. Though fashioned from styrofoam, the authenticity of the paint colors and placement of equipment hooks prompted visitors to ask if the dugout had been salvaged by the museum when the stadium was torn down.

The exhibition concludes with a section on the end of the Northern League and the demise of the Rox. Both were lost in 1971 to the squeeze between declining attendance and the realignment of professional baseball across the country. Prior to the 1971 season, the Rox even lost Municipal Stadium which was razed to make room for a shopping center. The exhibition pairs St. Cloud's loss of its minor league team with the achievement of major league dreams by players. Two prominent panels display photographic enlargements of baseball cards for major league players who were part of the Rox story. One panel honors Rox players who made it to the majors, and the other panel includes major leaguers from rival Northern League teams. These images combine with memorabilia such as a travel check made out to Lou Brock to end the exhibition on the positive note of major dreams come true.

Lines of Control: The PERT/CPM System

With the production of "Minor League, Major Dream," the Stearns County Historical Society initiated a new planning system for exhibition development. Over several years, the society's ten-person professional staff had developed an engaging permanent exhibition surveying Stearns County history, mounted interesting temporary exhibits, and earned national recognition through the American Association for State and Local History awards program. Despite these accomplishments, the museum staff felt the need for a better exhibition planning system, one that would help them manage time more efficiently. They adopted PERT/CPM, a hybrid project planning system developed in the 1950s by the U.S. Navy and the DuPont Company, respectively.[2] These combined acronyms stand for Project Evaluation and Review Technique/Critical Path Method.

The Stearns County Historical Society uses the PERT/CPM system to develop a schematic diagram of the planning process into five phases with checkpoints or milestones that mark the completion of each phase. The phases and corresponding milestones are:

Phase	Milestone
Idea	Topic Approval
Discovery	Feasibility Document
Development	Exhibit Scenario
Research	Label Text
Design	Scale Model or Drawing

The PERT/CPM diagram serves as a flow chart that includes the major activities required to move from one milestone to the next. The diagram incorporates the activities in a manner that represents which activities must follow each other in sequence and which activities occur independently. All of the activities in one section of the PERT/CPM diagram lead to the achievement of the next milestone. Fabrication follows the completion of the five planning phases.

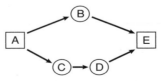

While lines and points define direction and space, time is often the most elusive element in exhibition development. The Stearns County Historical Society employs the PERT/CPM system as a method of scheduling and tracking the timely completion of activities in the exhibition planning process. The simplified diagram below shows how activities are tracked from one milestone to the next.

In this diagram, activities B, C and D must be accomplished to move from milestone A to milestone E. Task C must precede task D while task B operates independently. The lines on the diagram show these paths. If the time estimated to complete the work represented by the path A-C-D-E is eight days and the time to complete A-B-E is fifteen days, A-B-E represents the critical path. Any loss of time along path A-B-E will affect the schedule of the entire project. The A-C-D-E path could lose as many as seven days without affecting the schedule of the project.

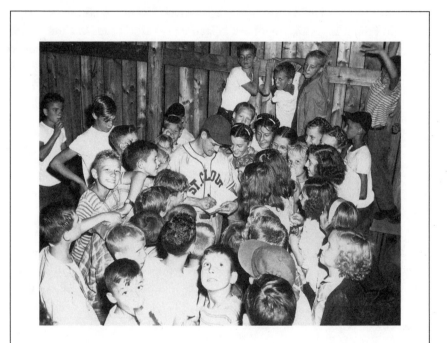

Hal Schact signs autographs for the "Knot hole gang" in 1946. Children and adults were part of the community spirit that supported the Rox.

Courtesy Stearns County Historical Society

In "Minor League, Major Dream" the Stearns County Historical Society staff set out to address, via a seventeen-hundred-square-foot exhibition, the twenty-six years of operation of the St. Cloud Rox. The staff chose to emphasize the human side of the story. Batting averages and ERA's played a lesser role in the exhibition's content than personal stories that could engage the community and touch its affection for the Rox. In addition to this interpretive goal, the exhibition process served as a training experience. Professional staff members, Ann Brown and Kevin Britz, guided the project; but Susan Clark, Susan Efta, and Cindy Lester, interns from local colleges, performed much of the work. With both interpretive and training goals, the exhibition's planning process translated into a long and complex PERT/CPM diagram. Each phase included several paths converging on the milestones leading to exhibit production. The diagram also included separate paths leading to ancillary ends such as stocking the museum's gift shop with Rox and baseball souvenirs, renting billboards to publicize the exhibition, and printing invitations to its opening.

The creative energy of jazz hardly springs to mind from descriptions of milestones, critical paths, and PERT/CPM diagrams. However, in the Stearns County Historical Society's planning process, the diagram serves only as a baseline along which to improvise. The organization relies as much on the informality possible with a small staff as it does on the structure of the PERT/CPM system in exhibition development. For "Minor League, Major Dream" the feasibility study (milestone 2) does not exist as a written document. The project interns presented an oral report to the staff in lieu of a written document. Throughout the planning process, the exhibition team—staff and interns—met almost daily for early morning discussions of the project. The conceptual evolution of the exhibition resulted from these meetings, not from the formality of the PERT/CPM diagram. The exhibition team employed the PERT/CPM system to monitor and control its use of time.

The Stearns County Historical Society adopted the detailed analysis of task and time through the PERT/CPM system to avoid piling too much work into the last stages of the exhibition process. In previous exhibitions, the society staff eliminated finishing touches at the fabrication phase because tasks that should have been completed in planning phases had carried over into the production period. The staff wanted to tighten control of time to address this problem. With the PERT/CPM diagram as a baseline, the exhibition planners hoped not only to preserve but also to add embellishments—their own improvised riffs and slides of exhibit production.

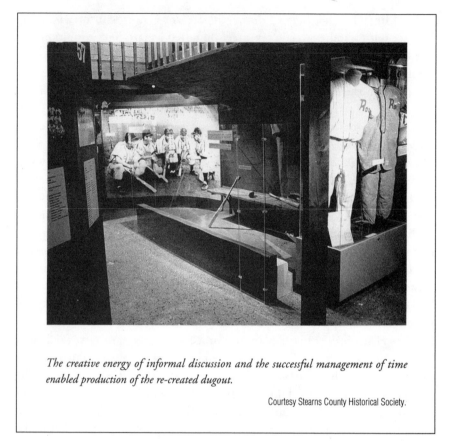

The creative energy of informal discussion and the successful management of time enabled production of the re-created dugout.

Courtesy Stearns County Historical Society.

Points of Improvisation

The Stearns County Historical Society followed its PERT/CPM diagram as a complexly articulated time line. The diagram led to the completion of "Minor League, Major Dream" comfortably on schedule. Moving the planning process along as schedule left time at the end of the project for the finishing touches that the museum felt it has lost in some earlier exhibitions. The museum allocated the time captured to creative improvisation in the exhibition's design and production. This allowed extras such as the re-created dugout. The staff had initially printed a small photograph of the dugout to include in the exhibition. One of the interns recalled considering the image for a photomural. Although others could not remember the suggestion in the free give-and-take of daily meetings, the idea quickly evolved to create a full-scale replica of the dugout. The creative energy of informal conversation and the successful management of time allowed what began simply as another small photograph in the exhibition to become a convincing re-creation and an effective change of pace in the exhibition's design.

The opening panel offers another example of creative improvisation in the exhibition's design. The written exhibit scenario envisioned an entry way simulating the main gate at Municipal Stadium. The planning team dropped the idea during its daily meetings. In its place, the staff made use of life-sized images cut from a photograph enlarged to mural size. The entry displays the figures of a batter, catcher, and umpire. The staff placed the cutouts in the spatial relationship they would have occupied on the ball field. A curved wall behind the figures adds a sense of depth to the scene and a rotating baseball, mounted on an electric motor concealed in the wall, lends the feeling of motion. Unlike most photographic cutouts, which only destroy the context of the picture and emphasize the flatness of the images, the technique works well on this opening panel and provides an engaging invitation to enter the exhibition.

The production of "Minor League, Major Dream" even managed to stretch the lines that defined the exhibition space. As the interns made connections with former players, a rich store of anecdotes about the Rox games and teams began to grow. These stories fed the exhibition's goal of focusing on people rather than scores and statistics. While the depth of the collection of newspaper photographs provided material to illustrate more of these human stories in the exhibition, the room to do so did not exist in the area allocated to the project. By staying on or ahead of its PERT/CPM schedule throughout the project, the museum found time to construct extra panels and expand the exhibition some two hundred square feet into an adjacent area.

As valuable as the exhibition team found PERT/CPM to be, the system clearly served to enable rather than to initiate creative improvisation. Adjustments and improvements to the exhibition made their way from thought to reality not along the lines of the PERT/CPM diagram but through the informal daily meetings of the exhibition team. Suggestions emerging in these morning discussions formed the basis for most changes. The ease with which these changes emerged demonstrates an advantage of the face-to-face contact and flexible working situations that small museums at their best encourage. Good suggestions over morning coffee need not die the slow death of memos and change orders mandated by bureaucratic lines of communication in some large museums.

The Stearns County Historical Society uses not only control of time through the PERT/CPM system but also control of fabrication to enable creative changes during the exhibition process. The museum staff performs virtually every element of exhibition fabrication, from building panels to developing mural-sized photographs. The ten person staff has mastered a wide variety of fabrication techniques through direct experience. The staff can incorporate a suggestion into the production of an exhibition even into the installation period because it controls the elements of fabrication. Turning a suggestion into a reality involves no negotiations with vendors, no shipping or handling time, and no rush charges.

The exhibition process in a small museum may demand every bit of the flexibility that is possible in such an organization. In this setting, significant new information and artifacts often emerge right up to the opening of nearly every exhibition. In Stearns County, the level of community interest in the Rox and the accessibility of the exhibition planners to this interested public only increased the availability of artifacts. Control of time and technique enhanced the ability of the museum staff to blend last minute information and materials into "Minor League, Major Dream."

Lines of Thought

The informal communication and flexibility possible in small museums played a central role in the intellectual development of "Minor League, Major Dream" from the project's inception. The idea emerged not from a formal planning process but rather from a comment by a staff member—made during the hectic rush to install previous exhibition—that the museum should do an exhibition about baseball. The staff developed that recommendation of a topical area into the idea for an interpretive, social history exhibition that would examine the reasons for the formation, success, and decline of the St. Cloud Rox. The exhibit scenario (milestone 3) presented the interpretive theme that the shift from community-based direction to bureaucratic direction from parent major league clubs was a primary factor in the team's gradual decline. As a second layer of interpretation, the scenario proposed that the exhibition would illuminate the human aspirations of community promoters, fans, and players that the team represented.

From idea to installation, the museum extended the physical lines defining the space allotted to "Minor League, Major Dream." However, the interpretive boundaries determining the content of the exhibition became more restrictively drawn. Often bounded by the lines of the playing field itself, the exhibition's content rarely reached beyond the walls of Municipal Stadium. The selection of artifacts reveals these tight boundary lines most clearly. The exhibition displays bats, uniforms, pennants, and dozens of baseballs, but it does not use a single artifact other than baseball memorabilia. The most unusual artifact is a seat cushion used in the stadium in the 1950s. The preservation of the utilitarian seat cushion comes as a pleasant surprise, but this artifact extends the exhibition's content no further than the stands.

The label text in "Minor League, Major Dream" makes a less restrictive presentation of the exhibition's content. Labels point to the tedium of long bus rides to out-of-town games and acknowledge "favorite watering holes" that entertained ball players in St. Cloud. Labels report declining attendance in the 1960s and the painful demolition of Municipal Stadium to make way for a shopping center. Yet, as all exhibition planners know, labels often speak with the softest voice of any element in an exhibition. This exhibition needs a plastic bag from the Shopko shopping center that replaced Municipal Stadium or a beer sign from one of the "favorite watering holes." The staff might have made a valuable investment of some of the time gained through the PERT/CPM planning process by making a trip to the salvage yard in search of an old bus seat. What the label text says, the visitor should see. An exhibition speaks more powerfully when labels, historical materials, and design deliver a coordinated message.

The fact that exhibition planners did not match artifacts to label text in some parts of "Minor League, Major Dream" suggests more than a breakdown in label-writing technique. Any historical episode has many sides, and good interpretive exhibitions almost always require a variety of artifacts to reflect this multifaceted nature of history. Exhibition planners can apply the rule of thumb that most interpretive exhibitions will contain some artifacts that seem dissimilar or unrelated until they are placed into the exhibition's story. Bus seats, beer signs, and Shopko bags do tell part of the story of minor league baseball in St. Cloud, Minnesota. "Minor League, Major Dream" does not meet the rule of thumb that most interpretive exhibits include some artifacts that seem dissimilar. The use of artifacts in "Minor League, Major Dream" reveals an exhibition in which the underlying function changed from interpretive to commemorative.

This critical shift in the exhibition's function began as a modification of focus. Through the interns' contact with former Rox players and supporters, the staff perceived that an exhibition that examined the team's decline in detail would focus too heavily on unpleasant memories. The museum staff felt that the educational value of such an exhibition could be lost in the reawakening of negative feelings about the demise of the Rox. These negative feelings in many ways distorted the overall story of success that characterized the Rox's twenty-six years of existence. The Stearns County Historical Society concluded that teaching visitors about the decline of minor league baseball would not serve the community as well as rekindling the spirit of the Rox. The staff and interns gradually refocused the exhibition on the community spirit that marked the history of the team. A modified exhibition topic emerged.

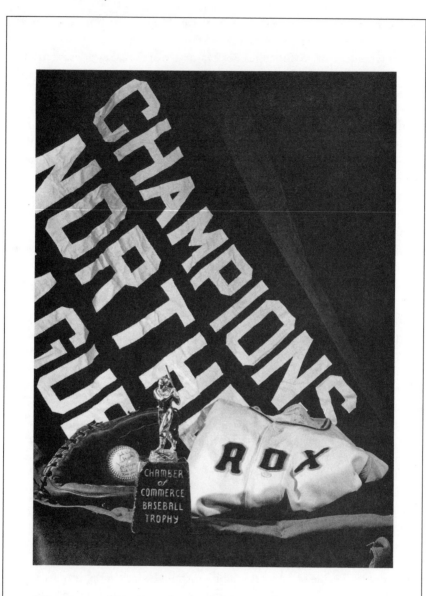

"Minor League, Major Dream" mixes the label text of an interpretive exhibition with the artifacts of a commemorative exhibition.

Photo by Sue Clark.
Courtesy Stearns County Historical Society.

Choosing a topic is the single most important step in planning an interpretive exhibition. Once a topic is chosen, exhibition planners face the second most important task: holding on to the idea.[3] Good ideas make good exhibitions as long as the ideas are not lost or obscured in all the other parts of the exhibition planning process. Unfortunately, the complexity of combining all the elements that make up an exhibition creates an ever-present danger of losing track of the basic idea or premise that started the project. In "Minor League, Major Dream" the museum did not lose the exhibition idea but did modify it. Equally significant—but less apparent to its planners—the modified topic changed the exhibition's function from interpretive to primarily commemorative. Ultimately, "Minor League, Major Dream" mixes the label text of an interpretive exhibition with the artifacts of a commemorative exhibition.

Commemorative exhibitions have valid roles in history museums. However, the change from an interpretive to a commemorative perspective requires a basic review of all the elements of an exhibition's content. In the case of "Minor League, Major Dream," this review should have revealed the disjuncture between label text and artifacts in several sections of the exhibition. The interpretive exhibit that began under the title "Minor League, Major Dream" envisioned the aspirations of St. Cloud's community promoters as one of the story's major dreams. De-emphasizing the outcome of that story recast the project and created an exhibition better titled "Spirit of the Rox." Whenever an exhibition idea is recast, the review that should follow may add or eliminate artifacts, suggest a new title, modify design, or change any of the exhibition's major elements.

The straight lines of a PERT/CPM diagram do not include the re-examination of purpose or method that can occur during an exhibition project. Review adds circular lines to an exhibition planning process. By envisioning these circular lines an exhibition team can create a planning process that is in part reiterative.[4] Reiterating an exhibition's basic premise during planning helps hold on to the idea. This reiterative part of the planning process also reveals the exhibition elements—title, artifacts, labels, design—that must change if the idea changes. Exhibitions do not always move directly A-B-E and A-C-D-E as shown on a PERT/CPM diagram. Changes may cause a return to point A and a new path to point E. The circular lines of review cannot be eliminated from exhibition development.

The underlying idea for "Minor League, Major Dream" evolved in response to the museum's perception of the community's attitude about the Rox. In a variety of other ways, community members transferred their interest in and feeling for the Rox to the exhibition. Ball players, bat boys, team directors, and fans searched their memories for information and their attics for historical

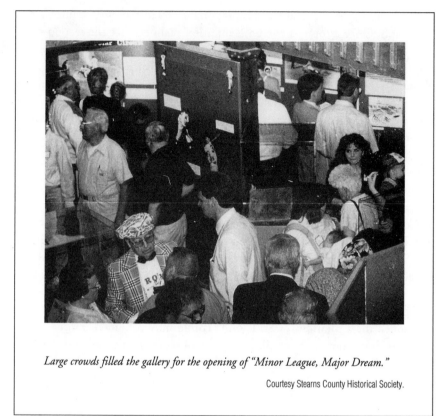

Large crowds filled the gallery for the opening of "Minor League, Major Dream."

Courtesy Stearns County Historical Society.

materials. People continued to bring Rox memorabilia to the museum even after the exhibition had opened. The first day of the exhibition turned into a major community event with people lined up outside the museum hours before the doors were unlocked.

By touching the feelings of people who cared about the team, features such as a re-created radio broadcast prepared by the former Rox announcer became part of the exhibition. That re-created broadcast describes an imaginary game played by a composite team featuring many of the Rox best players from the 1950s and early 1960s. Magic names like Lou Brock, Orlando Cepeda, and Tony Taylor fill the air but create images of a team that never existed. More critical to the presentation of history, such a team never cold have existed. The composite team includes seven African-American or Hispanic ball players, a number far in excess of baseball's unwritten but rigid quotas of the day.

In 1953, John Kennedy and Ozzie Virgil became the first African-American players on the Rox. In each remaining year of the decade, the team carried no

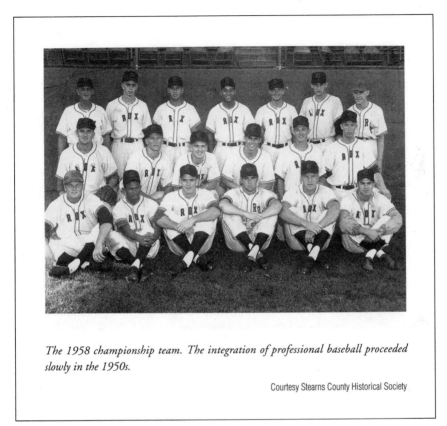

The 1958 championship team. The integration of professional baseball proceeded slowly in the 1950s.

Courtesy Stearns County Historical Society

more than three players of African-American or Hispanic descent. That period's attitudes about race dictated that integration would proceed slowly and would not be extended to rooming arrangements. Professional baseball teams arranged their number of African-American and Hispanic players so that they could room together.[5]

The exhibition observes, "The integration of the minor leagues fulfilled major league dreams for many black players." This observation mirrors the exhibition's title but not the realities of the time. Baseball's negotiation of the color line affected the "major league dreams" of players in different ways according to race. Major league teams, which stocked the minor league rosters, did not sign African-American or Hispanic players who were marginal prospects. Any African-American or Hispanic player judged less than an excellent prospect had no chance to dream the major league dream. Yet this color line shifted when teams took the field. Teams did sign white players of marginal ability to fill out minor league rosters. These players served primarily

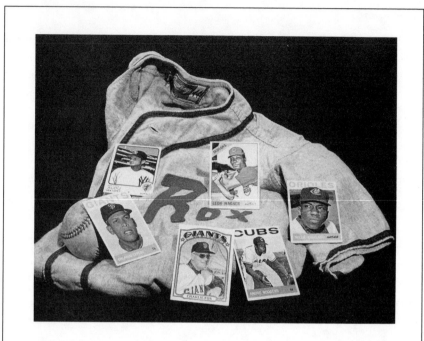

Baseball cards show the major league alumni of the Rox. Each African-American or Hispanic player actually assigned to the Rox represented a major league dream with an excellent chance to become a reality.

Photo by Sue Clark.
Courtesy Stearns County Historical Society.

for better prospects, white and nonwhite, to play and practice against. Many white members of the Rox held major league dreams that would forever be illusions. In contrast, each African-American or Hispanic player actually assigned to the Rox represented a major league dream with an excellent chance to become reality. Re-creating a radio broadcast with a Rox team featuring seven men of African heritage—Tony Taylor, Lou Brock, Orlando Cepeda, Willie Kirland, Ozzie Virgil, Andre Rogers, and Leon Wagner—ignored the tangled ironies of the color line that was wrapped around professional baseball in the heyday of the Rox.

Conclusion

Historical examination of the color line in professional baseball does not corroborate the presentation in "Minor League, Major Dream." This serves as a powerful reminder that the planning process for exhibitions in history museums has a more fundamental baseline than that established by a PERT/CPM diagram. The methods of historical study form that fundamental baseline. History museums should find the keys to the "art of exhibition development" not in the methods of art, the methods of science, or the methods of engineering, but in the methods of history.

Historical methods do drive the first phases of the exhibition development process at the Stearns County Historical Society. In conceptualizing an exhibition about baseball, the staff gathered historical data from the museum's collections and from the community. Using the data, the exhibition planners developed a historical interpretation that emphasized the parallels between the larger aspirations of the Rox players and those of the community of St. Cloud for their respective futures. The exhibit scenario proposed to trace this human story over time through the growth and decline of the Rox and the aspirations that the team represented. The exhibition's title, "Minor League, Major Dream," embodied this premise.

Research for "Minor League, Major Dream" drew heavily on oral history sources and brought into focus the continuing strength of the community's feelings for the Rox. The museum responded to its findings by shifting the exhibition's focus to commemorating the community spirit that supported the Rox. Three factors allowed the Stearns County Historical Society the flexibility to initiate change: the effective control of time through the PERT/CPM system, the daily communication of the exhibition team fostered by working in a small museum, and the in-house control of exhibition fabrication. Although the PERT/CPM system is the museum's formally delineated planning tool, daily communication and control of fabrication may make even greater contributions to exhibition development at the museum.

The lines on a PERT/CPM diagram move constantly forward in the planning process. "Minor League, Major Dream" reveals the need to include the circular lines of review in exhibition development. In the change from an interpretive focus on the aspirations represented by the growth and decline of the Rox to a commemorative focus on community spirit, inconsistencies developed between the story written in the words of label text and the story represented through the use of artifacts. Checkpoints to review the ideas in the exhibition might have identified these inconsistencies and prompted discussion of how to correct them. Regular re-examination of conceptual planning, either to identify change or to reinforce original ideas, strengthens the exhibition development process.

Baseball players understand that regardless of the strategies they develop for a game, what they do when they step between the lines of the playing field matters most to the outcome of the contest. Exhibition planners may apply a similar wisdom to their work. The Stearns County Historical Society staff has adopted the PERT/CPM system as a planning tool to manage the use of time in exhibition development. However, the performance of the tasks between points on the PERT/CPM diagram really determines the outcome of the exhibition. Both hits, such as the introductory panel for "Minor League, Major Dream," and misses, such as the exhibition's treatment of baseball's color line, can occur within the framework created by this planning tool.

Tracing the lines and connections of history that museums preserve in their collections and interpret in their exhibitions establishes a field as infinite in possibilities as the action on a baseball diamond. Those who play the game of baseball or practice the art of exhibition move constantly through complex sets of tasks and complex sets of decisions. Baseball players, despite the complex possibilities of potential action, follow one simple rule on every play—keep your eye on the ball. So too, exhibition planners might borrow the wisdom of a simple rule from which to initiate complex action—keep your eye on the idea.

Institutional Profile

Name: Stearns County Historical Society
Location: 235 S. 33rd Street, St. Cloud, Minnesota 56301
Size of Institution: 23,000 square feet
Date of founding: 1936
Number of professional staff: 10

Exhibition Data

Name of exhibition: "Minor League, Major Dream"
Dates of exhibition: May 1990–May 1992
Cost: $20,400 (excluding salaries)
Names and titles of exhibition personnel: Ann Brown, Curator; Kevin Britz, Deputy
    Director; Susan Efta, Intern; Susan Clark, Intern; and Cindy Lester, Intern.
Date of original conception: October 1987
Duration of exhibition development process: seven months
Sources of funding: In-house exhibit budget

Consultants: James Poff (content)
Number of objects exhibited: Approximately 200
Related programming:
Publications: Articles in Stearns County Historical Society
newsletter
Other: Exhibit opening featured baseball food and appearances by former
   players. Book signing by W.P. Kinsella, author of *Field of Dreams.*
Professional journal reviews: None

Notes

1. In the early years of baseball broadcasting, radio stations presented the home
games of local teams live from the ballpark. To save money, many stations broadcast
road games by re-creating them from the studio. Via telegraph or telephone, the
announcer in the studio received a brief description of the action. From this outline, the
announcer improvised an account of the game as if he were viewing it. See Curt Smith,
Voices of the Game (South Bend, Ind.: Diamond Communications, Inc., 1987), 26–30.

2. The descriptive information that follows about the PERT/CPM system has been
adapted from, Kevin Britz, "A Systemized Approach to Exhibit Production Management,"
Technical Leaflet 175, *History News* 45 (November/December 1990): 3–4.

3. Deborah Kmetz, "Applying Design Principles to History" (Presentation delivered
at the Exhibit Development Institute of the Regional Conference of Historical Agencies,
Troy, New York, 19 July 1989).

4. Nicholas Westbrook, "Historians and Designers Collaborating on Exhibit
Planning" (Presentation delivered at the Forty-eighth Annual Meeting of the American
Association for State and Local History, Rochester, New York, 14 September 1988).

5. Orlando Cepeda with Bob Markus, *High and Inside: Orlando Cepeda's Story* (South
Bend, Ind.: Icarus Press, 1983), 18–23; Henry Aaron with Furman Bisher, *"Aaron, r.f."*
(Cleveland: The World Publishing Company, 1968), 21–22; and Frank Dolson, *Beating
the Bushes* (South Bend, Ind.: Icarus Press, 1982), 107–111.

FORGING A BALANCE

A Team Approach to Exhibit Development at the
Museum of Florida History

Candace Tangorra Matelic

While many museums experiment with the team approach to
exhibition planning, few have acquired as much experience as the
Museum of Florida History. This essay analyzes the team process for
all of the permanent and temporary exhibits in a state institution with four
sites, nearly 80,000 square feet of museum space, and fifty acres. It is a
remarkable story. Perhaps more importantly, the team approach at the Museum
of Florida History has affected much more than exhibits. It is an exciting model
for the field and has as much to do with professional growth, understanding,
and respect as it does with the process of developing exhibits. My information
was collected during two day-and-a-half visits to the museum, in February and
April of 1990, which included both a questionnaire and discussions.[1] From the
findings, we can learn about effective organizational structure, both formal and
informal, and glean clues for thriving in even the bureaucratic environments of
state agencies.

The Museum of Florida History collects, preserves, exhibits, and interprets
the material record of human culture in Florida. In particular it focuses on how
people shape and react to social, political, religious, and cultural changes, and
how they interact with their natural and human environment. The museum, as
an agency of the state of Florida, is primarily concerned with interpreting those
events and conditions that are unique to Florida's population but also with
those events in which Floridians are part of larger national and global

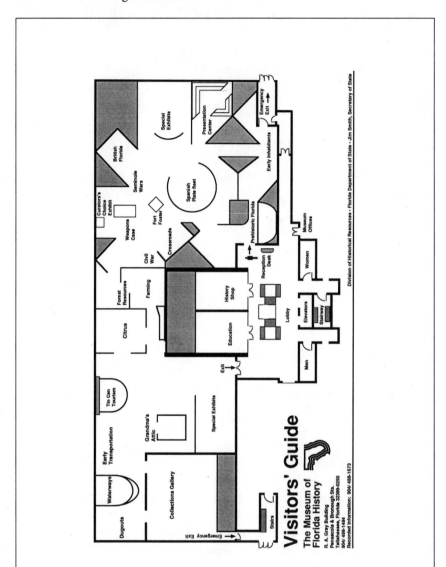

The exhibits in the Museum of Florida History's main gallery reflect both a topical and a chronological approach to interpreting the past. Two of the exhibits seen in this floor plan, "Prehistoric Florida" and "The Collections Gallery," were developed using the team system.

Courtesy Museum of Florida History.

communities. Along with educational programming, community outreach, consultation, and technical assistance, the museum's mission is accomplished through travelling, permanent, and temporary exhibits.[2]

In the main museum gallery, a space of approximately twenty-two-thousand square feet, visitors wander through at least a dozen areas covering prehistory through contemporary events and including topics such as agriculture, the citrus industry, tourism, waterways, and the peoples of Florida. The exhibit approach is as varied as the subject matter. For instance, there is a gallery area with a vaulted ceiling constructed with open beams as if to simulate grandma's attic which is filled with materials for visitors (not only children) to explore. The "Prehistoric Florida" area includes a re-created environment like those commonly found in natural history museums, and the "Waterways" area is enclosed in half of a re-created boat with two levels of exhibits. The exhibit on the citrus industry includes a section that shows the processing of fruit before it reaches consumers, and the "Collections Gallery" reminds one of walking into a storeroom filled with large shelves of artifacts. Interspersed among these exhibits are the more traditional panels and cases, a resource center, and two areas for changing exhibits. The variety in approach produces an exciting and refreshing overall effect. The floor plan indicates how these areas are arranged.

The goals of the museum are to produce educational and entertaining exhibits and make them as artifact rich as possible without submerging the interpretive message. Each topic is chosen to elucidate the museum's mission, and educational value is always a high priority.[3] The museum staff has developed a long-range exhibits plan, and in the best of circumstances, the exhibit topics originate from this document. But as director Diane Lewis notes, "there are occasionally instances where decisions are determined by political levels above the museum administration," which can cause frustration. However, this is part of life in Tallahassee, as are the seasonal shifts dictated by the legislature's sessions. Major exhibits usually open during the spring legislature session, a time when the museum is most busy.

The museum was opened to the public in 1977, and the staff has grown from seven to thirty-eight individuals. With growth has come additional bureaucracy and a clear recognition that "the institution is a political animal," a condition that has advantages and drawbacks. It is within this context that the staff has developed a team approach to exhibit development.

The team approach at the Museum of Florida History began in 1985 after several staff members attended a workshop on the team approach to exhibit development sponsored by the Kellogg Foundation. The initial road was a bit rocky as the staff moved from a more traditional mode of exhibit development dominated by collections, design, and the director. Within two years the staff had formalized the process with a thirty-six page "Exhibit Development Manual." Although they've "never had a meeting to consider whether they should stop it, it's now the norm." The staff continues to refine the process to improve efficiency, and most feel that it is worth the effort even with its pitfalls and problems. As Lewis expressed, " We know two things for sure. It is much easier to produce exhibits without the team process. The product, however, is much better with the team process."

To understand the complex issues related to both people and process, we must briefly consider how exhibits were produced at the museum before 1985 and how the current system has evolved. Some staff members describe "life before the team approach" as a scenario in which members of the collections and design sections and the director were "riding herd" over the museum. Curatorial research was completed independently, produced reams of copy, and was a "battle to cut." The historian dictated the terms of the exhibit. This product was handed to designers with no input from education and very little advocacy for collections care. The completion of the process was often "inevitably down to the wire because of disagreements and strong wills." During 1984 the museum staff experimented with a team for the "Waterways" exhibit and credited that experience for helping to sort out some major issues. It was a fairly large group of team members, and "the structure was pretty loose." The informality, some missed deadlines, a "strong willed researcher" (from the educator's perspective), numerous arguments, and a "down-to-the-wire," pressured production and installation phase, all pointed out the need for more structure.

I wish I could report that sending a team of staff members, made up of a designer, a historian, and an educator, to a Kellogg workshop in 1985 changed things overnight like a stroke of magic. It didn't happen that way. The museum did begin experimenting with the concept of "three equal voices, three people working as a unit."[4] By May of that year, the workshop team circulated a proposal that adapted the Kellogg guidelines to the specific needs of the museum, suggesting that the document could be altered to conform to the particular needs of individual exhibits. The proposal suggested that the benefits of the team approach included a greater knowledge of the total exhibit process; an enhanced personal interest in each stage of the project for team members; a better understanding of the problems of other museum professionals; and a system of checks and balances that guard against inappropriate copy, design, and educational objectives. During the summer of 1985, a short questionnaire was circulated to thirteen staff members to elicit some initial feedback. The staff responded to the process, even in this fledgling stage, enthusiastically.[5]

As I discussed this early period of experimentation with staff, people often referred to it as their "team crazy phase," noting that there were sometimes too

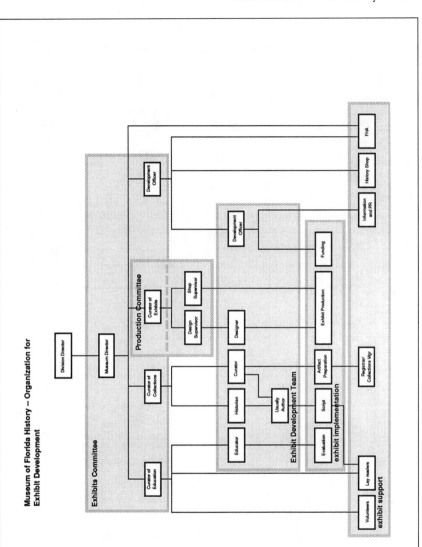

Museum staff compiled the "Exhibit Development Manual" to explain how the team process should work. This organizational chart, included in the manual, illustrates the roles of various museum staff members in exhibit production.

Courtesy Museum of Florida History.

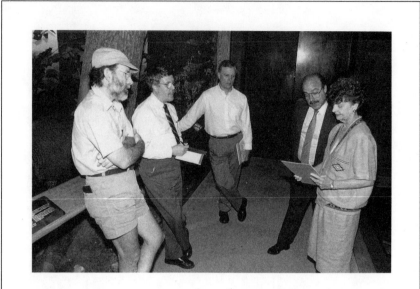

Team members Kermit Brown, fabricator, Erik Robinson, curator and historian, Lynn Rogers, designer, Alberto Meloni, development representative, and Terri Fox, educator, meet in the "Prehistoric Florida" exhibit.

Courtesy Museum of Florida History.

many meetings and too much detail in minutes, especially covering disagreements. Since team members naturally came to meetings with preconceived notions about research, design, collections, education, and how all of these elements fit into exhibits, they certainly had different viewpoints about the role of team members.

The "Old Capitol House" team exemplifies well the variety in perception and also illustrates some of the challenges the staff faced in the transition phase. As the team name implies, its assignment was an exhibit located in the House of Representatives Chamber of the Old Capitol building, one of the historic sites administered by the museum. In 1984, staff historian Erik Robinson, working independently, began research for the exhibit—before the team approach was adopted by the museum. In 1987, the first team was deactivated after the script was finished due to lack of funding. The second team began in November 1989. As the museum administrators recast the project in the team mode, adding an educator and a designer, they quickly realized that no one was working at the

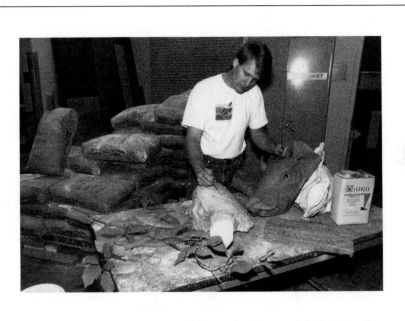

For "Prehistoric Florida," museum researchers and sculptors used fossil evidence from northern Florida to prepare a life-sized replica of the nine-foot-long Giant Armadillo.

Courtesy Museum of Florida History.

same level. Based on his previous experience, Robinson harbored preconceived ideas about the authority of the team and the decision-making process, particularly concerning research and authorship. The designer, Bob Burke, was new to the team process. He had recently returned to the museum after some time as an independent designer. Since his previous museum experience had been before the team approach, he viewed the team members as "consultants" to "his" design. The educator, Jane Brightbill, who had been on the staff since 1985, advocated consensus decision making in the team. Obviously, the group was both challenged and strengthened by different viewpoints.[6]

One other important factor helped the team approach take root at the museum. Time and again the staff mentioned the influence of the director's attitude and management style. As Albert Meloni, development section head noted:

In the beginning, because of the authoritarian management style of the director, the team process was not taken seriously by the administration, however the teams took themselves seriously. The next director (Diane Lewis), a participatory

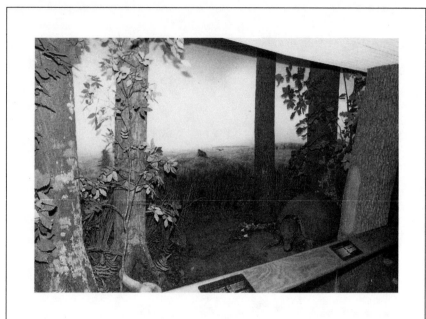

"Prehistoric Florida," which opened in May 1989, was the first permanent exhibit produced for the museum's main gallery to use the team approach.

Courtesy Museum of Florida History.

manager, supported it, and the management attitude became more tolerant of disagreement, willing to let the team work it out, both in personality and content issues. We have evolved from a far more dictatorial approach where the section heads stepped in more readily. The management style of the director clearly affects the credibility of the team.

The team process as it has evolved at the museum is described in the "Exhibit Development Manual." Let's start with the players. In the team approach, staff members from each discipline within the museum are assigned to work together as equals in the development of an exhibit. Each team member has a definite role and duties to accomplish the following charge: "Acting as advocates for the visitor, the historical information, the artifacts, the presentation, and the funding sources, members of the team present ideas and points of view, negotiate, compromise, and make decisions toward making the best possible exhibit based on the resources available."[7]

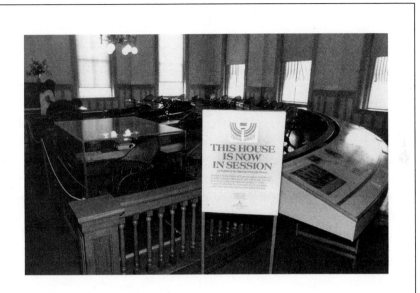

The Museum has produced several exhibits at The Old Capitol using the team approach. "This House is Now in Session" opened in 1990 in the historic House of Representatives chamber.

Courtesy Museum of Florida History.

The exhibit development team includes a curator, designer, development officer, educator, and historian. (On all recent teams a fabricator has also been added). Usually the historian or curator serves as the author, and one of the team members is selected to serve as team coordinator. Staff members normally work on two to three teams at any given time, quite possibly in different roles, depending on the subject matter, their expertise, and whether or not they have been selected to serve as coordinator or author. The normal time frame for a team assignment can range from a few months to several years. There is a separate production committee, consisting of the curator of exhibits, the design supervisor, and the shop supervisor. Each exhibit team calls on the staff in the museum's four sections (research and collections, education, design and fabrication, and development) for input and implementation. Exhibits may also use the services of readers, editors, and occasionally, specialists not on the museum's staff for additional support. An Exhibits Committee, composed of the four section heads and chaired by the director, coordinates administration and planning, reviews key steps in the process, facilitates communication, and resolves conflict if necessary.

There are twelve steps, or milestones, in the process, six of which require the approval of the Exhibits Committee before the team can proceed to the next step. The first step, an exhibit proposal, is presented by any staff member at any time, or it may be assigned by the Exhibits Committee. It describes the subject and type of exhibit, educational objectives, possible artifacts and graphics, possible related events, and funding sources. Once the Exhibits Committee has decided that an exhibit is feasible, a team is chosen, and it begins working on an exhibit concept. Including a proposed title, research survey report, statement of intent, working outline, artifacts list, graphics list, exhibit strategy, proposed budget and schedule, and formative evaluation strategy, the exhibit concept provides the conceptual basis for decisions about the organization, content, and

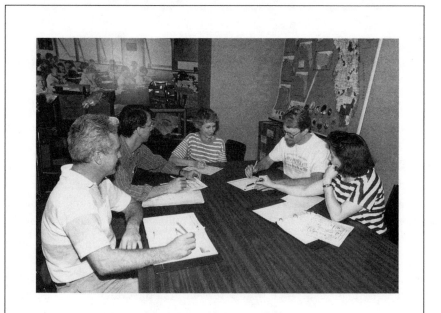

The museum uses the team approach to plan temporary exhibits, special events, and other projects. Kip Proctor, development representative, Bill Celander, designer, Wanda Richey, educator, Chip Bloyd, fabricator, and Anita Andrews Gregory, curator and historian, meet to discuss an incoming, temporary exhibit.

Courtesy Museum of Florida History.

design of the exhibit and ancillary programming. The historian prepares a separate research report that helps the rest of the team become familiar with the subject and serves as a foundation for the exhibit, educational programming, and related publications.

The team then proceeds to the next two steps, preliminary exhibit plan and the preliminary script. The designer responds to the exhibit concept by rendering a set of drawings, diagrams, and models in coordination with the shop supervisor and the team. The curator, historian, and designer prepare a comprehensive list of artifacts and graphics (with a 10 percent margin for the addition or subtraction of small artifacts), and a complete list of topics and subtopics that is coded to a diagram of the exhibit space. The development officer summarizes the current status of fund raising, and the educator writes a narrative description of programming plans. The author drafts the preliminary script (within 10 percent of a final script at this point), which is reviewed for content, accuracy, and structure. Staff members not serving on the team or as independent readers review the script to confirm that it can be understood by the audience. The "Exhibit Development Manual" provides a format and samples for the script as well as the exhibit proposal. The Exhibits Committee reviews and approves the preliminary exhibit plan, and the director approves the budget.

The Exhibits Committee uses the final exhibit plan to do a last evaluation of the concept, theme, content, design, and programming of the exhibit before committing major resources of the museum to the project. At this stage the exhibit development team produces a final design with scale elevations, floor plans, case layouts, and a scale model—if it is a large project. The team determines the specifications for graphics, headlines, label text and captions, lighting, and audio-visual components. Both an editor and the team review and approve the script, and they finalize programming plans. The production committee prepares the final budget and production schedule. During the production and installation phases, each museum section contributes the support necessary to prepare artifacts, build exhibit furniture, and install the exhibit. The education section coordinates the evaluation. If any alterations are recommended as a result of evaluation, they are taken to the Exhibits Committee for approval and then made by the design and fabrication section.

To facilitate communication about each project among all staff members, the team coordinator takes minutes of each meeting and writes them up within one week. He or she shares them with the director and team members. The director shares them with section heads who add their comments and notes to the document and return it to the team coordinator. Additional copies of the minutes are placed in a central location available to all staff members. The coordinator then circulates the revised minutes to team members. Team members also communicate verbally to the section heads and circulate other pertinent reports, such as the exhibit concept and preliminary exhibit plan.

The use of both research and collections vary according to the topic and approach of each exhibit. Research may be based on current scholarship by others or may be original findings produced by the team historian. If the necessary expertise is not available on staff, consultants may be contacted. Regardless of who does the research and writing, the credit for authorship goes to the team rather than to individuals. How central collections are to each exhibit also varies. At one end of the spectrum is the "Collections Gallery," which showcases artifacts with little interpretation beyond identification. At the other end is the "Prehistoric Florida" exhibit that has no artifacts but provides a purely interpretive, environmental context for the "Early Inhabitants" section that follows. Other exhibits fall between these two extremes. For permanent exhibits, the museum draws on its own collections, purchasing additional artifacts as

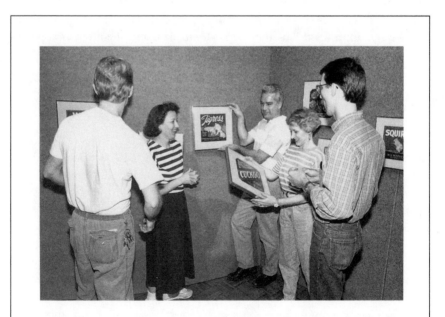

One team has been set up to oversee the museum's TREX (traveling exhibits) program. Here, team members discuss plans for "Florida Citrus Labels."

Courtesy Museum of Florida History.

needed and as resources allow. Loans are more often used in temporary exhibits. Exhibit teams work quite comfortably within these parameters.

Although this description does not include all of the details and responsibilities of team members at each step along the way, it provides a sense of the exhibit development process. While the "Exhibit Development Manual" was designed to formalize some aspects of the process for consistency and control and to define the limits of flexibility, it was also intended to evolve over time. The loose-leaf format facilitates modifications.[8] The staff uses "the written word" primarily as a reference in the early development phases to set up scheduling or to clarify various steps, particularly those requiring the approval of the exhibits committee. Team coordinators consult the manual to assist with planning, remembering the requirements of reports, or when they are unsure about duties or schedules. New staff members use the document to orient themselves to the process. Some people review it each time they receive a new team assignment, and of course, a few staff members never look at it.

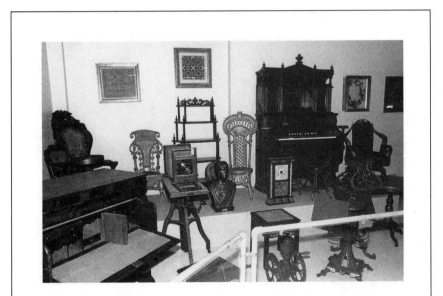

In 1991, the museum opened a new exhibit, "The Collections Gallery," in its main gallery. Artifacts from the museum's permanent collections will be rotated into this open storage area.

Courtesy Museum of Florida History.

I asked the staff members from design and fabrication, collections and research, and education sections to analyze the existing document, and numerous people had ideas about how to improve it. The original author, Mark Driscoll, then curator of exhibits, felt that it still seemed clear after a few years, but thought that since the interpretations of other staff were uneven, it could use an overhaul. Many staff members commented on the document's strength as an organizing tool and particularly appreciated the definition of responsibilities. Yet they were quick to point out that the actual process was less formal than prescribed. They modified the system to fit the situation at hand—varying the degree of emphasis or detail at a particular stage—and sometimes used shortcuts. Staff members defended some adaptions of the manual in that, on occasion, they needed to alleviate problems of personality conflicts, time constraints, and particularly difficult exhibit topics. The staff members' thoughtful critique of the manual included the following recommendations: add a brainstorming step early in the process; develop an exhibit outline to

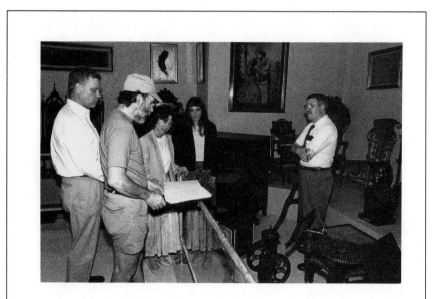

Several team members discuss plans for "The Collections Gallery" with museum director, Diane Lewis, Lynn Rogers, designer, Kermit Brown, fabricator, Diane Lewis, Jeana Brunson, curator, and Erik Robinson, historian.

Courtesy Museum of Florida History

cross-reference graphics, written content, and artifacts; articulate several alternative guidelines for different types of exhibits; revise the research report requirement since there is not always the luxury of doing it as described; and design a more user friendly format. They also requested more examples of completed steps, particularly an exhibit concept report and exhibit plan.

Does the team approach work any better than the old system? Is the product more effective now, and is it worth the extra time and effort? How does the system and staff deal with group dynamics? What happens when conflicts arise? Are there any burning issues on staff members' minds?

To explore answers to these questions, during my second visit, I developed with Lewis twenty questions which she distributed in written form to sixteen key staff members from the collections and research, design and fabrication, development, and education sections. I compiled the results from the questionnaire and coded the responses by section. These data were sent back to the museum for immediate feedback and its own internal self-study and added to my information for this essay. Both through the questionnaire and during our various discussions, I asked the staff to go beyond the analysis of the written manual and to think about the actual practice of the system in an attempt to answer these questions. Predictably the discussion got lively. Staff members often responded quite differently depending on whether they met in section groups or as team members. In their exhibit teams, the tone of conversation was extremely cooperative, even as we discussed concerns and conflicts, as if their bond as a team dictated a group life beyond any one of them individually. Back in the more traditional ambiance and support of their own sections, staff members talked about the benefits and trade-offs of the process as advocates for their respective sections. The educators clearly felt that they had gained significantly, the collections staff were much less defensive than I had expected, and the designers had the most territorial concerns.

The museum staff discussed a number of specific issues and aspects of the team approach. The issues seem to fall into three groups: those related to the process, as it has evolved over time and is currently practiced; those related to people, including group dynamics, relationships among committees, and individuals' roles; and those related to why the Museum of Florida History uses the team approach, the overall strengths and weaknesses of the system, and its effect on other areas and activities. As is quite common in the history museum field, there have been a few staff changes since this information was collected, and of course the exhibit development process continues to undergo refinement. So maybe it is best to think of this essay as a progress report.

During my visits I heard a lot of discussion about the authority of the teams and how recommendations are determined within the team. While most staff members agree with Mark Driscoll's comment that "decisions are subject to and framed by the higher order of sound museum practice and ethics, and everybody abides by those rules," there is a clear difference in opinion about how democratic the process should be. Some feel that teams should always reach consensus on decisions and vote when they don't agree. Others think that "voting formally" is unnecessary because there is a general willingness to compromise for the common good, usually leading to consensus. Still others feel that while consensus is desirable, team members should make final recommendations in their respective areas of expertise. For instance, should a team have the power to overrule a curator on an issue related to collections, one that could theoretically jeopardize the protection of an artifact? Similarly, what happens when "a panel is larger than the team approved?" Is this a design decision or a team decision? Staff generally agrees that the brainstorming step is very valuable because it promotes an awareness of the different areas of expertise. Staff members also share a general disdain for individuals who "exempt themselves from abiding by team recommendations and treat the team as no more than a medium of communication regarding their personal decisions." All in all, staff members are quite respectful of each others' expertise and advocacy roles but equally concerned about the authority and accountability delegated to the teams.

Staff members feel that the role of the team coordinator carries a great deal of responsibility and is very important to the success of the process. In addition to the communication responsibilities already mentioned, the coordinator serves as a liaison between the team and the Exhibits Committee, schedules and chairs meetings, keeps the process on track and moving forward, and shapes the experience positively or negatively. Jeanna Brunson, a member of the curatorial staff, notes that while the role may need more definition (there is not much discussion in the manual), it should remain flexible so as not to be limiting. She notes the extra time required for resolving conflicts, for "the care and feeding of individual team members, working with them to work out concerns." Other staff members who have served in the role of team coordinator agree with Brunson's perception. In fact the majority of the staff feels that the team coordinator should have more power to make decisions, especially when those decisions would help to keep the process moving. I should mention, however, that one member of the design and fabrication staff suggests that the team coordinator should always be a designer with the authority to designate duties and have the team's last word.

What happens when there is a conflict within the team that can not be resolved? Discord sometimes occurs over the issue of personal assignments versus the team process, or "when staff [members] fancy themselves experts in other areas." Clearly the design and fabrication staff members feel so constrained as if every team member were trying to design, without the training or understanding of translating verbal ideas into design language. They feel they have to act as "guardians of exhibits." This group also expresses the very legitimate concern that the team has no authority over members for missed deadlines, yet the fabrication department can not miss its deadlines. When team members can not work out a conflict by themselves, they take it to their section heads, either in the context of the Exhibits Committee or as individuals. They all realize that "sometimes this works, and sometimes not; ideas can be shot down." Yet, the appeals process is viewed as one of the important checks and balances in the system, and as Robinson notes, "that right should be exercised rather than always recognizing the authority of the team."

However, the majority of museum staff suggests that the teams ought to have more authority than currently accorded to them. Staff members note that as professionals who have knowledge and expertise in their fields, they should be given as much leeway as possible so that they can be as creative as possible. One member of the design and fabrication staff feels that the bureaucratic checks both confuse the team's authority and slow the exhibit development process. A curator repeats that staff members experience a great deal of frustration when the higher authorities in the state system hold opinions that run counter to those of the museum staff, essentially wiping out the staff's authority. They experience similar frustration when an outside consultant or designer is involved in a project because the lines of authority are not clear, placing an additional burden on the group, especially the team coordinator.

It is hard to talk about authority without touching on the relationship of the team to the Exhibits Committee, which staff members describe as similar to that of business to client or museum staff to board. Many feel that since only team members understand all the details of their decisions and recommendations, the Exhibits Committee should delegate the power to see those decisions implemented and hold the team accountable for its actions. Although, as a curator notes on this issue, perhaps the problem is not a matter of delegation as much as it is a need for communication from administration directly to the team rather than through the section heads. Some staff members feel that the "garbled transmissions of ideas" confuse the exhibits committee and recommend that a team member or the team coordinator participate in committee discussions, especially to interpret or edit brainstorming results. Mary Montgomery, collections and research section head (and a member of the Exhibits Committee), suggests that since the committee receives few formal reports from teams beyond meeting minutes, the committee might make "milestone field trips" to the exhibit space to hear the teams' informal presentations and discussions of the exhibit plans. Even within the Exhibits Committee, however, the process is one of continual "discussion, negotiation, and compromise."

At the "heart of the matter," of course, lie the ubiquitous issues of communication and group dynamics. These issues seem to be the make-or-break concerns because they can undermine even the most comprehensive system. As we know from any type of group activity, the dynamics change with each new combination of players, and the process will always be in a state of flux because of new people. We should also expect some "wasted motion in the system due to personal agendas."

When asked to describe the attributes of a good team member, staff members mention flexibility, patience, an open-minded attitude, responsibility, cooperativeness, ability to listen and contribute positively to discussion, and a good sense of humor. They discussed professional respect, for each other individually and for the role of each section in the exhibit development process. They talked about trust, diplomacy, and the care needed to accommodate strong or differing opinions. They included a willingness to work hard, to compromise, to think about all aspects of the exhibit, not just one specialty; a commitment to the idea that the goal of the team approach is to make better exhibits; and a conviction that those exhibits should inform, interest, educate, and entertain. While staff members are clear and consistent about these ideal attributes, they are realistic at the same time and readily admit that "both the strengths and weaknesses of teams are the personalities." Clearly, the process requires much individual effort, and "the team is only as good as its members."

Since we are really discussing a change in the professional behavior of staff members, the issue of whether or not team work is included in performance appraisals bears examination. Although there is normally a lag time between when a team is formed and when its work is reflected in written personnel evaluations, the issue is important because it represents the museum administration's real attitude towards the process. If one's work as a team member or coordinator is not included in his or her appraisal, the employee may view team participation as too risky and not worth the effort. When it is included as an integral and important aspect of one's job, staff members understand that team work must be taken seriously. At the Museum of Florida History, this attitude is beginning to happen as "many appraisals now recognize the norm of the team process."[9] Currently supervisors in the collections and education sections weigh employees' team participation more heavily than the supervisors in the design and fabrication and the development sections, and perhaps this contributes to the overall difference in staff attitudes towards the process. While all staff agrees that this area could be further improved, staff members feel that "standards are being changed to reward and acknowledge this work."

Another concern, or problem area, is the lack of consistent evaluation, either of exhibits or the team process. The evaluation of exhibits is outlined in the "Exhibit Development Manual" as a responsibility of the education section but is not implemented with any regularity or consistency. Bill Celander of the design staff clarifies that although little or no evaluation takes place after an exhibit is installed, the decisions arrived at by the team during the exhibit development process go through an evaluation in that team members question everything and all decisions must be justified in terms of the goals of the project. Interestingly, he describes the team approach as a "fiery process," with products that are "forged" by this continual decision making as a "tempering" force. Two collections staff members attribute the lack of exhibit evaluation to the absence of support from the administration and section heads for carrying out suggested exhibit modifications. In terms of evaluating the team process itself, Lynn Rogers, the successor to Driscoll as curator of exhibits, sums up the consensus that such assessment is done only informally because more structured appraisals usually judge personalities, not process. He notes that evaluating the process of teams on a regular basis could be very beneficial and that perhaps the museum should establish a formal procedure. In the meantime, staff members seem comfortable with individual self-evaluation, learning from mistakes, and trying to make the next assignment an even more productive experience.

Most members of the museum staff agree that the team approach, though not perfect, with time has evolved into an efficient process. Team members spend less time brainstorming and get to decision making faster, and the meetings overall are shorter. They are also better at "adjusting personal work plans to accommodate section and team priorities," although they quickly admit that to do so is a delicate balancing act. The delicate balance occurs on the macrolevel as staff tries to resolve the concerns of each section with the goals of the entire institution, and on the microlevel of the individual team, as it struggles to balance "allowing the process to work [with] maintaining efficiency." As Brunson notes, "the team process helps to expose and dissipate the stereotypical views of the sections," so that members can move beyond the old traditional roadblocks quickly to address the task at hand. For instance, the historians are much more efficient as a result of team input at the concept and idea stage and focus their research and writing. Members of the development staff feel that their colleagues now understand why they must be involved from the beginning of a project rather than their "jumping in at the very end to plan receptions and fund raise." Curators are much more sensitive to the needs of visitors, and educators have less trouble advocating that exhibits are teaching tools that actively engage visitors in the learning process. The designers recognize the value of meeting the concerns of the other sections, and some even suggest that their designs are better because of the process.[10] The entire staff appreciates that the team approach currently is quite effective in "dissipating the power games."

The staff also feel that the product is better because of the team approach. Creativity is enhanced by the input and brainstorming of the entire team, and the free flow of ideas often produces presentations and approaches that are more exciting than a mere assemblage of panels, cases, and labels. As team members discuss the content of each project, they naturally bring multiple perspectives to the subject. The process helps to ensure that the wide variety of audience interests and perspectives will be covered in the exhibit installation. In addition, since the representation on an exhibit team includes all divisions of the museum, the final product reflects the consideration of how exhibits can be a vehicle for visitor learning as well as communicating accurate scholarship.

We've touched on issues related to process and people, and throughout this discussion I've suggested numerous strengths and weaknesses of the system at the Museum of Florida History. The final topics I want to consider are why the museum uses the team approach and its effect on other areas and activities. First I'll look at the spill over of using teams for activities other than exhibits, and I'll close with some comments on why this is an instructive case study.

Because of the successes of the team approach, the staff has applied it to other tasks such as a 1988–89 collections inventory and several special events. The process has definitely moved beyond exhibits. As Al Meloni described, "it has reached the point that we seem to need a team for everything to keep everybody happy." He mentioned that there was not a team for a recent gala, and consequently, the staff felt uninvolved and disregarded. Probably the best example of the spill over of using teams at the museum occurred in 1988–89 when twenty-eight staff members participated in a team process to develop a long-range (ten-year) plan. Each person chose or was assigned to a topic area that corresponded to the exhibit sections in the main museum gallery, making a total of nine groups. Julia Hesson, a historian, served as the project coordinator, in addition to serving on two of the groups. (Note the use of new terminology, not to be confused with exhibit teams.) Some staff members concentrated their energies as the coordinator for only one group while others served on two or three groups. There was a careful effort to represent as many sections as possible in each group, without allowing any section to dominate, and to involve section heads, but not as coordinators. While the overall organization of this project was related to exhibits, the focus was clearly on coordination, planning, and establishing priorities rather than individual exhibit development. The planning groups were encouraged to talk with one another when they discovered areas of overlap. Following the meetings of individual groups, the group coordinators convened to discuss common problems, empty space, historical gaps, economics, and a ranked order of priorities. Finally the group coordinators met with the Exhibits Committee to develop a plan to implement the results. Even though the museum staff continues to deal with the frustration that the plan might change by an external mandate or a previously unforseen funding source, the overall result of the process was extremely positive. Everyone felt that the project helped to further educate all staff about other areas. It was the first time that the fabrication staff was included, and members are now on exhibit teams on a regular basis. Because staff members had invested intellectual and emotional energy into the project and the museum, they felt a sense of satisfaction.[11]

These feelings lead directly to the reasons why the Museum of Florida History uses the team approach. Many staff members describe the motivations in the same manner. They note the importance of input from all of the sections and suggest that the various points of view facilitate, as Terri Fox from the education section expresses, "an exhibit that is appealing to the visitor, imparts information in a usable manner, without compromising the integrity of the historical content or artistic presentation." The system works well when a number of projects are underway simultaneously, and it allows "the right people to know what is going on in a timely manner." Although the process takes more time, staff believes that the product is better because the interaction fosters creativity. "It does as much for interdepartmental communication as it does for the exhibit. Everybody grows, gains a better understanding of the museum's goals and functions. This helps to further professional respect and professional standards."

There is no question that the team approach to exhibit development costs time and energy. In most cases, it requires museum staff members to examine their own biases and stereotypical views of all museum functions. Such inspection may be painful. The process simply will not work without willingness and open minds, and, as in any process of change, it takes time. We know that organizations are naturally resistant to change, and people often follow suit, especially when it comes to adapting their behavioral norms. Yet I am certainly convinced by this case study that the results are worth the effort. Although I've argued with colleagues who purport that exhibits are the driving force in history museums, I now understand how exhibits can be a vehicle for improving communication, coordinating activities, and promoting professional respect. Such changes are occurring at the Museum of Florida History and lead me to agree with the staff prediction that the team process will change the nature of museum directors as time goes on. As they so poignantly express, "one can't really run a decent institution without this, it comes down to communication."

Let me end with a brief, forward-looking note. The museum staff continues to refine the team approach and has already adapted the milestones to better address the needs of temporary exhibits and special events. Staff members also plan to revise the "Exhibit Development Manual" to reflect many of the concerns addressed in this essay. Of course, as you probably guessed, they know that they will produce the best results for the revision by using a team approach.[12]

Institutional Profile

Name: Museum of Florida History
Location: 500 S. Bronough Street, Tallahassee, Florida 32301
Size of Institution: 80,000 square feet; 50 acres (4 sites)
Date of Founding: 1967; opened to public 1977
Number of professional staff: 32

Exhibition Data

Name of exhibition: Various exhibitions in the museum's permanent exhibits gallery
Dates of exhibition and venues: varied
Size of exhibition (square feet): varied
Cost: varied
Names and titles of exhibition personnel: Listed throughout the essay for various exhibits
Date of original conception: 1985
Duration of exhibition development process: Continuing
Sources of funding: State, private
Consultants: minor use for some exhibits
Number of objects exhibited: 0 ("Early Inhabitants") to 1,205 ("Collections Gallery")
Related programming: The museum provides a mix of gallery programming, publications, media coverage, gallery talks and lectures, workshops, special events, and exhibit opening programming for each exhibit.
Professional journal reviews: None

Notes

1. Throughout this essay, I have tried to attribute statements to individuals when I could identify them by names and when the issues and subjects did not seem controversial or sensitive. In some cases, I have not attributed a direct quotation because it was either a remark in a group meeting expressed by a number of people, or it was a written comment on a questionnaire without a signature.

2. This description was paraphrased from the museum's mission statement as published on page 1 of the "Exhibit Development Manual," 1987.

3. Goals were stated by Diane Lewis, museum director, in a set of notes that answered questions posed by the author. They are paraphrased as stated in the text.

4. The Kellogg Foundation funded a series of workshops on exhibit development using the team approach from 1982 to 1988.

5. Copies of the internal questionnaire and memos related to the initial team who attended the Kellogg workshop were shared with me by Terri Fox, educator, who was one of the original team. For the record, Bob McNeil represented collections. Design and fabrication was represented by John Locastro and Ed Jonas. Locastro was unable to complete the workshop, and Jonas replaced him.

6. This summary is based on a discussion with this exhibit team and on supplementary written materials, particularly the exhibit proposal.

7. "Exhibit Development Manual," by Mark Driscoll, former curator of exhibits, with input from other Museum of Florida History staff, 1987, page 1.

8. My summary of the process was excerpted from the descriptions in the "Exhibit Development Manual." Page 2 provides a list of the milestones, pages 3–9 and 12–13 provide more detailed descriptions of steps, pages 16–17 outline the job responsibilities of all project personnel, and pages 10–11 show an exhibit development flow chart. The appendixes, pages 20–36, include sample documents and forms for scheduling and budgeting. The organizational chart from page 36 of the manual is reprinted as part of this article.

9. A number of staff graciously shared portions of their most recent performance appraisals to prove this point.

10. There is not a consensus of support in the design and fabrication section for the team approach. However it should be noted that the majority of the sections are generally in favor of the process.

11. Summary based on written materials provided by Julia Hesson and on discussions with staff. Of particular use were the written proposal dated 8 July 1988 and the chart of planning group assignments dated 14 July 1988.

12. This prediction is based on a conversation with Diane Lewis, museum director. I am extremely grateful for the openness, candor, and cooperation of the Museum of Florida History staff throughout the preparation of this essay.

A PRIORITY ON PROCESS

The Indianapolis Children's Museum and "Mysteries in History"

Cynthia Robinson and Warren Leon

Some of the best history exhibits are in children's museums rather than in history museums. Although some children's museums are merely glorified toddlers' play spaces, the best ones deserve serious examination and careful emulation. They demonstrate a subtle understanding of the exhibit medium and of their audience's needs. By appealing to children's desire for novelty, fun, and involvement, children's museums also captivate and educate adults.

Children's museums' ability to produce creative, exciting, and successful exhibits resides partially in their exhibit planning process. This essay examines the making of one exhibit, "Mysteries in History," at the Indianapolis Children's Museum, to see what history museum professionals can apply to their own work. That "Mysteries" is only partly successful despite a fundamentally sound premise and production process shows how difficult it is to create an outstanding exhibition. But before inspecting this particular exhibit, let's consider the context in which children's museums operate.

Children Are a Demanding Audience

Those who try to educate children in a museum or other noncoercive, voluntary setting discover quickly whether or not they are reaching their audience. Most children do not suffer in silence. When they are bored or uninterested, their attention wanders; they chatter and whine. Faced with a museum exhibit they do not like, they will impatiently pester and pull their adult companion to leave.

Observant museum staff members soon learn that their first task is to capture the attention and interest of their audience. It does not matter how sound or important an exhibit's content is if it is not presented in an appealing, engrossing manner. Children judge a museum visit on the quality of the experience rather than on the quality of the staff's scholarship.

Children's museums therefore often place more emphasis on presentation than content, especially when compared to history museums. Sometimes the resulting exhibits rely so heavily on gimmickry and activity-for-the-sake-of-activity that the content gets lost. Yet, on balance, children's museums are right to place priority on presentation. For history exhibits aimed at adults as well as children, a well-thought-out presentation that is designed to capture and keep the audience's interest is essential to success.

Children Change So Exhibits Can Remain the Same

Visitors to a children's museum are ever changing. For example, if the museum's core audience comprises children aged six to ten, there is a complete turnover in audience every five years. There are always fresh children coming of age who are ready to take advantage of the museum's offerings. Even though an exhibit may have been in place for ten years, a newly arrived six-year-old will experience it as a new installation. Consequently exhibits at a children's museum can have a long life span.

Permanent exhibits succeed even with repeat visitors to children's museums. Children like the idea of re-experiencing favorite activities. They enjoy hearing the same story or watching the same movie many times, and they like to return to a museum exhibit if they enjoyed it the first time. Part of their continuing fascination is that they unconsciously experience the exhibit differently the second time around. Their intellectual ability, social skills, and knowledge change so rapidly that after even a few months' absence they can get whole different levels of meaning from the same museum objects and activities.

The best exhibits in a children's museum can therefore be experienced on a number of different levels and reward return visitors with new insights, more complex ideas, and varied activities. But the creation of such exhibits takes considerable resources, planning time, and coordination.

An exhibit—either aimed at children or adults—is such a complex and difficult medium that rushed, underfunded efforts are not likely to succeed. By focusing on the production of a relatively few long-lasting exhibits, the staffs of children's museums increase the chances of their educational success. An exhibit scheduled to last for ten years rather than ten weeks can be planned carefully. Significant production expenses and staff time commitments can be justified.

Even more importantly, staff has time to revise and modify the exhibit once it has opened and the reaction of the public has been measured. Staffs can use evaluation as a tool for improvement and fine tuning rather than for postmortem exercise.

When a history museum staff tries to mount a major temporary exhibit every few months, the result is likely to be disappointing. Yet many history museums feel obliged to emphasize such exhibits because their audiences are unchanging, and they perceive new exhibits to be the vehicle for encouraging visitors to return.

The changing nature of the audience at children's museums therefore gives such museums significant advantages. The Indianapolis Children's Museum has embraced an exhibit development process that builds on these advantages. The process emphasizes exhibits based on extensive research, staff travel, and evaluation. A carefully chosen team receives an unusually generous amount of time and money to complete its work. Information gained from ongoing evaluation provides a framework for new exhibits and is used to revise existing exhibits over a period of years.

The museum's history exhibit, "Mysteries in History," was initially installed in 1985 when the museum was just beginning to develop its current approach to exhibit planning. Parts of the exhibition have undergone revision several times, and it will likely remain in place for at least ten years. The story behind "Mysteries in History" and the Indianapolis Children's Museum's subsequent elaboration of its exhibit development strategy holds useful lessons for those working in history museums.

The Evaluation and Death of the Americana Gallery

Staff members at the Indianapolis Children's Museum did not initially set out to produce a new history exhibit, and they were certainly not proposing to design an exhibit based on the themes in "Mysteries in History." "Mysteries" instead emerged gradually as an outgrowth of a larger project—a two-year evaluation of the museum's educational effectiveness that was conducted by professional evaluators.

At first glance, the Indianapolis Children's Museum would have seemed an unlikely institution to consider such a comprehensive evaluation. By the standard ways in which museums measure success, the Children's Museum was phenomenally successful. Few American museums had as much popularity, centrality, and respect within their community. Indianapolis residents were proud of the Children's Museum and bragged about it to outsiders. When it moved to a new 203 thousand-square-foot building in 1976, it became the world's largest children's museum. Attendance skyrocketed from 180 thousand in 1972 to over one million visitors in the first fourteen months after the move.[1] An unusually strong funding base enabled the museum to employ 150 staff members, including fifty professional staff, and to attract over five hundred volunteers.

Shortly after the move to the new building, a number of factors led the museum staff to embark upon a major evaluation project. During the move the staff devoted an enormous amount of attention—out of necessity—to the physical aspects of the museum. The education programs and philosophy, however, had not received the same internal scrutiny and had been transported, unchanged, into the new building. Education staff members questioned the appropriateness of the old programs and goals in the new facility and wanted the move to be a catalyst for examining the institution's educational goals and methods of achieving them. As the last of the permanent installations neared completion, there was neither a plan for future exhibits nor a long-range plan for the museum's overall direction. Staff members decided to take a hard look at what they had just created at their new site.[2]

The people at the Eli Lilly Endowment were instrumental in shaping the evaluation study. They promoted the use of a qualitative model of evaluation, where visitors' perceptions, feelings, and knowledge are explored through in-depth interviews and observations. They also introduced the museum staff to Barbara Tymitz and Robert Wolf of the Indiana Center for Evaluation. In 1977 Wolf and Tymitz began to work with the staff at the Children's Museum. They collectively designed a two-year study, funded by the Lilly Endowment, to analyze the effectiveness of the museum's programs.

The evaluation team chose the museum's Americana Gallery as one of its study subjects. This eleven-thousand-square-foot exhibit was the museum's one history gallery, and it focused on Indiana's past. Museum staff had noticed that although the gallery attracted as many visitors as other areas of the museum, it had little holding power. Wolf, Tymitz, and museum staff members observed visitor behavior and interviewed people of all ages. They concluded that live interpretation in the gallery was successful but that the artifacts and labels did not engage visitors for long.[3] Those visitors who encountered an interpreter not only stayed longer in the Americana Gallery but the encounter with a museum staff member "apparently stimulated the visitor to pause longer at other displays. . . ."[4] Visitors who had observed interpreter demonstrations were also more specific in their descriptions of life in the past than people who had viewed the same displays without interpreters. Those visitors who had asked questions of the interpreters demonstrated even greater ability to retain and articulate information. Regarding the educational value of gallery interpreters, the report concluded:

> The demonstrations stimulated increased interaction between visitors. Children asked more frequent questions of their parents; adults spoke more with each other; and there was little hesitancy on the part of most visitors to question the person presenting the demonstration.[5]

Since the exhibit labels and the artifacts themselves had limited appeal or holding power, the interpreters were essential. But live interpretation only occurred at scheduled intervals. The authors of the report noted that:

> [Visitor] criticisms seem to be leveled not at the programs themselves but at their scarcity. In conducting the interviews on several days and under the three conditions . . . static display, quasi-static display, and dynamic display, it was significant that the Hall seemed to come alive on those times when programs were in operation.[6]

Not surprisingly, the gallery's evaluators recommended expanded use of gallery interpreters. But they also suggested ways to make the inanimate parts of the exhibit more appealing. They recommended adding more touchable objects, revising the labels to "present contrasts and curiosities" in the form of questions, and presenting more information about children' lives in the past.[7]

Although the evaluators suggested strategies for salvaging the Americana Gallery, their data ultimately produced a stronger reaction. They reported that "there were *no* visitors who expressed a clear understanding of the relationship between various areas of the Hall," and quoted one visitor who called the whole gallery a "hodgepodge."[8] Since the Americana Gallery was intended to be thematic, this was damning information. Rather than revise the exhibit, with its host of problems, the museum staff decided to scrap the gallery and start all over again.

Staff received support for its decision from the new director, Peter Sterling, who had come to the museum in 1982. Sterling wanted to shake things up. He had observed that the Children's Museum had "a self-satisfaction that within its walls it had the answers."[9] Sterling instead felt that the broader museum world and material culture scholarship were shifting rapidly in ways that the Children's Museum needed to consider. "I thought we should start from the point of view that we knew very little about this," he recalls, "and that our job was really to seek out the best solutions."[10] The museum's use of trained, outside evaluators like Wolf and Tymitz matched his vision of how to find those solutions. The new history exhibit that would replace the Americana Gallery would be the first major exhibit at the Children's Museum since Sterling had become director.

Developing a Plan for a New Exhibit

The evaluation of the museum's various exhibits suggested that the most effective ones had strong input from educators, according to exhibit planning director Nikki Black.[11] This finding was a catalyst for developing a team approach to exhibition planning and for creating a new staff position, the educator/curator.[12] In 1983 Mary Latham, educator, Alex Black, designer, and Robert Johnson, educator/curator of American materials, were given responsibility for proposing and planning a new history exhibition. They reported to the Exhibits Committee, a group of department heads and Executive Director Sterling.

The opening date for the new exhibit was set for two years in the future. Alex Black and Johnson estimate that they initially spent about 60 percent of their time on this particular project; the percentage rose to 80 percent as the opening date loomed closer.[13] Latham had recently had a child and thus spent her entire twenty-hour work week on the project.

The team was given conceptual freedom within a few unchangeable parameters. The exhibit they designed was to incorporate most of the recommendations made by the Wolf/Tymitz evaluation. They were to target eight- to twelve-year-olds as a primary audience since Indiana children study state history in the fourth grade. Because school groups constitute only 15 percent of the museum's visitation, the team had to consider the needs and interests of all age groups, including adults, who constituted 40 percent of the visitors to the Children's Museum.

The most significant restriction to planning was physical. A full-sized log cabin had been installed in the Americana Gallery and it could not be moved.[14] All conceptual plans had to include it as a historical topic, and all floor plans had to be designed around it.

Early in the planning, the team came up with a proposed budget of one-half million dollars, a figure that included the team's time and all construction and installation costs, as well as revision expenses that would be identified through evaluation of the finished exhibition. The museum received the entire amount from the Krannert Charitable Trust.

The exhibit team's first proposal was similar in content to the existing Americana Gallery. They suggested a chronological presentation of Indiana history from first contact between natives and Europeans to the present, with a focus on technology. Johnson recalls: "We originally wanted to do twelve settings, starting with a French fur trading post and coming all the way up to

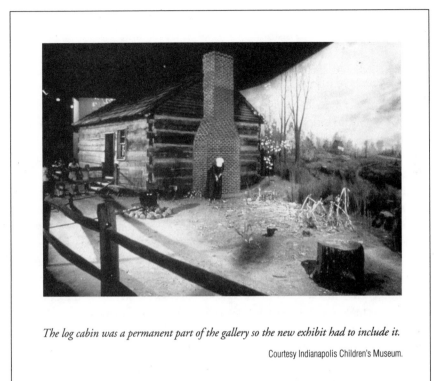

The log cabin was a permanent part of the gallery so the new exhibit had to include it.

Courtesy Indianapolis Children's Museum.

the present. Through these twelve settings we would also be following a family that started with the French fur trader and an Indian maiden all the way to the present. There would be genealogical links all along as well."[15] But the Exhibits Committee rejected this approach, as well as various variations on this theme that followed.

The team struggled with conceptual ideas for about a year. Towards the end, they wrote an eleven-page proposal for an exhibit to be titled "Clues in Your Attic" and mailed it to scholars and museum professionals outside the museum. In it, they identified seven objectives, proposed a floor plan, and described eleven re-created settings from different periods in Indiana's history.[16] They felt this proposal overcame one of the Americana Gallery's major weaknesses—its detached approach to the past. Visitors had difficulty relating to and getting excited about the various impersonal icons of the state's history that were displayed. The exhibit team therefore proposed a more personal, more accessible version of the past. To keep the history on a personal level and to "encourage visitors to investigate and appreciate their own personal and family histories more fully," each setting was to "represent a scene from the daily life of a child in a fictitious, but historically plausible, family unit."[17]

The Exhibits Committee still did not feel that the exact right approach had been reached, and some of the outside reviewers agreed. In the most extensive and provocative of the reviewers' critiques, David Parke, the associate director of the Farmers' Museum, suggested a different goal for the exhibit. In his view, a history exhibit for young people "should mainly be concerned with developing one's perception of the past in general—providing the visitor with some methods of looking at the past." According to Parke, Indiana's history should be of secondary importance. "Before the museum visitor can really begin to understand distant time periods, he or she must be able to perceive the existence of the past in our daily environment. . . . What clues are around us in our daily lives to shed light on the past?" Parke worried that the proposed exhibit's re-created settings would oversimplify history and provide pat answers to complicated questions. He argued that the excitement of history was that "there are so many mysteries, so many things yet to discover."[18]

Echoing ideas in Parke's critique, Peter Sterling proposed using the exhibit to help visitors understand the process of how people find out about the past. Sterling wanted to look at visitors from an unconventional perspective: "not just as absorbers or consumers of information, but as partners in understanding how one goes about learning about one's history."[19] By focusing on process rather than content, a young audience that had only a few years of personal experience to look back on would for the first time understand the meaning of the concept "history."

So the exhibit, now titled "Mysteries in History," finally had a conceptual focus. But because it had taken some "pushing and tugging for that idea to emerge," there were only ten months left before the new exhibit was scheduled to open.[20] The team reworked their ideas to design an exhibition that would teach visitors how to investigate the past. Many of the exhibit sections—an archaeological dig, a street scene, most of the vignettes in a section on oral history and of course the log cabin, traced their origin back to the original proposal developed by the exhibit team. Johnson recalls, "we felt so strongly about the visual impact of those settings that we never let them go."[21] The resulting exhibition plan incorporated process sections into Indiana history sections that had survived through the changes.

Although today the Indianapolis Children's Museum builds travel research for team members into the planning process and solicits input from outside consultants at various points during the exhibit planning process, in 1984 the museum was just beginning to incorporate these elements into its approach to exhibit planning. There were consequently few vehicles for gathering input from outside the museum. By the time the final idea for "Mysteries in History"

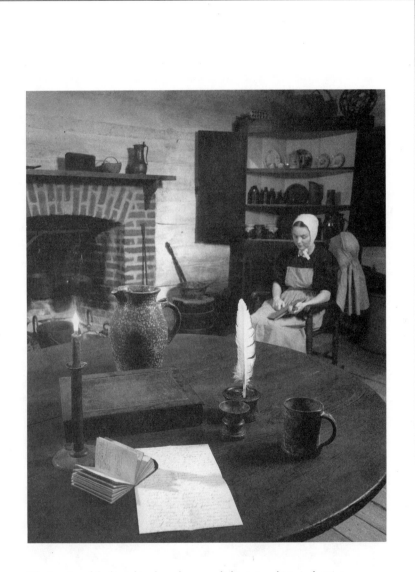

The interior of the log cabin shows letters and objects in a historical setting.

Courtesy Indianapolis Children's Museum.

emerged, the time frame was too tight to include further outside consultation anyway. Moreover, the focus on historical process was so unique that other museums could provide few relevant models. Nevertheless, the exhibit script was sent out to twelve professionals for their responses. The large size of the museum staff enabled team members to solicit ideas and feedback from their colleagues.

The First Incarnation of Mysteries in History

"Mysteries in History" opened in June 1985 and was divided into four clue sections, each highlighting a different process for investigating the past. Each section was divided in two: a "now" area that taught methodology used by historians, followed by a "then" area that presented a historical experience through reconstructions and artifacts.

"Dug Up Clues" featured an archaeological dig site in the "now" area where visitors could sift through dirt to find artifacts. A round diorama showed an archaeological dig, while a computer game allowed visitors to simulate one. In

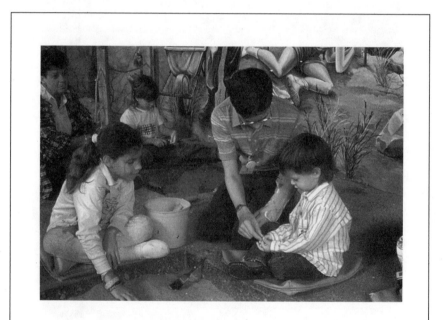

A mock archaeological site allows visitors to find artifacts and learn about archaeology as a source of knowledge about the past.

Courtesy Indianapolis Children's Museum.

the "then" area, a reconstructed fur trading post showed archaeological finds in their original setting.

"Written Clues" presented an attic area with documents and artifacts, the immovable pioneer log cabin, a covered wagon, and a computer simulation game, "Load a Wagon." The attic objects and documents introduced visitors to historical sources about everyday life in the past. The furnished cabin then allowed visitors to step into the past. Its exterior was realistically landscaped and a painted backdrop carried the scene into the distance. Beyond the yard was a pair of life-sized oxen and a Conestoga wagon. A circular diorama of a pioneer river village of the early 1800s put the cabin and its yard into a larger perspective. Visitors could pick up earphones to hear a young woman describing the community depicted in the diorama.

"Visual Clues" introduced the built environment as an information source through back-lit transparencies of architectural house styles, touchable architectural elements, and historical photographs. A re-created, turn-of-the-century commercial street, complete with trolley tracks, building facades, and street lights provided the "then" portion of "Visual Clues." Sound effects of horses' hooves, trolleys, and other street noises heightened the sense of stepping back in time. Visitors could enter three stores on the street.

"Spoken Clues" focused on oral history. Five scenes—a Vietnam veteran's bedroom, a cemetery, a circus act, a 1930's kitchen, and a one-room schoolhouse—were set behind glass. Recorded voices described memories associated with each scene.

In response to visitors' favorable reaction to the live interpretation in the old Americana Gallery, the exhibit was staffed with interpreters. Some led visitors in activities that explored historical methodology, while others dressed in costume and engaged in first-person interpretation of the past. The first-person interpreters were stationed in the re-created French trading post, the log cabin, and the turn-of-the-century stores.[22]

Initial Evaluation

The Indianapolis Children's Museum was committed to extensive evaluation of "Mysteries." Sterling and key staff members wanted the exhibit's development and evaluation process to be a model for future projects. They were especially anxious for staff members to collect evaluation data. As Nikki Black notes, "If the exhibit process was going to be a developmental tool for the staff, then they really needed to spend time out in the exhibit galleries after an exhibit opened to compare their expectations with the actual visitor behavior."[23]

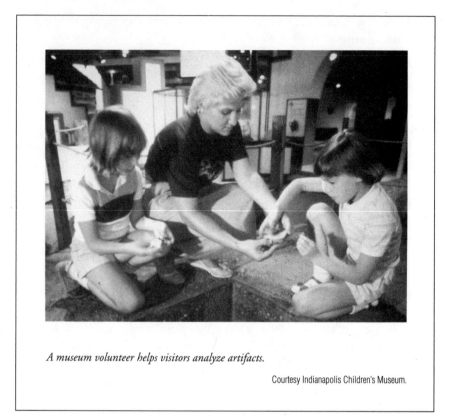

A museum volunteer helps visitors analyze artifacts.

Courtesy Indianapolis Children's Museum.

With funding from the Kellogg Foundation, Barbara Tymitz was again hired to organize and oversee the evaluation. "Mysteries in History" was the museum's first exhibition to provide written conceptual and behavioral objectives for the various exhibit components, and the evaluation tried to measure their success.

Tymitz, Indiana University doctoral students, and the staff conducted six separate one-month studies using a variety of information-gathering techniques. Staff members first observed the paths, stops, and length of time visitors spent at exhibition components. The collected data helped them develop questions about visitors' behavior for use in an interview portion of the study. The staff also studied the effectiveness of labels, the achievement of behavioral objectives, adult/child interactions, and the impact of activities upon visitors' understanding of the past.

Not surprisingly, the evaluation confirmed what was apparent to the casual observer—visitors were attracted to "Mysteries in History" and found it interesting. But the evaluation also provided less obvious information. For

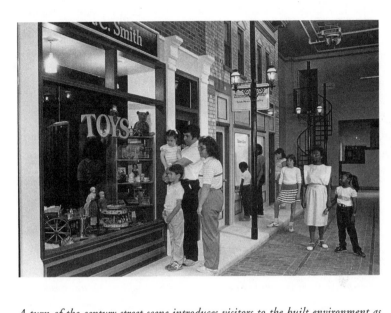

A turn-of-the-century street scene introduces visitors to the built environment as source of information about the past.

example, the staff found it revealing to learn which subjects and sections of the exhibit visitors found most interesting and to assess the effectiveness of the content, style, and placement of labels. Learning visitors' reactions did not always help the staff know how to improve the exhibit, however, since, as Nikki Black points out, evaluations only measure the effectiveness of what is present; they do not suggest solutions to the problems.[24]

When the exhibit's budget was first established, the staff had set aside 10 percent of it to cover the cost of postopening revisions. Some of the necessary changes were minor. For example, when the evaluation was just starting, the staff disconnected the oral history reminiscences in the "Spoken Words" section because the vignettes stirred visitors' own memories and stimulated them to share family and personal stories with each other. Over time, specific labels were also changed.

The evaluation also identified two general problems with the exhibit. First, visitors did not use the intended flow pattern—moving to the right, rather than the intended left, after the first section. Because visitors went through most of the exhibit backwards, they did not always see section introduction labels, and they had a hard time seeing the exhibit as a coherent, logical whole.[25]

The traffic flow situation was linked to a second, much more important problem—visitors did not focus on the central theme of the exhibit. When evaluators first asked visitors what they thought the museum wanted them to take away from the exhibit, only 11 percent "described the exhibit as one in which a person could learn about the past from clues in the present." Almost all visitors thought the gallery was about what life was like in the past or about the progress that had been made since the nineteenth century.[26]

"Mysteries in History" Five Years Later

In the five years since it opened, "Mysteries" has undergone many changes. To persuade visitors to travel in the intended direction, the museum staff tried everything from barriers to oversized signs. But when visitors climbed over barriers and ignored signs and arrows, the staff conceded defeat and placed introductory labels at the ends of each section for visitors traveling backwards.[27]

Ironically, the museum abandoned first-person interpreters—an innovation that had seemed to be a logical response to the evaluation of the Americana Gallery and to visitors' stated preference for live interpretation. The first-person interpreters had helped to confuse visitors about the purpose of "Mysteries in History" since they were placed primarily in the "then" parts of the exhibition. By 1990 the gallery floor was instead staffed by paid employees, interns, and volunteers. Primarily stationed in the "now" sections of the exhibit, supplying live, but not first-person interpretation, they led visitors in a variety of activities that introduce historical methodology.[28]

A number of more specific changes were made as well. The attic area is now "Samantha's Attic," and a computer simulation game, "Samantha's Search," allows visitors to acquire and practice new knowledge. In the log cabin, a sound-and-light show centering on diary entries directs attention to the significance of the cabin's furnishings.

Assessing the End Result

"Mysteries in History" seems like every history museum educator's dream—an exhibition that combines an investigation of historical process with a format that invites participation. The exciting concept plus the museum's substantial investment in evaluation and revision should have ensured a highly successful exhibition. Yet six years later, "Mysteries" has still not reached its full potential.

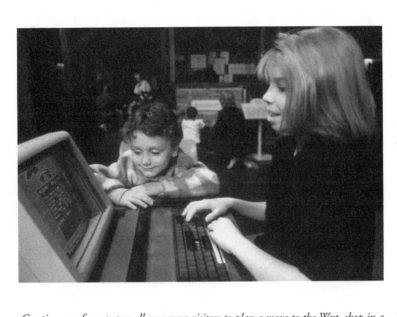

Creative use of computers allows young visitors to plan a move to the West, shop in a frontier general store, or trace a family's history.

Courtesy Indianapolis Children's Museum.

Despite all the evaluation and revision, museum staff members are not yet completely satisfied.

Part of the problem is that the staff has still not resolved the two central dilemmas identified in the initial evaluation—visitors' unwillingness to flow through the exhibition in the intended direction and their inability to perceive the theme of historical methodology.

At first glance, the flow pattern problem would seem minor, and the museum's solution of placing introductory labels at the ends of sections would appear to be satisfactory. Yet the solution undermines the structure of the exhibition—to introduce historical methodology and then apply it by "stepping back in time" in the historical re-creations. Visitors who enter the re-creations first may miss the exhibition's conceptual framework since the re-creations by themselves pose no questions about historical methodology. Moreover, when the "now" sections on methodology are entered after the re-creations, they seem irrelevant.

In part, the message of the exhibit remains murky because "Mysteries" has never had a strong story line. In fact, some of the changes over the years may have blurred what story line there was. By attacking the exhibit's problems through revisions of individual components, "Mysteries" has been left disjointed and confusing. We suspect many first-time visitors still can not figure out the purpose or central message of the exhibition.

Yet, "Mysteries in History" has considerable strengths as well. Its use of a mix of communication techniques, including staffed and self-directed activities, computers, audio tracks, and games, provides the visitor with many stimulating alternative ways to enjoy the exhibit. Visitors are encouraged to use all their different senses, and visitors of all ages participate in the wide-ranging activities.

Many of the individual activities are creative, appealing, and educational. "Load a Wagon," a successful computer game, is representative. Players are given a limited budget, then told to "buy" supplies for a westward journey. The wisdom of their purchase decisions is tested in the subsequent journey, and many players "die" on route. Younger visitors can practice the same skills in a low-tech version of the game in which they hang wooden supplies on the side of a Conestoga wagon cut-out. A diary account listing actual migrants' supplies is mounted by the side of the two games for observant visitors to analyze.

In general the computers and other advanced exhibit technology are attractive to visitors. Unlike many museums, the Indianapolis Children's Museum recognizes the need for constant monitoring so provides enough staff and money to keep the components working almost constantly.

The individual labels in "Mysteries in History" are quite successful too, in great part because there is much less text than in most history exhibitions, and all of it is in large, readable type. The staff has considered the purpose of particular labels and written them accordingly. Guidance labels tell adults how to use a particular activity with their children. Labels directed at children are simple and clear. One-line question labels stimulate thought and encourage discussion.

Why Didn't "Mysteries in History" Turn Out Better?

"Mysteries" certainly has considerable strengths but also fundamental weaknesses. One would have expected something more. After all, the concept was exciting and meaningful, the museum's staff was talented, evaluation was thorough, and the financial resources were ample.

Several factors account for the exhibit's mixed results. The exhibit took an unconventional approach and, although that adds to its appeal, the planning team had few models or precedents on which to draw. It was hard for them to anticipate how the public would interact with the exhibit since formative testing had not yet been integrated into the exhibit development process. Path-breaking, innovative exhibits are likely to have significant weaknesses. Yet this is not an argument against creativity. If a museum can show that its reason for innovation is to try to please the audience, visitors likely will be understanding and will tolerate weaknesses in the exhibit.

No matter what approach the Indianapolis Children's Museum staff had taken (or any other museum's staff chooses to take for that matter), it would have had difficulty producing a fully successful history exhibit without some revisions, since so many elements contribute to the final product. Neither an intriguing premise, solid scholarship, an attractive design, exciting activities, nor an engaging presentation is enough. Instead, each element must be successful, and all must be combined in a way that connects to the audience's needs and interests.

"The chemistry of doing an exhibit is very complicated," Sterling acknowledges. "I don't think anyone's ever come out of one of our exhibits thinking completely like we just cracked the code of the Rosetta stone."[29] Because Sterling understands the complexity of exhibit development, in the years since "Mysteries" he has put greater resources into exhibit research and exhibit development.

Much more than most other museums, the Indianapolis Children's Museum has invested significant money—thousands of dollars each year—into what businesses would call "R & D." The exhibit planning process has been lengthened, evaluation has become even more intensive, and staff members are expected to travel widely to museums and other educational sites before they complete their plans for a new exhibit. Outside experts and members of the intended exhibit audience are consulted and always play an important role in shaping exhibit plans. After a new exhibit opens, there is the expectation that it will be examined and revised several times over a period of years. The museum continues to allocate 10 percent of each exhibition budget to postopening evaluation and subsequent gallery revisions. The museum staff has become experienced at conducting these postopening evaluations.

The Children's Museum now places greater emphasis on the sort of formative evaluation that takes place before an exhibit opens and is pioneering the inclusion of the audience in the exhibit planning process. Exhibition planners use children of museum members, walk-in visitors, community groups, specially designed museum classes, and child advisory committees to test exhibition concepts and components. Informal evaluation strategies are as simple as "borrowing" young visitors from their parents for short periods of time on weekends to test prototypes or to ask opinions. Among the most elaborate testing strategies are focus groups run by marketing consultants. The focus group discussions are videotaped and watched simultaneously by staff located in another room.[30]

The Children's Museum has made audience research and exhibit evaluation intellectually challenging and absorbing tasks. Other museums would be wise to follow the Children's Museum's model when they produce permanent exhibits and, as the Children's Museum has done, use a modified version of the model for the development of temporary exhibits as well.

But money and time are not enough to produce excellence in exhibitry. The planning process must be structured carefully. The Children's Museum had never used a team approach to exhibit development before "Mysteries," and, unsurprisingly, the process was flawed. Over time, the staff has refined its approach to team planning. When embarking on a new exhibit, the Indianapolis Children's Museum now chooses team members differently. Priority is put on creating teams with balanced personality styles. In fact, in an interesting innovation, but one we do not necessarily recommend, prospective team members take a personality test to identify the ways in which they receive and process information.

During the development of "Mysteries," team members' roles were unwritten and loosely defined. On exhibit development teams today, each member's tasks and responsibilities are clearly spelled out. Moreover, the respective roles of the planning team and the Exhibit Committee have been delineated to diminish confusion and conflict.

The Team Approach and the Vision Thing

In general, the team approach to exhibit planning has proven to be better than the traditional, linear style (curator to designer to public) of exhibit development still in use at many museums. The team approach taps the skills and ideas of more than one person from the inception of the process, and the process of articulating ideas forces team members to clarify and support their opinions. For these reasons, increasing numbers of museums have adopted the team approach.

Yet the team approach also has limitations. Even with all the best intentions of combining the skills and talents of several people, the team can become just another bureaucratic committee producing exhibits by consensus rather than by vision or conviction. A team structure can confine creative staff members and prevent them from developing novel ideas. Staff may offer only those ideas that will win quick acceptance from a diverse committee and that can be easily implemented. Moreover, team members may unconsciously sacrifice their ideas to maintain smooth working relationships, thus subtly changing the group's goals from exhibit planning to the fostering of interpersonal relationships. This dynamic can be compounded by hidden relationships among the theoretically equal team members: a team member holding a low-ranking museum position may feel intimidated by a team member from the higher echelons; a shy team member may be unwilling to express opinions to a more assertive team member.

Team slots are generally designated by department (for instance, a team may have an educator, a curator, and a designer). The sameness of each team's composition can mean that a team's collective voice has little chance of sounding unique. By using the team approach, a museum risks perpetuating the traditional "institutional voice" through its exhibitions, even as other history museums experiment with "authored" exhibitions that more clearly reflect opinions and schools of scholarship.

In the worst circumstances, the team approach to exhibit development can result in orphan exhibits for which no one feels ownership and no one takes responsibility. Staff members may not feel motivated to work hard when they do not receive recognition for their own personal creation.

To succeed, team exhibit planning must be carefully orchestrated. Museums can choose a democratic team model or one which gives more authority to a designated team leader. No matter which approach, however, the team must be structured differently than a committee in which each participant plays an equal role in all decisions. Instead, each team member must be given a clear and distinct sphere of responsibility within the team, and the combined skills and talents of team members must be appropriate for the project goals. Even within the constrictions of teamwork, there needs to be a way that the creative individual with iconoclastic ideas can triumph over pedestrian colleagues. Everything should not be decided by majority rule. Just as important, team members should receive individual credit and recognition for their work.

History museum exhibits are still not creative or exciting enough.[31] No matter what planning style is employed, the exhibit development process should place a premium on creativity and vision. The Indianapolis Children's Museum recognizes that only through vision can exhibits become truly exciting learning experiences. Sterling calls "Mysteries in History" "an unfinished piece of business" that has still not reached its potential. In analyzing the exhibit's shortcomings, he points out the ultimate problem with most history exhibits: "It has never had a good vision of where it could go."[32] Luckily, with the Indianapolis Children's Museum's emphasis on the exhibit development process, on exhibit research, on evaluation and on its audience, it is a likely setting for fostering such a vision.

Institutional Profile

Name: Indianapolis Children's Museum

Location: 3000 N. Meridian Street, P.O. Box 3000, Indianapolis, Indiana 46206

Size of institution: 325,000 square feet

Date of founding: 1925

Number of professional staff: 150 full-time, 100 part-time

Exhibition Data

Name of exhibition: "Mysteries in History"

Dates and venues: Opened July 1985, permanent exhibition

Size of exhibition: 10,000 square feet

Cost: $500,000 (including salaries)

Name and titles of exhibition personnel: Mary Latham, Educator; Robert Johnson, Curator/Educator of American Materials

Sources of funding: Krannert Charitable Trust

Consultants:

Content consultants: Ivor Noel Hume, Thomas J. Schlereth, David L. Parke, Jr., Mark P. Leone, Barbara Jackson, Kenneth Cutler, Mary Ellen Brown, Liliane Kresean, Fred Schroeder

Design consultants: Edward Green, George Gardner, Arminta Neal, Elaine Gurian

Number of objects exhibited: 2,700

Related programming: A variety of hands-on activities that take place in the "Mysteries in History" galleries including Archaeological Dig, Artifact Activity, The Remember Box, When I Was a Kid, Shutterbug Sleuthing, Stereoscopes and Stereographs, House Wanted, Log Buildings Tour, Cemetery Symbols, Document Game, Create Your Own Document, Quilting Bee, Garbology, Trading Post, Print Shop Ladies Emporium, Danner's Variety Store.

Notes

1. The postmove attendance figures far exceeded expectations. Museum staff had hoped to be able to draw 800,000 visitors by the end of the century (Nikki Black, phone interview with Cynthia Robinson, 13 November 1990). By 1986, more than 1.5 million visitors came to the museum annually ("The Children's Museum History," press

release, Indianapolis, Children's Museum, August 1989). As a result of its popularity, the museum has added several additions.

2. Nikki Black, phone interview, 13 November 1990.

3. Barbara Tymitz and Robert Wolf, "The Americana Gallery: A Study of Program Impact on Visitors," unpublished report (Indianapolis Children's Museum, n.d.), 23.

4. Ibid., 9.

5. Ibid., 22.

6. Ibid., 23.

7. Ibid., 23.

8. Ibid., 25.

9. Peter Sterling, interview with Cynthia Robinson, Indianapolis, Indiana, 26 March 1990.

10. Ibid.

11. Nikki Black, interview with Cynthia Robinson, Indianapolis, Indiana, 25 March 1990.

12. With this new job definition, the educator/curator became responsible not only for a collection, but for its educational value and potential. The educator/curator's office was placed in the gallery so that he or she could interact with and observe visitors. The issues of teaching and learning became the educator/curator's major research field, and the subject area of the collection became second.

13. Alex Black and Robert Johnson, interviews with Cynthia Robinson, Indianapolis, Indiana, 25 March 1990.

14. The early nineteenth-century log cabin had been installed when the museum was still under construction. "The logs of the dismantled cabin were so long that the only way to fit them into their new home on the museum's fourth level was to hoist them by crane over museum walls before the museum's fifth level was ever built" ("Log Cabin," press release, Indianapolis Children's Museum, n.d.)

15. Robert Johnson, interview, 25 March 1990.

16. [Clues in your Attic Conceptual Plan], (Indianapolis Children's Museum, [1984]), passim.

17. Ibid., 2.

18. David L. Parke, "Evaluation of Concepts," memo to Indianapolis Children's Museum Staff [1984].

19. Peter Sterling, interview, 26 March 1990.

20. Nikki Black, interview with Cynthia Robinson, Indianapolis, Indiana, 26 March 1990.

21. Robert Johnson, interview, 25 March 1990.

22. Descriptions of the exhibition's appearance are included in Barbara Tymitz, "Case Study of an Evaluation Process: A Kellogg-Smithsonian Demonstration Project," unpublished report (Indianapolis Children's Museum, October 1986), 2–4; Alice Taylor Reed, "Digging into History," *The Christian Science Monitor* (30 August 1985): 27; George Gonis, "History in the Making," *History News* 40 (July 1985): 12–16.

23. Nikki Black, interview, 25 March 1990.

24. Ibid.

25. Tymitz, "Case Study of an Evaluation Process," 15.

26. Ibid., 11.

27. Robert Johnson, interview, 25 March 1990.

28. Current descriptions of "Mysteries" are based on observations and data gathered by Cynthia Robinson, 25–26 March 1990.

29. Peter Sterling, interview, 26 March 1990.

30. For a detailed description of some of the museum's evaluation strategies, see Linda A Black, "Create a Space," *Children's Environments Quarterly* 4 (Spring 1987): 46–50.

31. Suggestions for innovative history museum exhibits are contained in Warren Leon, "A Broader Vision: Exhibits that Change the Way Visitors Look at the Past," in *Past Meets Present: Essays About Historical Interpretation and Public Audiences*, Jo Blatti, ed. (Washington, D.C.: Smithsonian Institution Press, 1985), 133–52.

32. Peter Sterling, interview, 26 March 1990.

TELLING A STORY

"The Automobile in American Life"

Carroll Pursell

The first time I watched the film "Car Culture" at the exhibit's drive-in theater, I saw no couples cuddling: but then, of course, no one has ever called the Henry Ford Museum and Greenfield Village a passion pit. One woman in the sparse audience did remark that her kids never fell asleep in the car as she always planned for them to do. Neither did the exhibit, "The Automobile in American Life," turn out to be anything like what Henry Ford planned for his museum of collections.[1]

The Henry Ford Museum and Greenfield Village has one of the acknowledged great collections of the world, if it is not yet one of the world's great museums. Dedicated in 1929 by Henry Ford himself, the museum and its collections reflect the personality, wealth, and political biases of the man himself. They began, and to some degree still remain, eccentric, lavish, idiosyncratic, and bathed in nostalgia and hero worship. The village is a collection of historic buildings displayed and interpreted as part of an outdoor, living history experience. A generation ago the critic of technology, Siegfried Giedion, expressed surprise that Ford had not saved an archival record of his revolutionary contributions to mass production. Instead, as Hugh Kenner has remarked, he "had elected to restore Greenfield Village, a kind of museum of procedural archaisms."[2] The visitor to the Ford Museum itself enters a replica of Philadelphia's Independence Hall and winds up in an eight-acre space that resembles nothing so much as a Ford factory of the late 1920s.[3]

Ford apparently collected by whim, instinct, and interest rather than according to any intellectually coherent policy or plan. Thus his passion for steam led to one of the great steam engine collections to be found anywhere in the world. Automobiles were, not surprisingly, among the favored objects, while other subjects, such as mining and lumbering, were virtually ignored. Concentrated between 1830 and 1910, the artifacts were originally displayed on the eight-acre floor of the museum in rectangular enclosures, set off by parallel aisles crossed perpendicularly at regular intervals by other aisles. Set behind velvet ropes and identified only by small labels giving minimal specifications, the collections were arranged more as open storage than anything resembling exhibits.

For the three decades after 1940, visitors to the museum saw pretty much the same things on display, and those in the same taxinomic manner. Even into the late 1960s, the museum had "almost no curatorial staff," a fact, along with the displays, that reinforced and perpetuated its "image as a provincial, out-of-step institution."[4] Then in 1979, as part of its fiftieth anniversary celebration, the museum reopened its Mechanical Arts Hall (the "factory" building), redone and renamed the Hall of Technology.

The newly redesigned space now contained four exhibit areas: home arts, agriculture, power and shop machinery, and transportation. Of these four, the last took up nearly half the floor space. By way of introduction to these areas, an interpretive center was installed at the entrance, consisting of eighteen hundred graphics, seven hundred artifacts, and an equal number of text blocks, all organized into either "time capsules" or "curatorial areas," and all squeezed into thirty-two thousand square feet of floor space. The "time capsules" were intended to suggest periods of general American history while the "curatorial areas" introduced the major collection areas on the main part of the floor.[5]

Reviewing the new Hall of Technology in 1980, Larry Lankton found it only a limited improvement over its predecessor. In the transportation section, for example, he discovered that "the locomotives and rail cars are queued up as before on old tracks, and the 175 automobiles continue to resemble a large parking lot." The rectangular arrangement of aisles had been abandoned in favor of a "Washington-like street plan," with diagonal aisles leading to such "focal points" such as the 1930 Auburn Phaeton sedan, which spun on a turntable all day, introducing motion and a place to sit down for museum viewers. Lankton complained that there was "no exhibit [that] examines the impact of the automobile on the American culture or economy." Indeed, he insisted, "the Hall of Technology, although tidier than its predecessor and a little more informative, still begged the question" of what all these "things" meant.[6]

The coming of Harold Skramstad, as museum director, from the Chicago Historical Society and the Smithsonian Institution's National Museum of American History symbolized a critical turning point for the Michigan museum in 1981. He quickly appointed a Curriculum Committee to report on the "unique historical resources" of the Edison Institute and to address the question, "how should these resources be most effectively interpreted and made accessible to our many publics?"[7]

Since Ford's time, the museum and village had been presenting history as nostalgia, patriotism, progress, trivia, and consensus. In place of that approach, the committee advocated history as inquiry and meaning. A "Proposed Henry Ford Museum Plan," appended to the report, listed as its third and last "phase," a redoing of the transportation exhibits, including a need to "redesign and install transportation collection, i.e. extend rail collection, move horse drawn vehicles to near community area, reinstall commercial vehicles and automobiles, establish special exhibits area. . . ."[8] For the museum as a whole, a new mission statement was worked out that boiled down to the question: "How has America been transformed from a nation based on farms and villages to one based on cities, factories, and offices?"[9] Most importantly, a conscious decision was made that the mission of the museum and village was not merely to exhibit objects, but to "tell stories."[10] Greenfield Village offered the best opportunity to implement the new plan, and changes took place there first. Edison's Menlo Park laboratory, for example, which Ford had moved to the village, was rethought and redone between 1985 and 1987 to provide a more sophisticated interpretative experience as well as to add critical new dimensions, such as gender, to the exhibits.

When the attention of the new director turned to the Hall of Technology, the large and still uninterpreted transportation portion of the museum cried out for new treatment. Again Skramstad appointed a committee. All the members had been on the staff before his arrival, but all supported the new departures to which he was committed. The first idea proposed treating transportation as a whole. Although such modes of transport as streetcars and water craft were, in general, missing from the collection, the large and impressive 600 thousand-pound locomotive (one of the few objects on the floor that did not seem out of scale in the factorylike premises) could not be ignored. Originally the staff envisioned thematic areas, with such titles as "Moving People and Goods," "Breaking Barriers of Times and Space," and "Getting Away From it All."[11] The plan evolved into a rather more limited one of reinterpreting and reinstalling the automobile collection alone.[12]

The planning group for the transportation exhibit was chaired by John L. Wright (in 1991 director, Public Programs Division) and included people from collections, public programs, exhibits, and public affairs. The group adopted the new belief of the museum that, rather than already knowing the story and wanting only to see the objects, visitors needed to be *told* the story, through an interpretation of the objects. At the end of a year's work, Skramstad took the group's plans to the institute's board with the recommendation that the exhibit be scaled back to deal principally with the automobile. Staff agreed with Skramstad's recommendation, and there is evidence that all individuals felt relief in the reduction of subject. Some on the staff did, however, worry that an initial, major exhibit on the automobile alone might reinforce whatever misperception the public had that the Henry Ford Museum was merely a showroom for cars.

There were several good reasons for scaling back. First, the automobile collection was arguably the most important single element in the overall transportation holdings. Second, for a first effort at the entire museum, the automobiles must have seemed a sufficiently formidable challenge. Also, the transportation collection had gaps that would have made a comprehensive

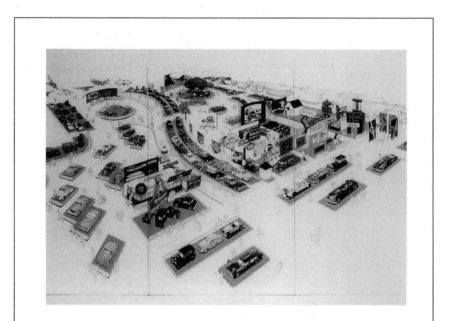

Conceptual rendering, done during the planning process, shows the exhibit area.

Courtesy Albert Woods Design Associates.

exhibit extremely difficult. Finally, by happy accident, the state of Michigan wanted an important automobile element in its planned sesquicentennial celebration. That goal placed a severe time constraint (a bit less than a year) on the exhibit's development but at the same time provided badly needed funds.[13] In the classic manner, the paint was still wet when the six million dollar exhibit opened in November 1987.

Museum leaders realized that such a large and ambitious exhibit could not be managed in the institution's usual manner; a new management style was needed. Thomas Elliott was designated project manager and, since this was his (as well as the museum's) first experience with such responsibility, he was sent to Michigan State University to study project management. Having himself discarded his normal staff responsibilities for the new job, Elliott had authority to pull other staff members from their regular duties to be members of his team. He was also able to use other staff people in their normal capacities and to hire new people that he needed.[14]

Another management innovation was the creation of a review team, chaired by Elliott and including Skramstad, Steven K. Hamp, chairman of collections, Wright as director of public programs, and G. Donald Adams, director of external affairs. The committee, made up of people with the authority to make decisions, met weekly, putting the exhibit on the fast track.[15] The track, in fact, proved to be somewhat too fast for comfort. Once all the work was completed and the exhibit was opened, staff harbored the conviction that budgets and timetables can be unrealistic and unduly constraining if hardened too soon in the planning process.

As project manager, however, Elliott's responsibility was to bring the exhibit in on time and within budget.[16] Teams searched out appropriate objects, and Hamp, as concept coordinator, oversaw curators who put together concept (or position) papers on various subjects which were brought to the review group. Albert Woods Design Associates of New York, the exhibit design specialist, was brought into the process very early, as was James J. Flink, the nation's leading automobile historian and a professor at the University of California, Irvine, to be a scholarly consultant.

The overall conception of the new exhibit called for replacing the former display—"a parking lot under a roof," one museum official called it—with a new "landscape" for the automobile. The designer remarked that "the Henry Ford had been sort of skipped over by the interpretive movement." The head of collections promised that "we're going to redo the whole place in terms of telling a story," and that the "Automobile in American Life" was to lead off.[17] Museum officials harbored some concern that automobile enthusiasts would resent the new exhibit, but apparently that public, too, likes the story being told. Indeed such groups as the Society of Automobile Historians and the Antique Automobile Club of America have given the show awards. Perhaps in part because the museum's revenue comes mainly from attendance fees and memberships, it remains very concerned about audience reactions. For "The Automobile in American Life," a professional marketing consultant was engaged to do focus group interviews.

Exhibit planners decided to divide the area—nearly one-third of the museum's total floor space—into eight principal spaces: "The Evolution of the Automobile and Its Industry," "The Car as Symbol," "Automotive Landscape," "Designing the Automobile," "Advertising and Promoting," "Driving for Fun," "Getting Away from It All," and "Bicycles and Motorcycles."[18]

Although the staff was proud of what it considered the finest collection of American automobiles in the country, long-standing museum policies had shaped the collection in ways that, during the exhibit's development, proved unhelpful. The museum had an abundance of richness, touring cars of the 1920s, for example, but very few cars from the post–World War II period. The exhibit helped the museum to slough off a "collector's" mentality and to devise a collection policy that addressed needs of specific exhibits.

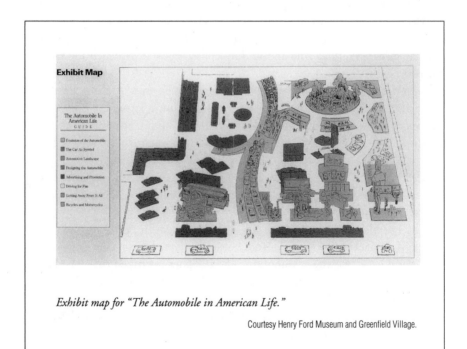

Exhibit map for "The Automobile in American Life."

Courtesy Henry Ford Museum and Greenfield Village.

The old display area contained 180 cars, while the new has only 108. Of these about thirty, mostly from the post–World War II period, had to be newly acquired for the collection.[19] In addition, artifacts were acquired that reflected and symbolized the roadside environment. Staff acquired a 1937 tourist cabin to be placed alongside an archetypal 1960's Holiday Inn room. A 1936 Texaco service station and a 1960 McDonald's hamburger sign were picked up, along with the marquee for the Douglas Auto Theater (opened 1955) and Lamy's Diner, built in 1946 and restored by the museum for $75,000. The designer referred to the collecting process as "editing the collections to eliminate redundancy and acquire important missing vehicles" as well as other artifacts.[20] In addition, the designer has claimed that "for the first time, an exhibit environment was created that allowed the display of rich supporting materials from the museum's archives."[21]

Woods's purpose was to "support and enhance the museum's fine collection of artifacts, bring them to life, and place them in context using a collection of vintage film footage, sound, and memorabilia."[22] In more concrete terms, as the designer later wrote, "our role, as designers, was to deal with the environmental and architectural problems of the building and to design interpretive exhibit

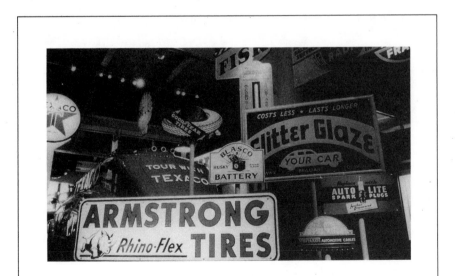

A scene from the "Automotive Landscape" section, showing "Gas and Auto Services."

Courtesy Albert Woods Design Associates.

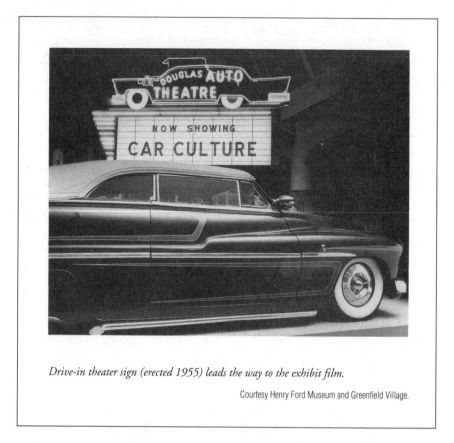

Drive-in theater sign (erected 1955) leads the way to the exhibit film.

Courtesy Henry Ford Museum and Greenfield Village.

experiences to replace the previous noninterpretive display that has characterized the museum."[23]

The museum space presented two problems of particular importance. The first is one of scale. The great factorylike expanse of eight acres rises at least forty feet to the roof, which is held up by rows of concrete columns forty feet apart. Someone remarked years ago that in the old transportation section, only the 300-ton locomotive looked to be in anything like the right scale.[24] The space dwarfed all other artifacts. Woods realized that cars resting on the museum floor, or even raised on platforms, would present a sea of horizontal objects in a powerfully vertical space. The drive-in movie's tall screen, forcing viewers' eyes upward, was a deliberate attempt to bring some relief to the prevailing flatness. Happily, the drive-in provided as well a welcomed place to sit down for twelve minutes of excellent movie viewing. The strong and familiar neon signs of McDonald's hamburgers and the Holiday Inn accomplished the same purpose. Originally designed to be seen among the welter of other signage, and far enough down the road that speeding drivers could react in time, they still cut the horizon like church steeples in New England or grain silos in the Midwest.

A second problem involved lighting. The factory loft contained monitors to let in natural light. Such light, of course, was often too little or too much for the unnatural purposes of a museum, and the ultraviolet radiation from the sunlight posed significant problems for the preservation of exhibited artifacts. The designer has written that "steps were taken to control the direct sunlight that had made effective lighting impossible," as well as "acoustic measures" to "allow the use of sound sources without building walls that would visually divide the space."[25] For the new installation, the designers sealed off the monitors and installed about 700 pinpoint lights. "We consider this a sculptural show that emphasizes the lights, not the building," Woods claims, "and spots do that best."[26]

The early inclusion of a designer in the planning process worked well according to museum staff. Woods not only gave dimensionality to the story, he and his staff also found ways in which the story could be told differently, sometimes combining ideas in such a way that they could be expressed by the same objects. Having a design firm so far away as New York City proved difficult at times, but today's FAX machines will overcome much of the inconvenience associated with distant designers.

In fact, the experience may have been a learning one for all concerned. The not quite identical notions that the exhibit should "narratize rather than analyse," and that exhibits are by their very nature sensual rather than intellectual experiences, caused some tension. The design firm was used to dealing with clients who gave it the vision and then left the firm with a freer hand in realizing it. Telling a story implies a beginning, a middle, and an end and the need to encourage the museum visitor to "read" the exhibit front to back.

As visitors approach the exhibit from the museum entrance, they cross a row of automobiles illustrating "The Car As Symbol." Here, six superb specimens illustrate freedom, style, power, youth, individuality, and success. Ahead lies "The Evolution of the Automobile," two parallel rows of cars (fifty of the exhibit's 108) and six television monitors cleverly set along a raised pathway designed as a "highway" to be traveled.

The first vehicle displayed is, in fact, the first (1982) Honda made in the United States, and the last is an 1893 Benz Velocipede, the world's first production car. The order is, of course, deliberate, taking visitors from the present (a worldwide auto industry) and familiar (a Japanese car) to the

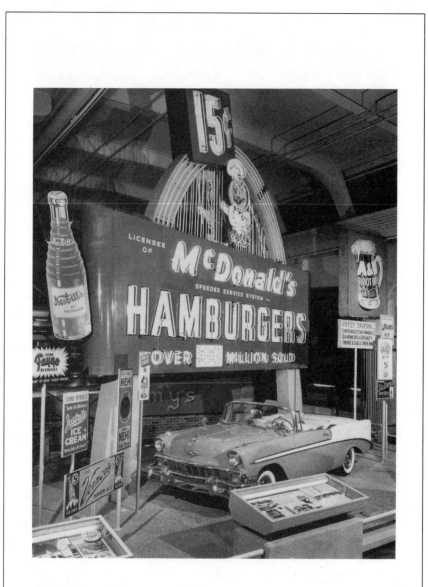

A 1956 Chevy Bel Air is parked beneath a 1960 McDonald's sign in the "Automotive Landscapes."

Courtesy Henry Ford Museum and Greenfield Village.

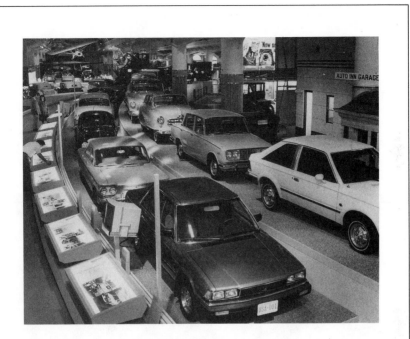

"The Evolution of the Automobile" follows a highwaylike path past videos, exhibit cases, and the cars themselves.

Courtesy Henry Ford Museum and Greenfield Village.

unfamiliar past.[27] The television monitors tell the story of automobile manufacture period by period, through excellent vintage film.

To the left and right of the 1982 Honda lies the "Automotive Landscape," certainly the most spectacular part of the exhibit. From left to right one sees Lamy's Diner and the McDonald's sign, an old service station and the newer Texaco one, the drive-in theater and miniature golf link, and the Holiday Inn and a tourist cabin. These splendid artifacts, all acquired for the show (and raising the thorny question of collecting the twentieth century), dominate the visitors' attention and give the exhibit its reputation for glitz and excitement.

Behind the Texaco station and drive-in, visitors encounter "Advertising and Promotion," with small artifacts (magazines for example) and television monitors showing clips of a range of activities, including commercials and newsreels and film clips of auto events that were little more than staged promotions.

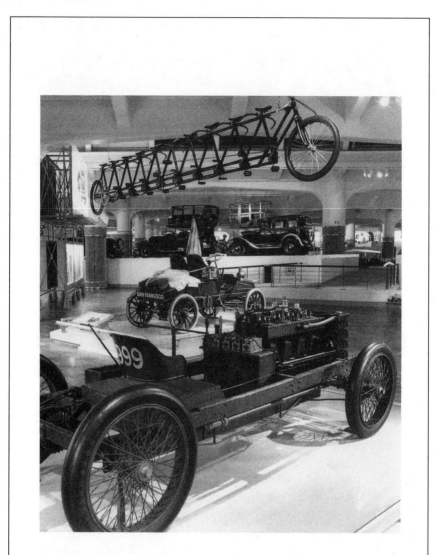

The "Advertising and Promotion" section features three promotional vehicles: Henry Ford's 999 racer (1902), Packard's Old Pacific (crossed the country in 1903), and a ten-person bicycle (1896).

Courtesy Henry Ford Museum and Greenfield Village.

To the right, then, is "Driving for Fun," that attempts to conjure up "the lure of the open road, the exhilaration of speed, and the freedom associated with motion."[28] Here an MG TC (1949), a Ford hot rod (1932/54), a soap box derby car (third place, 1939), and a 1941 Harley Davidson with sidecar, illustrate the point though in a very static setting. Behind the group and extending to the right is an area devoted to bicycles and motorcycles, offered as precursors of the automobile though also evolving parallel to it. At the rear one finds "Getting Away from It All," a wooded area with a Volkswagen camper (1959), an Airstream mobile home (1949), the obligatory Burma Shave signs, and related vehicles and artifacts.

Finally, to the extreme left, is "Designing the Automobile," featuring the last remnant of the despised parking lot with specimen cars (1959 Caddie convertible and 1955 Chevy Bel Air) and a series of television monitors featuring famous designers. Images of eight designers, such as Raymond Loewy, appear on a touch screen menu, and by touching the appropriate portrait

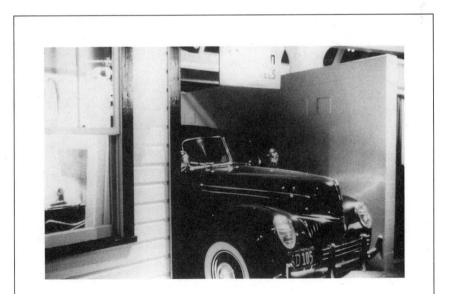

All is quiet at the 1930's tourist cabin. Photo by Eric Breitbart.

Courtesy Albert Woods Design Associates.

visitors see a brief film of the individual's work. Some films include interviews with the designers.[29]

The exhibit appears to be singularly free of mistakes, though some inevitably intrude. The old Packard wagon, fitted out for camping in the "Getting Away from It All" area is identified as having been used in the Mexican-American War rather than during Pershing's 1916 punitive expedition against Pancho Villa. The slick metal benches provided for those who want to sit and watch "Advertising and Promotion" propel one forward and, without braced legs, perhaps onto the floor. In Lamy's Diner, visitors expect food service, but despite a costumed waitress who welcomes visitors into the diner, no food is available. (One wonders if at least the smell of fresh coffee might make the experience better—or even worse?)

More serious is the fact that "The Evolution of the Automobile," "The Automotive Landscape" and "Getting Away from It All" work so well, the other sections, especially "Bicycles and Motorcycles" and "Driving for Fun" seem left behind in the dust of the old parking lot. To a significant extent, even the "Car As Symbol" and "Designing the Automobile" suffer from the same defect. They

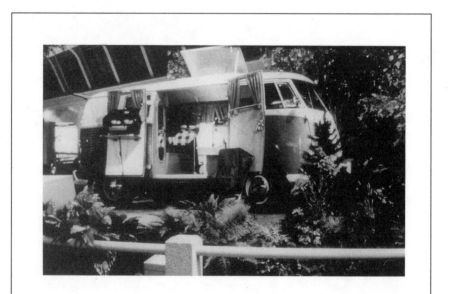

In "Getting Away From It All," a Volkswagen camper is set up in a sylvan environment.

Photo by Tom Ancona.
Courtesy Albert Woods Design Associates.

seem elegantly frozen in a context so thin as to be hardly detectable. Car buffs will no doubt enjoy the sections, but aficionados presumably enjoyed the Transportation Hall before its transformation.

Curiously, people were left out of the story told. The diner is empty except for the waitress. The tourist cabin has small ants on the window sill and a soda bottle, but the people are off somewhere. No one is playing golf, and there is no smiling face at the Texaco station. No voices of wrangling parents and whiny kids exit from the camp trailers, and while the trunks of three marvelous cars lie between visitors and the movie at the drive in, no one seems to be making out or going for popcorn. Whether manikins and hidden audio recordings would have worked or not is an open question. But the absence of people, other than the visitors, is palpable.

The highway of evolution is beautifully done (though a broken white stripe down the center might have been a good idea), but the notion of traveling from the recent models to older ones is equivocally handled. Although the entire exhibit is designed to be entered and exited at any one of a number of points, the design plan encouraged visitors to walk up the highway into the past. In fact, on one day I observed, most visitors moved the other way, from the 1893 Benz down to the 1982 Honda. We expect to be taught from the past to the present, and that habit appears hard to break. More surprisingly, the exhibit's guidebook itself lists the seven eras of development in their chronological order, rather than in the order they appear in the exhibit.

Most significantly, "The Automobile in American Life" is a very positive exhibit. Except for an open copy of Ralph Nader's *Unsafe at Any Speed*, exhibited along the evolution highway (fittingly near a Chevrolet Corvair), the hard questions of our automobile culture are hardly mentioned. The Nader book rests in a small case (labeled "The Government Steps In") with mention of auto exhaust problems and the energy shortage, but there the matter rests.

Could one ask a museum, founded by Henry Ford, in its exhibit paid for in part by the state of Michigan to celebrate the area's signature industry, to introduce mangled bodies, crumpled cars, inner city children retarded by the fumes of leaded gasoline, abandoned rail and trolley lines, and the like?[30] At the same time, the lack of any such questions reinforces the absence of people in the exhibit and undermines the exhibit's obvious seriousness of purpose, to place the automobile in the context of American life. One reviewer has found in the drive-in film "a brilliant and perfect corrective to the more celebratory and progress-oriented stories narrated around the great collection of cars," but this is not obvious to every observer.[31] Except for one jarring and tense car chase (from *The French Connection*), the exciting music and mix of movie and television clips is a triumph of nostalgic good feelings.

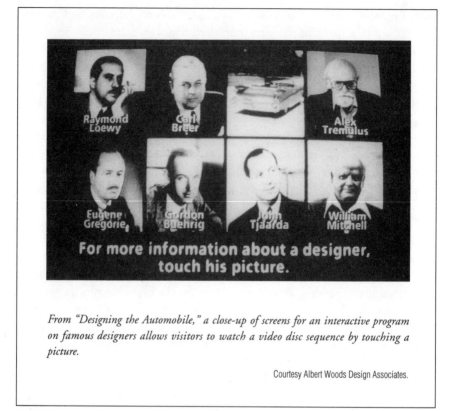

From "Designing the Automobile," a close-up of screens for an interactive program on famous designers allows visitors to watch a video disc sequence by touching a picture.

Courtesy Albert Woods Design Associates.

The most important adjunct to the exhibit is the twelve-minute film shown in the drive-in. Made by Mary Lance and Eric Breitbart of New Deal Films, it has a voice over narration but no clear didactic message. Instead, a marvelous and evocative montage of period songs (mostly rock and roll) and film footage from movies and other sources reinforces the unforgettable fact that the automobile framed and colored the coming of age of many Americans. Doubtless many visitors sat down to rest and watch the film once during their visits, then just before leaving, watched it one more time. It's that good.

The museum's staff extended the educational value of the exhibit by holding a conference on "Americans and the Automobile" at the museum 4-6 November 1988. Sponsored by the Society for Commercial Archeology, the meeting, opened to the public, featured sessions entitled "The Restoration of 'The Automotive Landscape': A Close-up Look," "Auto Geography," "Auto Arts and Literature," "Forms of Commerce," "Curating the Car Culture," "Roadside

Architecture," "The Auto in the City and Suburb," and "Shaping Consumers." A collection of papers selected from the conference has been published.[32]

While (in 1990) there is as yet no proper exhibit catalog or monograph for "The Automobile in American Life," the staff has produced a handsome, full-color, thirty-two-page guide to the exhibit.[33] It would be a service to at least some scholars and teachers if the twelve-minute film seen in the drive-in theater were also available for purchase or loan.[34]

Like many museum gift shops, that at the Henry Ford Museum operates at least as much as a source of revenue as an educational adjunct to the main mission of the institution. Along with the inevitable arts, crafts, souvenirs, and memorabilia, several shelves of books tempt the visitor who is interested in the subjects of the exhibits. Although books for car buffs were well represented on one day, serious monographs were scarce. No copies of any of the definitive works of James J. Flink (ironically one of the scholarly consultants for the project) on the automobile were available. When this was called to the attention of staff members, they were surprised and insisted that the works should have been there.

The "Automobile in American Life" is an exciting and first-rate exhibit, both because it provides a context worthy of the Henry Ford Museum's unparalleled collections and because it marks, at last, the beginning of modernization for the whole museum. Already (in 1990) the museum staff is beginning to plan the next segment of an ongoing process, the superb machine tools and prime movers that will renovate the old area called "Power and Shop Machinery." The overall decision to interpret rather than simply display artifacts was more overdue than surprising, but it has already begun to revolutionize the museum—promising to make it at last what it always might have been, a world-class institution.

Institutional Profile

Name: Henry Ford Museum and Greenfield Village
Locations: 20900 Oakwood Blvd., Dearborn, MI 48121
Size of institution: Henry Ford Museum—12 Acres of exhibit space
Date of founding: October 21, 1929
Number of professional staff: 270 full-time employees,
    approximately 100 professionals

Exhibition Data

Dates and venues: Opened 7 November 1987, long-term exhibition
Cost: $5,100,000 (excluding salaries)
Names and titles of exhibition personnel: Steven K. Hamp, Chairman of
  Collections Division; John L. Wright, Director of Public Programs Division;
  Randy Mason, Curator of Transportation; Thomas Elliott, Manager of
  Design and Production, Exhibits Division; G. Donald Adams, Director of
  External Affairs; George May, John and Horace Dodge Curator of
  Automotive History; Harold K. Skramstad, President
Date of original conception: February 1984
Duration of exhibit development process: November 1985–April 1987
Sources of funding: Michigan Equity Grant program, private foundation grants,
  corporate gifts, and individual donations.
Consultants
Content consultants: Richard Gutman, Chester Liebs, James Flink,
  Bill Porter, Dan Vieyra
Design consultant: Albert Woods Design Associates, Inc.
Other consultant: Clark Malcom, exhibit text editor
Number of objects exhibited: 105 large vehicles, 50 smaller vehicles, 50 signs, 6
  architectural installations, 400-500 artifacts used to populate settings, 800-
  900 two-dimensional artifacts from library and archives collections
Related programming:
Publications: The Automobile in American Life, a souvenir booklet;
  The Automobile in American Life, a book by George F. May.
Media: Film "Car Culture," produced by Mary Lance, written by Eric Breitbart,
  for Henry Ford Museum & Greenfield Village. Nine video disc loop
  productions used in the exhibit; one interactive video disc.
Other: Self-guided tour titled "Car Trek"
Professional journal reviews:
Joseph J. Corn, "The Automobile in American Life," *The Journal of American
  History* 76 (June 1989): 221–24.
Charles K. Hyde, "'The Automobile in American Life,' An Exhibit at Henry
  Ford Museum, Dearborn, Michigan," *Technology and Culture* 30
  (January 1989): 105–111.
John M. Staudemaier, S. J., "The Automobile in American Life",
  The Public Historian, A Journal of Public History 10 (Summer 1988): 89–92.
Roger M. Williams, "Tin Lizzies in a New Landscape," *Americana Magazine* 16
  (March–April 1988): 36.

Notes

1. I am very much indebted to staff members of the Henry Ford Museum and Greenfield Village for their cooperation with my many requests for interviews and materials. I am particularly indebted to Harold Skramstad, Steven K. Hamp, and John L. Wright.

2. Hugh Kenner, *The Mechanic Muse* (New York, 1987), 39–40.

3. These observations are based in part on Larry Lankton, "Something Old, Something New: The Reexhibition of the Henry Ford Museum's Hall of Technology," *Technology and Culture* 21 (October 1980): 594–613.

4. Ibid.

5. Ibid., 602. The Interpretive Center was contracted out by the museum because it lacked an adequate exhibits staff.

6. Ibid., 611, 602.

7. The Edison Institute, Henry Ford Museum & Greenfield Village, "Report of the Curriculum Committee, 1981," 1. John Wright chaired the committee. The other members were G. Donald Adams, John L. Bowditch, Peter H. Cousins, Sheila F. Ford, Candace T. Matelic, and Henry J. Prebys.

8. Ibid., 18–24, 29–31, 105.

9. Steven K. Hamp and Michael J. Ettema, "To Collect or to Educate?" *Museum News* 68 (September/October 1989): 42.

10. Not all staff approved of this radical shift in philosophy, of course, and there are indications that some felt left out at this point.

11. Albert H. Woods to author, 10 May 1990.

12. Ibid.

13. Roger M. Williams, "Tin Lizzies in a New Landscape," *Americana* 16 (March/April 1988): 36.

14. Using teams is now routine at the museum for large and small exhibits.

15. This review committee was so useful that it was made a standing committee. It still meets and, because of its top-level membership (including Skramstad himself), has the power to decide, not just recommend. The museum used as its model the Ford Motor Company's handling of its new Taurus model car.

16. Although Gantt flow-charts were not used on this exhibit, it showed the need for them, and they are now routinely employed.

17. Williams, 34.

18. In some literature, the eight themes become six with the elimination of "Driving for Fun" and "Bicycles and Motorcycles." See, for example, the announcement for the 1988 conference, "Americans and the Automobile."

19. Williams, 36.

20. Woods to author, 10 May 1990.

21. Woods to author, 7 March 1990.

22. Promotional booklet distributed by Albert Woods Design Associates of New York City.

23. Woods to the author, 7 March 1990.

24. Lankton, 601.

25. Woods to author, 7 March 1990.

26. Quoted in Williams, 40.

27. Joseph J. Corn, review of the exhibit in *The Journal of American History*, 76 (June 1989): 221–24.

28. *The Automobile in American Life*, 24.

29. The other designers are Carl Breer, Alex Tremulus, William Mitchell, John Tjaarda, Gordon Buehrig, Eugene Gegorie, and Harley Earl.

30. See the review of the exhibit by John M. Staudenmaier in *The Public Historian* 10 (Summer 1988): 89–92.

31. Exhibit review by Corn, 224.

32. Jan Jennings, ed., *Roadside America: The Automobile in Design and Culture* (Ames: Iowa State University Press, 1990).

33. It sold for $4.95 in the spring of 1990. In 1990, George May was preparing a monograph to accompany the exhibit.

34. Apparently the problem of permissions and payment of fees to reproduce and sell all the various film clips involved would be prohibitive.

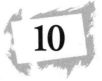

"BROOKLYN'S HISTORY MUSEUM"

The Urban History Exhibit as an Agent of Change

Michael Frisch

A Complex Mission

Planning and realizing a permanent exhibit is a demanding challenge for any city history museum. By definition it requires a searching examination of the institution's identity and role. It requires an assessment of the museum's collections and its real and potential audiences. It requires a range of activities and resources: board support, fund raising, design and content consultants, and audience development. And it requires the development of a strategy for representing the museum's identity, for developing its collections, for mobilizing and utilizing its resources, and for reaching its audience—all in a way that advances the central objectives of the institution.

Such an agenda further burdens the already demanding exhibit development process with additional dimensions of complexity and delicacy. Consider how this complexity is then squared or cubed when the institution mounting the permanent exhibit is itself in dramatic flux, when its identity, mission, audience, and collections are in the midst of being redefined and reconfigured. In such circumstances, designing the exhibition becomes the crucial fulcrum of all the forces at work in the institution. Initiated and propelled by the changes under way, the exhibit becomes itself a major agent for change. It defines and represents the institution to the public in its newly emerging role and form, and it generates momentum capable of redirecting the path of the institution's future development.

Such has been the experience of the Brooklyn Historical Society, which between late 1985 and 1989 mounted a major, permanent exhibition on Brooklyn's history, designed to propel the transformation of a long-established but sleepy and conventional historical society into a major, revitalized institution intimately involved with the community around it. Some of the challenge is captured in the fact that the exhibit ended up with no title, as such. The exhibit has been publicized and marketed as "Brooklyn's History Museum"—quite literally, the exhibit is the institution as it has presented its new self to a new public.

To realize the ambitious and complex aims, the staff of the society developed a highly original approach to its presentation of Brooklyn's history. Staff members abandoned traditional conceptions of narrative and organized the historical interpretation instead around five overlapping "symbols" of Brooklyn life. The innovative approach imposed its own unique burdens and challenges that had to be discovered, understood, and resolved before the potential of the exhibit strategy—in terms both of historical substance and audience development—could be realized.

Taken together, such institutional and intellectual considerations made for an exhibit development history that tested every dimension of institutional process. The lessons of these various struggles had perhaps as much to do with the ultimate success of the exhibit as did the historical and design choices themselves and the broader institutional context within which they were made. In surveying the story of the exhibit, I hope to convey what has made "Brooklyn's History Museum" such a unique, exemplary model of how an exhibit can engage and address complex problems. But I also hope the essay will illustrate some more general and representative dimensions of the historical exhibit development process as confronted by a wider range of institutions in a wide range of contexts.

Process and Problems

Brooklyn was the third largest city in the United States until it became a borough of New York City in the area's consolidation of 1898; even today, its 2.3 million people constitute a population larger than that of eighteen of our nation's states. And yet until quite recently, Brooklyn had no museum devoted to its history and no museum of any kind in its downtown heart.

It did have a historical society, however—the Long Island Historical Society, founded in 1863. Like many such institutions founded in the nineteenth century, it was a combination plaything and storage attic for the community's Victorian elite. Housed in an elegant Queen Anne structure built by the

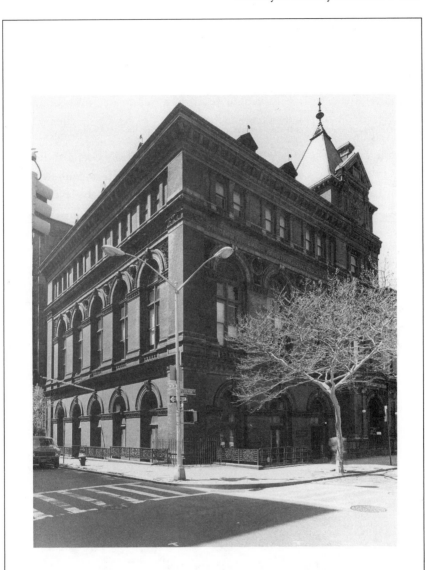

The Brooklyn Historical Society building sits on Pierpont Street in downtown Brooklyn. The founders of what was then called the Long Island Historical Society erected the structure in 1878-1880 for the use of the society.

society's founders in 1878, the institution assembled an impressive collection of art works, graphics, and artifacts and maintained a substantial library, the whole constituting "the most comprehensive collection of Brooklyn-related materials in existence."[1] But by the mid-twentieth century, the society had virtually ground to a halt. Its large first-floor auditorium subdivided into commercial rental space, the society operated just the library—or rather, the library pretty much was the society.

In the late 1960s, some energetic new members of the board of directors began to revive the Long Island Historical Society. Reflecting an awakened sensitivity to local history and its potential place in the borough's revitalization, efforts gathered momentum, after a halting start, with the hiring in 1982 of an energetic young director, David Kahn. By 1986, annual funding had risen from under $200 thousand to some $650 thousand; the staff had grown from nine employees to twenty, thirteen of them full-time; and a small exhibit program

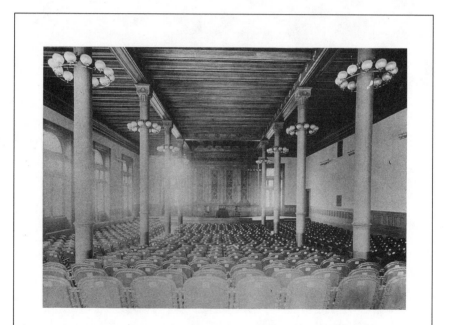

The auditorium of the Long Island Historical Society building as it appeared around 1900. The three-thousand-square-foot space now houses the "Brooklyn's History Museum" installation.

had been launched. The institution itself addressed the confusing anachronism of its name—which had reflected the city's earlier orientation to an increasingly suburban Long Island—by becoming, in 1985, the Brooklyn Historical Society. Also in the mid-1980s, museum officials made a commitment to confirm institutional changes in public form by developing a major, permanent exhibit. The proposed exhibit followed a decision to renovate the former auditorium— with its elegant twenty-foot ceilings and large windows—into a three-thousand-square-foot exhibition space, with an additional five hundred square feet for rotating, smaller exhibits.

The project did not get off to a great running start. It began with a vague determination to mount an exhibit that would be something other than the story of city fathers and eminent leaders. Its planners decided instead that the exhibit would have to involve the diversity of Brooklyn's people and their lives over time, and it would explicitly seek out connections between Brooklyn's past and its complex present. The society had the interesting idea of hiring a young anthropologist to give its impulse substance and focus, thinking that an anthropologist rather than a historian might have the best "take" on the kind of holistic social history it sought. Hiring an anthropologist was a fine idea, but it didn't quite work, in a sense because the hunch turned out to be almost too correct. The anthropologist had wonderful ideas, many of which survived in the final exhibit plans. He was so committed to weaving detail into an overall picture of Brooklyn as a "society," however, that he was reluctant to leave anything out, a fatal problem generally but especially for an exhibit limited to 3,000 square feet. "The result," Kahn recalls, was that "conceptually things started to spin out of control."[2]

Exhibit planning was brought back under control in 1986, owing to the finalization of the exhibit team: Kahn, Project Director Ellen Snyder-Grenier, Curator of Education Jane Emmet McDonough, and a carefully selected group of academic consultants who met with staff frequently. During that year, the staff completed enough preliminary planning to permit the preparation and submission to the National Endowment for the Humanities of a successful project implementation grant proposal for the refinement of the script and for the design and fabrication of the exhibit.

The crystallization of a nonnarrative conception of the exhibit built around five distinct symbols of Brooklyn provided the key breakthrough for the exhibit planning process. The five symbols—the Brooklyn Bridge, the Brooklyn Navy Yard, Coney Island, the Brooklyn Dodgers, and the powerful cultural image of the "Brooklynite" as a "type"—encapsulated the essence of Brooklyn's story. The idea came not from the consultants, who proved most useful in helping to refine and focus it, but rather from the staff. Indeed, it has been emerging

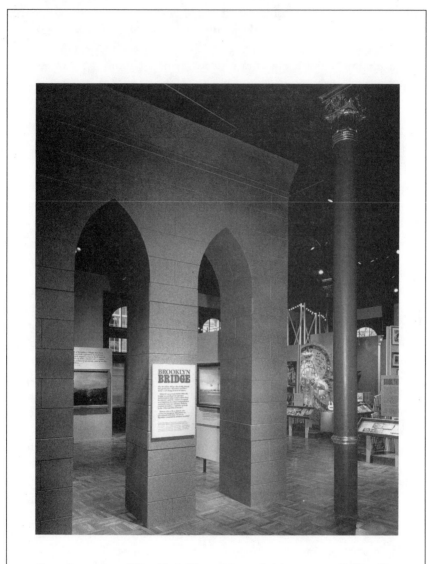

From the entrance of "Brooklyn's History Museum" visitors can see the "Brooklyn Bridge" section. The roller coaster construction that rises over the "Coney Island" section is visible in the rear.

Courtesy Brooklyn Historical Society.

gradually in the process of assembling materials for the exhibit. Finally, as Kahn tells it, "Ellen came into my office one day and said, 'Look, some of the things we talk about all the time, no matter what list or what perspective, there's general agreement that the exhibit cannot go forward unless it's got the Brooklyn Bridge in it, unless it's got the Dodgers, unless it's got Coney Island—there's this short list of things that absolutely have to be there; whatever else we could eliminate from the project, these things cannot be eliminated. So why not make them our focus?'"[3]

Making a virtue of necessity turned into a powerful and original organizing concept that worked on several levels. Each symbol was to be used as a base for building broader interpretations of a particular dimension of Brooklyn history, for comparing myth and reality, and for linking past to present. Each involved artifacts and images already familiar to visitors, anchors to which they could connect personally, emotionally, and intellectually, a ground on which challenging and less familiar material could be received and digested. And by releasing the exhibit from the hold of a single, linear or chronological narrative, the five somewhat independent yet interlocking components would allow visitors to browse the exhibition in a sequence of their own choice and to experience multiple points of encounter and reference, a goal consistent with the objective of attracting new and curious visitors bringing diverse experiences and perspectives to the exhibit.

The concept was sharpened in an intensive year of research and planning that culminated in the powerfully argued and supported NEH implementation proposal noted above, which was submitted at the end of 1986. The five symbols shaped the research and collections assessment as well as the exhibit content, strategy, and design approach. The plan that resulted seemed fully ready for implementation. Throughout the process, society staff had successive meetings with the original consultant team. And as the implications of each symbol's treatment became clearer—Coney Island, for example, broadened into a general interpretation of leisure and recreation over the course of Brooklyn's history—an additional tier of experts was added to the advisory group.

Looking back, the staff believes that the consultants played a cumulatively substantial role, but in a somewhat surprising way. The academic advisors proved less valuable for their professional expertise—as assessors of historical evidence, refiners of historical interpretations and judgments, and guarantors of the accuracy of the content—in other words, the academics were less helpful as an academic counterweight to the exhibit planners' orientation toward artifacts, communication, and even entertainment. Rather, the academics proved most helpful in offering intellectual lift, not ballast, for what one staff member playfully called "cosmic" insights—that is, for help in seeing interesting connections among diverse historical ideas and materials and in imagining how the exhibit might handle such content, link such ideas, and communicate the complexity the research and exhibit concept together were helping to crystallize. Rather than a division of labor, then, between historians and interpreters, scholars and designers, and consultants and staff, the development process featured a dialogue focused squarely on the overall conception of the exhibit as the driving force behind both content and treatment. The staff feels this imagination centered dialogue bears much of the credit for whatever success attended the exhibit's installation. As we shall see, the impress of the process is quite evident in the exhibit visitors now encounter.

But the process also bears the credit, in a certain sense, for the single greatest problem that emerged in the development of the exhibit, one that tested profoundly the resolve and leadership of the project staff. An early expression of the commitment to an integral project team approach was the notion of bringing the exhibit designer on board very early on. As explained in the NEH proposal: "Prior to the first consultants meeting the society hired [X, name omitted] as the project's exhibit designer. The staff felt it was important to have a designer participating in planning activities from the very beginning. [X] has a particularly good reputation with history museums and it was felt could offer excellent advice on the present project."[4] Indeed, the designer participated actively in the development process through 1986, and the NEH proposal included detailed drawings and design specifications, helping qualify the project for major implementation rather than planning funds.

The very intimacy of the process, however, led project staff members gradually to discover that they were uncomfortable with the designer they had chosen. With every iteration, it became increasingly evident that although the emerging plans promised a handsome and professional exhibit, staff and designer were simply not on the same wavelength. "We had an idea of what we wanted this thing to look like," Kahn recalls, "and that idea either did not get relayed to the designer or he was incapable of following through on it."[5]

The differences centered first on the handling of space. The designer's plan never seemed to take full advantage of the dramatic possibilities the high ceiling presented for evoking the powerful symbols on which the exhibit was based. Instead, the designer's dividers and panels of uniform height seemed likely to become a "rat maze" very much at odds with the flow and visual variety the staff hoped to encourage. More substantively, the staff grew increasingly uneasy about the treatment of artifact display as the plans developed. They sensed "a basic misunderstanding about what the artifact was supposed to do in this exhibit," in that the proposed design seemed to spotlight evocative but ordinary objects "as if each thing were a work of art, you know, like a Faberge egg, that they were all these beautiful objects. And you look at that stuff down there in the exhibit—the chewing gum and the souvenir plates are not inherently fabulous artifacts. That's not why they're down there. He would have had a lunch box sitting up here on the shelf with a spotlight on it, and then down here, a helmet—it was just a total misunderstanding of what the exhibit's all about."[6]

And so, for all the professionalism of the proposed design plans, with the project so far along in its development, and with the implementation plans pending before NEH, Kahn and his staff decided to release the designer and to start over. The controversial decision was as courageous as it was dramatic, since the intimate collaboration with the designer from the start of the project meant that the designer's removal involved more professional embarrassment and implied far more self-criticism than would have been the case otherwise. Indeed, the crisis represented a grave challenge to the staff's self-confidence and its capacity to build support and funding for an exhibit still steaming along on a fast track.

But the ability to make such a difficult decision seems only to have confirmed and deepened the staff's confidence in the vision driving the project. That they rose to the occasion became clear later, in the results and in the fact that the exhibit was completed not terribly far behind the initial schedule. But it was evident almost immediately in the process as well. Learning from their mistakes, the society's team improvised an approach to selecting a new designer that was as dramatic a departure from convention as was the decision to fire the former one so far along in the exhibit process. Rather than repeating the error of hiring a designer on the basis of reputation and portfolio, the staff decided on a course rarely chosen in history exhibits. They allocated scarce resources to fund what was in effect a design competition. Three candidates were invited to compete and paid a thousand-dollar honorarium each to submit a design plan responding to the exhibit concept and materials already developed.

A creative process led to an equally creative result. Finding no one submission fully satisfactory, the project staff proposed a unique collaboration between two of the competitors: an architectural firm that had shown tremendous imagination in its approach to handling and shaping space and a design-graphics firm that had seemed the most imaginative in its ideas about arranging objects and presenting information. The combination clicked immediately, and the project moved forward swiftly with a great deal of the collaborative dialogue among staff, consultants, and designers originally intended. Among other things, the dramatic crisis and its resolution demonstrate the indispensability of vision and leadership. Productive notions of collaborative dialogue can thrive on, and

In the "Coney Island" section, interpretive material is set within the playful, impressionistic roller coaster construction.

may indeed require, a clear sense of where the project is headed and why and a firm determination to hold to that course.

Before we turn to the exhibit itself to see what all this has meant in practice, one final feature of the development process is worth considering—one which at first glance may seem inconsistent with the confident, "inner-directed" approach evident in the firing of the first designer. Toward the end of the process, the society convened a series of focus group meetings, which involved extensive explorations with carefully selected publics. Each meeting's discussion began by exploring the group's interests and leisure activities generally, moving on to an examination of feelings about museums and historical societies in general and the Brooklyn organization in particular, to discussions about what interested people about history in general and about Brooklyn and community history in particular, and finally—against this broader background—to responses to the exhibit plan and specific exhibit designs and materials. Four groups were convened: a representative sample of existing museum users, a group of nonusers demographically matched to the user profile, a sample of black nonusers, and a sample of white working-class nonusers.

The use of focus groups sounds more like an advertising or marketing approach than an exhibit development process, and indeed that is exactly what it was. The society was explicitly not seeking feedback to inform fundamental modifications to the exhibit plans. The focus group meetings took place early in 1988, a bit more than a year before the exhibit's opening. The major decisions had already been made, and research and design were well under way. Rather, the staff's explicit concern was outreach, and it hired a marketing firm to conduct the extensive study. "The purpose was to see how the exhibit might be most appropriately described and marketed to diverse audiences here in Brooklyn," Kahn notes. "Specifically, we wanted information about how to talk about this thing, whether in press releases or in public appearances or in posters or in whatever we did."[7]

The results were very substantial in marketing terms. The study revealed that hardly anyone knew that the Brooklyn Historical Society existed, much less what historical societies in general were or what they did. As a result, the staff decided to project the exhibit as "Brooklyn's History Museum," as a way to jump start the institution and exhibit, in the public's eye, from a position of near total inertia.

But the study proved even more important in confirming the exhibit's overall intellectual strategy and approach. The discussions revealed that most nonusers had relatively indifferent responses to formal questions about interest in "history." With the slightest probing, however, members of the focus groups expressed enormous interest in things historical. They responded with excitement and ideas to the planned exhibit materials, especially those bearing on the history of ordinary people and everyday life, on their own neighborhoods and groups, and on the broader issues in the life of Brooklyn and its various communities. The focus groups showed enthusiasm for precisely what the exhibit was designed to emphasize. (It will be of interest to many readers to note that the only unhelpful and unproductive focus group was the existing users. They proved the most unable to move beyond a narrow conception of history as details and objects, the most rigid in their conceptions of what life in the past must have been like and how it must be presented in an exhibit, and in general the most cranky and resistant in facing new ideas and approaches.) All in all, the focus groups proved extremely helpful to the staff in some last minute decisions concerning the inclusion of particular artifacts and illustrations and on some revisions of the script and design components. But the main effect of the focus groups comments was to accelerate and energize the final stages of preparation, encouraging among staff a deepened confidence as the institution turned to addressing its broad public for the first time.

Reading the Results

Let us join that public in a closer look at the installation. Having seen much of what went into the development of the exhibit, the best way to continue an exploration of the overall process will be to read crucial decisions back from realized results rather than forward from intentions and plans.

The physical announcement of the major organizing symbols greets visitors even before they enter the exhibit. Rising above exhibit cases and panels and marking the distinct areas of the gallery are dramatic, huge, theatrical mock-ups of the Brooklyn Bridge towers, of the Coney Island roller coaster, of "wags" at the navy yard, of the facade of the Dodgers's Ebbets Field, and a large photo mosaic of Brooklyn's people. The effect shouts excitement and fun—a jumble of initial confusion that gives way to clarity as the organization of the exhibit becomes evident. Right from the start, the staff's crucial gamble to switch designers seems to have paid off in exactly the ways intended.

The physical treatment and graphics announce the exhibit's orientation in another sense. The mock-ups are almost defiantly playful and unrealistic, as if making clear that the exhibit does not intend to instruct solemnly about "real" historical objects but does intend to offer comfortable, recognized symbols of the known, familiar, and loved emblems of Brooklyn. Each symbol provides a point of focus and a point of departure for the exhibit's subsequent explorations.

The role of each symbol becomes evident in the substance of each segment, especially the two that, in the room's layout, are the most likely to be the first examined by visitors—the bridge exhibit, opening to the left as one enters, or the navy yard, opening to the right. Some visitors may be surprised to discover that the exhibits are not actually *about* the symbols at all. The story of the building of the Brooklyn Bridge, for example, is by now familiar to many in Brooklyn and elsewhere, especially after the celebration of the structure's centennial in 1983. So the exhibit presents relatively little about the Roeblings, the cables, and the construction. Rather, the exhibit moves quickly from the bridge to its broader historical function—the long history of the water crossing between Brooklyn and Manhattan, why the need for a fixed link grew, and how it made a difference once it was there. The focus then widens to take in the history of New York's transportation, and how changes in modes and organization affected the history of the city and its peoples. Finally, the exhibit presents the dynamics of urban change and growth such as property and real estate development in Brooklyn—aspects shaped and stimulated by the impact

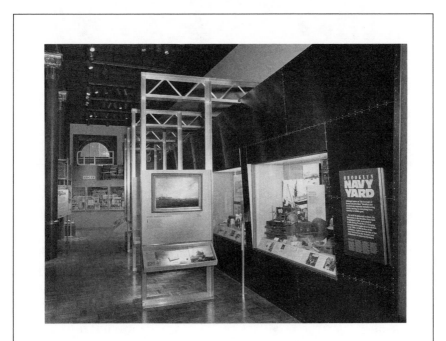

View into the "Navy Yard" section. Ebbets Field seats and the opening of the "Brooklyn Dodgers" section are visible in the rear.

Courtesy Brooklyn Historical Society.

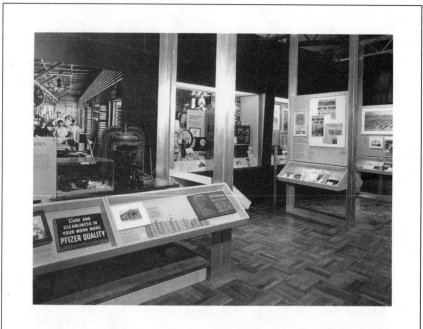

The "Navy Yard" section, looking from the area titled "The Worker's World" towards a case (rear) of objects made in Brooklyn and a case (center) on the closing of the navy yard.

of the bridge, by the link to Manhattan, and by developments in transportation, but hardly defined by them entirely and hence worthy of an independent exhibit section.

Within a quite brief compass, then, the focus on the symbol of the bridge permits examination of a wide-ranging and complex history, introducing broad and abstract ideas of urban change. In one sense the bridge and related references provide a bouncing-off point for this wider historical exploration; in another, they represent a constant anchor of familiarity and authority with which visitors can engage the less familiar and often more abstract discussions of urban change in the smaller, sidebar exhibit sections.

The strategy is similar in the navy yard treatment, where the facility, in both its rise and fall, becomes the ground for a complex examination of the dynamics of urban industrial history. The navy yard, now closed, serves both to evoke a

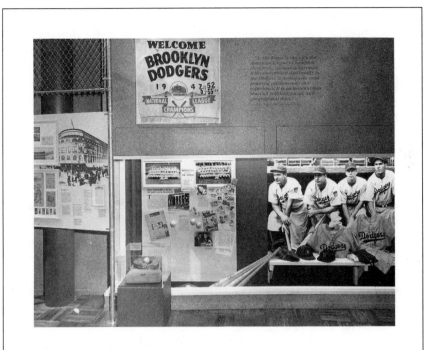

In the section on the Brooklyn Dodgers, material on the teams of the 1940s and 1950s is set in a "dugout" construction.

proud history for many Brooklynites and to support a more difficult and painful confrontation with the implications of modern deindustrialization. Similarly, the rise and fading of Coney Island, fact and image, provides the backdrop for reflections on deeper processes of change in the social history of urban leisure and consumption. Ebbets Field offers a departure point for thinking about the community function of professional sports and the nature of collective urban identities. The Brooklynites section of the exhibit is a frame for reflecting on the history of diverse communities and the meaning of Brooklyn as a whole—both as mythic stereotype and as changing reality.

Within the bounds of this general approach, the exhibit sections unfold an interesting variety of narrative techniques. In some areas, the symbol is simply the point of entry, with the focus widened in time and scope, but not all that dramatically altered, once the subject area is entered. The navy yard and Coney

Island are good illustrations of such use of symbols. Elsewhere, the symbolic and metaphorical aspect becomes the vehicle of development—as in the use of the concept of bridge or link in the Brooklyn Bridge component or the daring use in the Dodgers segment of the sardonic yet stubbornly hopeful fans' plaint from the 1950s, "Wait 'Til Next Year." The section reflects on the crushing disappointments of corporate logic so central to the Dodgers's 1957 departure, on Brooklyn's more general decline in the 1960s and 1970s the team's leaving seemed to have foreshadowed, and on Brooklyn's stubbornly resurgent hopes now for revitalization and renewal. In the "Brooklynites" exhibit interpretation starts from both ends—from the vitality of Brooklyn's diverse neighborhoods as evoked in a series of ethnic group portraits, and from the powerful yet limited popular and media stereotype of the Brooklynite "character," here epitomized by Jackie Gleason's "Honeymooners," whose actual props and re-created set are presented in one of the exhibit's more dramatic and compelling displays. The two vantages frame the contested, problematic meeting ground between changing realities and constructed images.

As even these brief sketches suggest, the themes of the exhibit sections are not entirely independent of one another. Each presents important resonances and interconnections, not surprising since each of the five symbols separates out for historical examination aspects of a community's history that are necessarily intertwined in reality and human experience. One of the most interesting dimensions of the installation is the care and subtlety with which it suggests these connections and encourages visitors to notice and follow threads and links throughout the entire exhibit. Label text can do some of this explicitly, but more striking are the more implicit choices that reinforce the point. The industrialist described in the navy yard segment—isn't that the same name as the real estate developer over there in the panel on suburban growth in the Brooklyn Bridge display? Doesn't the discussion here of the Dodgers's move echo the struggle over the closing of the navy yard described over there?

The interconnections, of course, are not accidental. The NEH grant proposal made clear, for example, the importance of including the black community's history in every component of the exhibit—because it is central to every aspect of Brooklyn's modern history—rather than being itself treated as a segregated "topic." Thus, the "Brooklynites" section presents the black dimension in everything from slavery under the early Dutch to recent West Indian immigrant communities. "Brooklyn Bridge" includes the formation of black neighborhoods in the displays on property and community development processes. The "Navy Yard" focuses on racism in employment and the black industrial migration more generally. "Coney Island" treats racism in New York's entertainment and leisure. And, of course, "The Dodgers" discusses Jackie

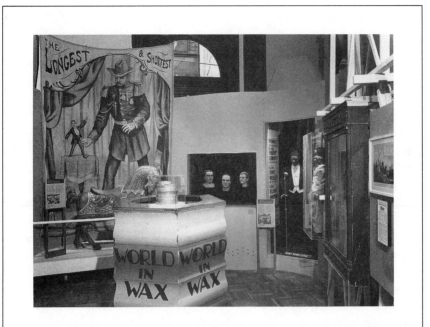

The "Coney Island" section features the barker's stand from the World in Wax Musee, a carousel horse and banner used to interpret the world of work at Coney, and a dummy, at right, once used by a black vaudevillian.

Courtesy Brooklyn Historical Society.

Robinson and Brooklyn's role in major league baseball and Bedford-Stuyvesant community organizations after the demise of Ebbets Field. Similarly, the dynamics of property and neighborhood development explained in some detail in "Brooklyn Bridge" are echoed from a different angle in the treatment of ethnic communities in "Brooklynites" and in the focus of modern redevelopment in "The Dodgers."

That such echoes and resonances come through so clearly owes much to decisions made about the exhibit's organization and presentation, which consistently features a playful and refractive rather than a solemn or didactic tone. The tone is reinforced by providing visitors with a map of the exhibit space rather than a prescribed path and by having the thematic areas wrap around walls and virtually spill into each other. The exhibit's floor plan courts some visitor confusion as to which component one is in order to make the point that, indeed, one is necessarily in more than one dimension at any given time or space. And the approach is well fitted to the constricted three thousand square feet available for the entire exhibit. In a larger space the thematic approach would have invited more separate spatial treatment for each theme and made more difficult the discovery of resonances or echoes—to go back to see, for example, if this industrialist here really is the same person identified as a developer over there.

The label texts reinforce the same spirit and tone. There are four levels and sizes of text, from general themes to specific object identification. Consistency in focus and presentation encourages visitors to examine the exhibit at various levels of detail and to follow the main themes and their cross-connections from area to area. Conversely, detached case study displays in each area allow visitors to investigate particular points and themes, without having to weave the sidebars into the overall interpretation. The organization of labels permits another point of entry for the visitor who prefers to move from particular to general or object to theme, rather than in the reverse order. (Given the conventional wisdom that people simply won't read detailed labels, it is gratifying to pass on reports from the staff that such behavior doesn't seem to have been the case. Shortly after the exhibit opened, for instance, a visitor complained that a small label identifying a navy yard worker's lunch pail was grossly in error. Everyone in Brooklyn knows, he pointed out, that those things are called lunch boxes, not lunch pails.)

Finally, the techniques used to display the artifacts also contribute to the exhibit's playful and nondidactic tone, implying a view of history as a mediation between then and now, between historical fact and historical memory, rather than as a solemn genuflection before relics of the past. The manner in which objects are presented recalls Kahn's comments about differences with the initial designer. The exhibit's installation succeeds in conveying precisely the alternative Kahn sought.

The tone of the exhibit is, perhaps, most apparent in the section on the people of Brooklyn. The large photo mosaic of scores of famous Brooklynites appears without any key or index to their identities. The collage is offered less as instruction than as a more open-ended invitation to visitors to use their own experience and knowledge in identifying the faces and to think about what the assemblage suggests in the context of the exhibit's focus on Brooklynites.

And beyond the prosaic, contemporary objects displayed, the exhibit includes some objects clearly not part of the museum's collection, nor worthy of acquisition. Often borrowed from families, fans, or private collectors, these items, however, take on a historical significance in that they become the lines to understanding an unfamiliar past. Thus it seems historically consistent for the

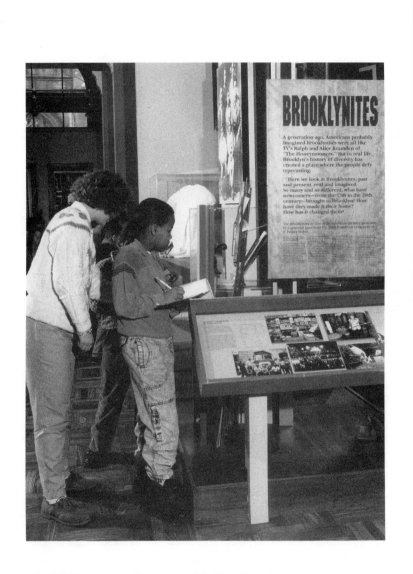

School children examine the entrance of the "Brooklynites" section.

Courtesy Brooklyn Historical Society.

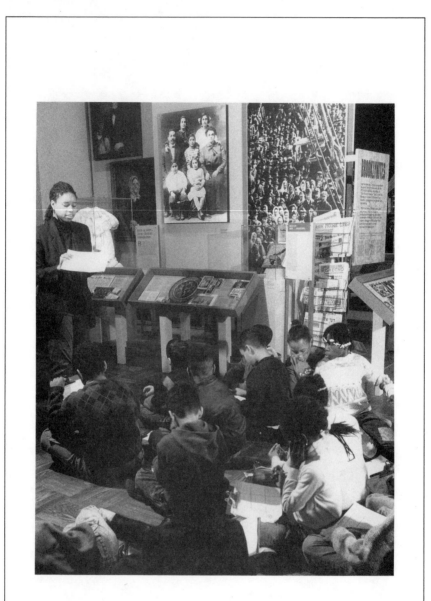

School group program is underway in the "Brooklynites" section.

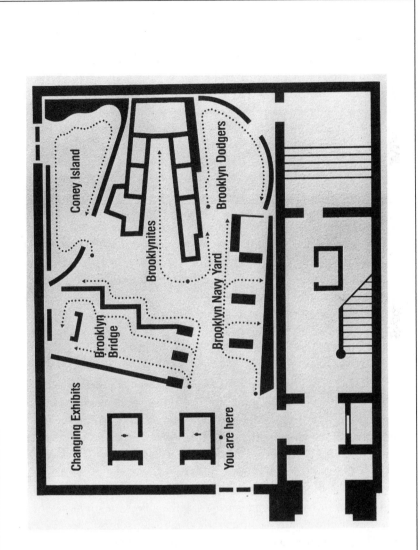

Orientation map of "Brooklyn's History Museum" exhibition is displayed near the entrance (lower left) and on a pocket card.

Courtesy Brooklyn Historical Society.

274 / Michael Frisch

"Honeymooner" set, which when used to broadcast the television series was a "living" artifact constantly in historical motion, to be in the exhibit a loose combination of objects that were "really" part of the set's fictional, mythic apartment. Even more poignant are the borrowed Ebbets Field seats, which upon demolition of the field, had been given to the New York City's Department of Corrections and were elaborately refinished by prisoners in the Bronx. Stained and varnished, they look nothing like they did in the ball park, but their present appearance is more suggestive of the complex historical relationships between past and present that the exhibit examines than if the seats had been restored to their ball park condition.

Brooklyn/Particular and Urban/General

Clearly the "Brooklyn's History Museum" succeeds in realizing its complex goals. It is no surprise to learn that the exhibit has been extremely popular and well received by its Brooklyn audience, an audience virtually created by the exhibit and carefully nurtured by a variety of ancillary programs and educational activities.

What remains is to consider the implications of Brooklyn's exhibit planning process and installation in the context of the issues of contemporary historical interpretation. Many of the points already discussed bear on a wider inquiry, of course, especially as they involve an approach to narrative and audience. But there is one dimension grounded more in historical content itself, which we have not yet considered very directly: the tension inherent in urban history between exploring a city's particular experience and exploring urbanization as a set of complex processes given expression in the place and time under consideration.

This tension parallels, but is not identical to, the exhibit's literal orientation around a broad instead of a narrow construction of historical topics—that is, the Brooklyn Bridge as the epitome of the history of transportation and communication in New York rather than as the object itself. Put another way, whether focused on object or thematic dimensions, how does the exhibit manage the dilemma of showing what is special and unique about Brooklyn's history while at the same time placing its uniqueness within the context of urban history as a more general phenomenon visitors might find interesting— and need to explore, because, in truth, we all live in worlds and dimensions hardly bound by locality alone. How successful, in this sense, is the exhibit in challenging the parochialism of even the best local history exhibit?

To this author, the exhibit suggests the answer: pretty successful. One comes away with a sense of far more than just the richness and complexity of Brooklyn's own history. It is hard to imagine that local residents would not be

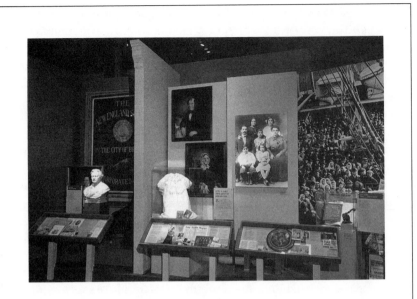

The section on Brooklynites includes, right, a discussion of nineteenth- and twentieth-century immigrants and, left, a sidebar "Focus on" section on New Englanders.

Courtesy Brooklyn Historical Society.

drawn by the exhibit to think intensely and in very broad, synthetic ways about the processes of growth, decline, and change, as well as dimensions of family, ethnicity, and community in American urban society more generally. My overall impression, however, is a composite one. It is interesting, and suggestive, to note how differently the individual components of the exhibit engage or do not engage this issue.

To this historian's eye, the major introductory sections on the Brooklyn Bridge and the Brooklyn Navy Yard are the most sophisticated and innovative in linking particular and general, in moving from Brooklyn's history to more abstract and hence transportable insights into urban process and structure. Such issues, indeed, are central to the construction of each of these components. The larger issues are less apparent, however, in the Coney Island and the Dodgers segments.

Though the baseball segment makes efforts to broaden its narrative beyond Brooklyn's own story, such attempts appear overwhelmed by the powerful, affecting particularity of Brooklyn's, and baseball's, legendary "Bums." And in fact it was precisely efforts to move beyond that story that generated some of the exhibit's only heatedly negative responses. The exhibit seeks to show that the Dodgers's move open insights into urban dynamics more complex than simply the greed of the heartless owner, Walter F. O'Malley, who took the team to Los Angeles when he could strike a better deal for a new stadium. But for at least some visitors for whom the wound still hurts, this contextualizing seemed only a kind of apology for the still hated O'Malley. The critics were quick to notice—again demonstrating that visitors read the fine print on labels—that the credits for the component begin: "The Brooklyn Dodgers section of the exhibition has been sponsored by a generous gift from Mr. and Mrs. Peter O'Malley. . . ."

The Coney Island unit is less controversial in contextualizing its topic in the broader history of leisure in New York and elsewhere, but the approach here is more literal than in other exhibit sections. Some tempting opportunities for broader references in time and space are passed by. Discussion of the turn-of-the-century evolution of Luna and Dreamworld—self-enclosed concept environments developed within and in opposition to aspects of the larger Coney honky-tonk environment—for instance, might have easily encouraged comparison to Disneyland, Disney World, and more recent theme parks as a way of invoking contemporary experience with which modern audiences are familiar. Such comparisons could have helped to provide a less localized base of familiarity and authority, beyond shared myth or New York local experience, for thinking about the issues Coney Island's history presents.

Of the five components, "Brooklynites" is perhaps the least innovative and challenging in the sense I am discussing. That it is also perhaps the most attractive and popular of the exhibit's components is therefore an instructive paradox, especially given our interest in the urbanization process. The approach taken in "Brooklynites" seems not a falling short or a flagging of the kind of interpretive energy demonstrated elsewhere, but rather a deliberate choice made relatively late in the course of developing the exhibit. The Brooklynites component is the only part of the installation that departs in a major way from the conception outlined in the NEH grant proposal.

The original idea focused squarely on the tension between the stereotyped "Brooklynite" of legend and lore, a white and usually male working-class image—Jackie Gleason's Ralph Kramden or William Bendix—and the complexity of Brooklyn's communities over time. In the NEH proposal and in an early mock-up, the tension would be evident from the exhibit's floor plan. The stereotype and legend would occupy the center of a large space, with the corners devoted to four distinct groups chosen for their capacity to illustrate broader themes about change and adaption in different eras of Brooklyn's history: the Dutch, New Englanders (a daring multicultural gesture, suggesting that the dominant culture is in moral and social senses just another "ethnic" group), Jewish Hasidim, and West Indians.

In the "Brooklynites" installation, however, the emphasis found in the proposal had been inverted. The exhibit highlights the barrage of images of Brooklynites, of ordinary people and the famous faces, and of the diversity of communities. The tension between the imaginary Brooklynite and the process-revealing four community profiles are still there, with African-Americans replacing the West Indians in this section and all reduced to a series of special "focus" modules. A series of displays on individual immigrant groups old and new—Irish, Germans, Italians, East Europeans Jews, Scandinavians, Poles, West Indians, Hispanics, Soviets, Asians—occupies the center of the exhibit area. Clearly, the demands of inclusion and representation ended up overwhelming, or at least enwrapping, the initial commitment to a leaner, theme oriented, analytic approach.

The staff generally does not seem to regret the shift, or to view it as much of a retreat. They concluded, in the exhibit planning stage, that the intended points about the image of the Brooklynite were too abstract to serve well as the central

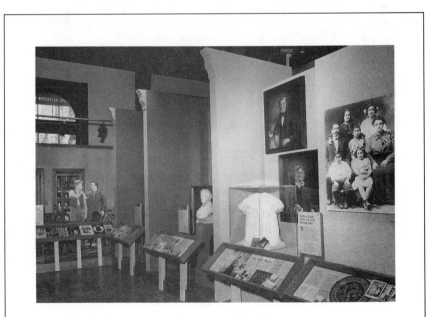

View in the "Brooklynites" section, with "Honeymooners" set in rear.

Courtesy Brooklyn Historical Society.

pivot for the whole interpretation, and that they ran a heavy risk of appearing to portray Brooklynites in a negative, condescending way. The broader diversity was not merely a matter of the staff responding to a multicultural imperative or an appeal to specific audiences. Rather, the change in the exhibit's emphasis seemed necessary to deal with what is emerging as a powerful theme of Brooklyn's contemporary history: the dramatic impact on concentrated urban areas of closely spaced, overlapping waves of immigrants as spectacularly diverse in terms of culture and conditions of emigration as anything seen in the "classic" immigration of the nineteenth and early twentieth centuries.

The modification of the imaginative original conception is certainly understandable. But it is still possible to regret the retreat it implies, especially in the light of recent presentations of real and mediated Brooklyns.

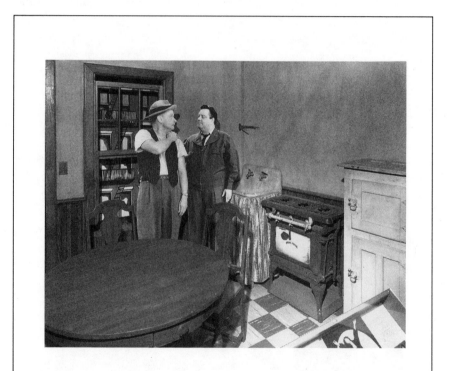

The re-created "Honeymooners" set in the "Brooklynites" section, combines "real" props as used on the television program set and items constructed or provided for this exhibition.

Courtesy Brooklyn Historical Society.

Bensonhurst, Yusef Hawkins, *Moonstruck*, *Do the Right Thing*, and *Jungle Fever* have brought the Honeymooners and Brooklynites right up to the present, placing at the center of intense public awareness and debate precisely the stereotypes of neighborhood, race, and ethnicity that the historical society had initially sought to highlight. Timing is everything, and it is possible, given this recent history, that had the original intent been maintained, the exhibit would have ended up seeming less exotic and sophisticated than the staff had feared, and indeed more prescient, relevant, and accessible.

But surely a historical society should be accountable primarily for its assessment and presentation of the past, not the future. On this score there is little to regret about the direction taken in the final installation of its ambitious plans. Without question, the "Brooklynite" component engages the most diverse audience, in immediate and profound ways. History here is personal, real, accessible, and textured in ways that seem to draw school children, families, and a range of visitors who enter the exhibit space.

And this quality, in turn, helps to suggest how successfully the installation as a whole represents the overall goals driving the exhibit development process. For if the intent was not so much to lecture an audience on historical correctness but rather to engage visitors in a more relaxed, shared exploration of history's relationship to a community's present, one in which the interests and experience of visitors could be actively engaged, then there is something quite appropriate in the fact that some exhibit components approach this interface from the end of historical explanation, while others approach it by addressing and confirming what visitors already recognize and know. The exhibit as a whole thus combines diverse modes of experience in a way that each visitor is able to modulate and control simply by the paths he or she chooses in wandering through the hall—a process made possible, as noted above, by the small size of the room and the clever, almost seamless way in which the exhibit segments fit together.

Agent of Change for an Institution

"Brooklyn's History Museum," then, is a strong exhibit and an even stronger example of an exhibit process driven from start to finish by the changes underway in its host institution. Perhaps the best confirmation of the depth and organic nature of this relationship is the fact that the exhibit is proving not only a product of change but an ongoing agent of change. Having chosen to represent in its name the institution as a whole, "Brooklyn's History Museum" now drives other projects the Brooklyn Historical Society developed to complement the institution's new image.

One outgrowth, for instance, is an ambitious documentation project on the Hispanic community designed to make sure current collections fully represent a complex period of transformation that will be inaccessible very shortly, as founding generations recede into the past and ongoing substantial and quite distinct patterns of Hispanic immigration are inscribed on the community.

Less direct an outgrowth, but nonetheless an expression of the same animating spirit, was the society's next major NEH proposal: an exceptionally ambitious and well-developed plan to computerize the library's extraordinary print, graphic, and photographic collections. The project combines data base archiving, video disc technology, and xerography in stations making the entire collection accessible to every visitor and researcher. Currently most of the images are uncataloged and grouped loosely in folders—anyone searching for a particular image or kind of image (street vendors, for example) would be unlikely to know where to look and unable to browse freely because archival protection precludes random physical access. Under the new system, every image will be photographed for video disc and be coded for any number of variables (so that a architectural photo showing a famous office building and a street vendor's stall would be coded for the vendor and hence instantly retrievable by a researcher assembling images of street level commerce). The computer-video disc station will permit flexible searches and screening of all located images, and a button will produce a photocopy of those selected. With this kind of total public accessibility, the archival copies will be given the kind of protection they require and accessed only as needed for publication or display.

The Brooklyn Historical Society's experience suggests that the long-term responsibilities of a historical society and the needs of a contemporary audience driven institution need not be incompatible, and indeed may be complementary. To the extent this is happening in Brooklyn, the process owes a great deal to an ambitious exhibit that showed how scholarly interpretation and emotionally satisfying encounters with personally relevant historical materials could be combined for local audiences.

As this essay has sought to demonstrate, the historical society's success is no accident. Accomplishments in Brooklyn trace to an exhibit development process propelled both by a clear vision and by the wisdom to alter, modify, and adjust a chosen path in response to experience, always the best teacher but especially so when the goal is a complex interaction with the public rather than simply an expression of what one sees from within.

Institutional Profile

Name: Brooklyn Historical Society
Location: 128 Pierrepont Street, Brooklyn, New York 11201

Size of institution: 3,500 square feet
Date of founding: 1863
Number of professional staff: 11

Exhibition Data

Name of exhibition: "Brooklyn's History Museum"
Dates and venues: Opened October 1989, permanent exhibition
Size of exhibition: 3,000 square feet
Cost: $600,000 (including salaries)
Names and titles of exhibition personnel: David M. Kahn, Executive Director;
Ellen M. Snyder-Grenier, Project Director; Jane Emmet McDonough,
Curator of Education
Date of original conception: Winter, 1985–1986
Duration of exhibition development process: Winter 1985–1986 to October 1989
Consultants:
Content consultants (during planning): Ronald J. Grele, Kenneth T. Jackson,
Margaret Latimer, Thomas J. Schlereth
Content consultants (added during implementation): Michael Ettema, Joshua
B. Freeman, Henry Glassie, Barbara Kirshenblatt-Gimblett, Kathy Peiss,
Steven Allen Reiss, Robert W. Snyder, Michael Wallace
Design consultants: Breslin Mosseri Design, Keith Ragone
Number of objects exhibited: 1,200
Related programming:
Publications: Visitor's guide, as handout; catalog in preparation
Media: Video documenting the making of "Brooklyn's History Museum"
is in preparation
Gallery talks: Elementary school programs, "Many Faces, Many Ways: The
Multicultural Diversity of Brooklyn"; Brooklyn Life Associates programs:
recollections and demonstrations by Brooklynites with experiences
related to the exhibition content; monthly programs of folk arts and
traditional storytelling
Professional Journal Reviews:
"The Definitive Brooklyn," *Humanities* 11 (March/April 1990): 36.
Richard Lieberman, "Brooklyn's History Museum," *Journal of American
History* 77 (June 1990): 225–32.

Notes

1. Brooklyn Historical Society, "The Brooklyn History Gallery," grant proposal to the National Endowment for the Humanities, 11 December 1986, 2.
2. Transcripts of interviews with David M. Kahn, executive director; Ellen M. Snyder-Grenier, curator; and Jane Emmet McDonough, director of education; Brooklyn Historical Society, with author, Brooklyn, New York, 6 June 1990, 16. Tapes and transcripts in the possession of the author.
3. David M. Kahn, interview, 6 June 1990, transcript, 59.
4. "The Brooklyn Historical Gallery", grant proposal, 4–5.
5. David M. Kahn, interview, 6 June 1990, transcript, 7.
6. Ibid., 75–76.
7. Ibid., 17–18.

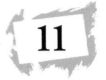

FUELED BY PASSION

The Valentine Museum and Its Richmond History Project

Lonnie Bunch

I n the 1942 film, *Casablanca*, Richard Blaine, a character played by
Humphrey Bogart, meets Victor Laszlo, the husband of his former lover, for
the first time. During an exchange of strained pleasantries, Laszlo comments
on Rick's prominence in Casablanca. To which the Bogart character replies:
"And one hears much of Victor Laszlo everywhere." Everywhere in the museum
world today, it seems, one hears much of the Valentine Museum and its
Richmond History Project, whether in the columns of *History News*, at sessions
of annual museum or historical association meetings, or during informal
gatherings of museum colleagues.

Since the mid-1980's arrival of its talented and driven director, Frank Jewell,
the Valentine Museum has generated much attention and garnered much
acclaim. Such notice stems from a variety of achievements and exhibitions that
have forced visitors to confront more controversial aspects of the Richmond's
history, like racism and industrial exploitation and the implementation of an
innovative and comprehensive plan for staff enrichment and development. In
addition, granting agencies like the National Endowment for the Humanities
have sanctioned the "Valentine method" by providing consistent and extensive
funding, enabling the museum to influence the profession through the creation
of meetings such as the 1990 conferences in Chicago, "Modes of Inquiry" and
"Venues of Inquiry," which explored the state of urban history in the nation's
museums. The willingness of the Richmond History Project to embrace the
notion of a "works-in-process" and to suggest a new paradigm for exchange

between scholars in universities and scholars in museums, also helps to explain the institution's visibility and prominence.

An Institution in Transition

That the Valentine Museum has assumed such an important role among the nation's cultural institutions is surprising in light of its history. The museum began to serve the public in 1898, when Mann Valentine II turned his home and his personal collections into a private museum for the city of Richmond, Virginia. For much of its existence, the Valentine Museum was seen as a small southern entity, known primarily for its celebration of regional culture through its extensive holdings in costumes and the decorative arts. Traditionally, the institution's centerpiece has been the 1812 Wickham-Valentine House, a three-story building well suited to interpret the lives of Richmond's elite.

In the early 1980s, a financial crisis led the museum's board of trustees to establish an informal long-range plan and to recognize the need for greater professionalism in the museum's staff. Concurrently, the city of Richmond underwent a revitalization that stimulated discussions about the need to raise the institution's profile and stature. These desires coalesced in 1984 when the museum hired Jewell as its executive director. In many ways, Jewell's vision for the institution and his passion and commitment to scholarly excellence fit quite nicely with the museum's desire to upgrade its image.

Immediately, Jewell began to assess the institution's strengths and problems and to reshape the museum's mission and supporting infrastructure. In order to accomplish the assessment, the Valentine Museum embarked in 1984-1985 on a rigorous and extensive institutional self-study that was shaped and implemented with the assistance of numerous scholars and museum professionals. Experts such as Harold Skramstad, president of the Henry Ford Museum and Greenfield Village; David R. Goldfield, professor of history at University of North Carolina, Charlotte; Barbara Carson, lecturer in American studies at the College of William and Mary; Edward L. Ayers, associate professor of history at the University of Virginia; and Donald Meinig, professor of geography, Syracuse University, worked with the museum for several years to help develop long-range administrative and exhibition plans. In addition, content and area specialists like Linda Baumgarten, curator of textiles at Colonial Williamsburg Foundation, Patricia Chester of Chester Design Associates, Eugene Genovese of the University of Rochester, and numerous others provided support and direction for specific collections, restoration, or exhibition related projects.

This impressive array of consultants demonstrates Jewell's desire to immerse the Valentine Museum in the main currents of museum and historical

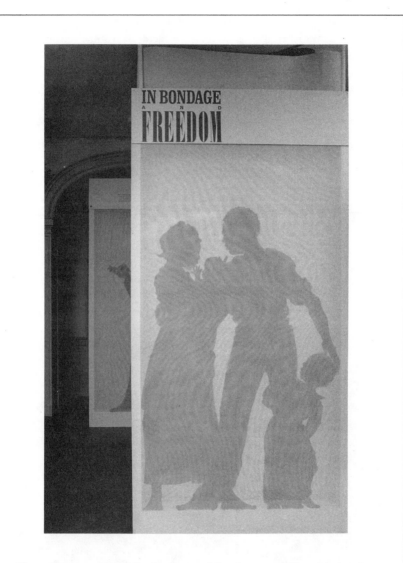

The opening in 1988 of "In Bondage and Freedom: Antebellum Black Life in Richmond, 1790–1860" cemented the growing national reputation of the Valentine Museum. This exhibit explored the urban experience of African-Americans—both slave and free—in prewar Richmond. The final shape of the Richmond History Project—an interdisciplinary team structured around the project historian—evolved from the process of crafting this exhibit.

Courtesy Valentine Museum.

scholarship and to ensure that the intellectual isolation that affects so many smaller historical museums was no longer a factor at his institution. The desire to be a part of the mainstream of historical thought and scholarship has been one of the guiding tenets of the museum since Jewell's arrival. Jewell preaches "that the museum, no less than the academy, creates history. Its work in this respect is subject to the same critical, scholarly standards as the work of any historian." Thus the Valentine Museum's reliance upon extensive scholarly consultation is an outgrowth of this belief. While all cultural institutions are not able to arrange such an august body of consultants, it is important and practical for museums to emulate the thoughtful analysis of the Valentine Museum's self-study.

Out of this self-study came many of the tenets and a five-year plan that were to guide the Valentine Museum and shape its most ambitious endeavor, the Richmond History Project. Most clearly, the self-study confirmed the museum's willingness to have its staff, educational programs, collections, and exhibitions

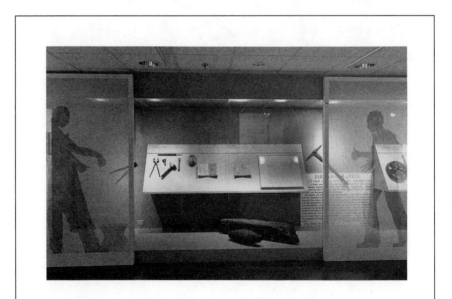

The use of theatrical scrims is an important design element in many of the presentations of the Valentine Museum such as this setting from "In Bondage and Freedom: Antebellum Black Life in Richmond, 1790–1860." These scrims help "people" the exhibit and provide additional context to the objects on display.

firmly grounded in and completely informed by the historical scholarship coming primarily from the nation's universities. Additionally, the plan called for a complete evaluation of the museum's holdings that would lead to deaccessioning of inappropriate materials and the identification of areas of future collecting. The self-study also demanded the development and implementation of effective management systems for collections, financial, and human resources, and emphasized the need for more effective staff recruitment and development. Finally, the plan encouraged the complete restoration of the 1812 Wickham-Valentine House and the creation of a strategy to increase visitation and to attract new audiences, especially from black Richmond.

More importantly, the five-year plan established an intellectual framework for the institution that the museum calls a "scholarly point of view." According to Jewell, the museum examines Richmond as "a case study of American social history and interpreted within the context of urban history." Two of the most dynamic areas of American historical inquiry, the "new social" history and urban history, serve, therefore, as the prism through which the Valentine Museum explores the history of its local community. To implement this "scholarly point of view," the Valentine Museum embarked on the Richmond History Project.

The Richmond History Project, an extremely ambitious endeavor, seeks to blend rigorous scholarly standards and innovative perspectives of urban and social history with "cutting edge" museum and exhibit concerns of audience, exhibition development, and institutional mission. The project will culminate in a number of elements including a major catalog, video presentations, and educational "school packs," but the centerpiece of the project will be a ten-thousand-square-foot exhibition, presenting a new interpretive history of Richmond.

The project will attempt to interpret over three hundred years of the Richmond's history by exploring a plethora of periods and issues. The scope of the exhibition will range from topics such as the development of Richmond's colonial economy to the enduring legacy of the recent struggles for racial integration, from the intellectual history of the "Lost Cause" to the effects of advertising on mass consumerism, and from the role of Richmond's women in the work force to the impact of industrialization on the city. The parameters of the Richmond History Project are indeed broad.

The exhibition will be installed in the Tredegar Iron Works in spring 1992. The site, located on the James River near the heart of downtown Richmond, is an important national historic landmark. The site's history speaks volumes about the Civil War, industrialization, and race relations in the South. There is no better site in which to interpret the history of Richmond.

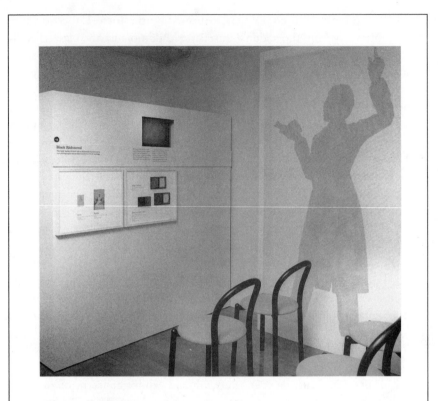

The exhibits of the Richmond History Project seek to create an environment where sound, word, image, and idea convey aspects of the interpretive context. Here, a theatrical scrim, an audio-visual component, and historical objects converge to explore daily life for blacks in antebellum Richmond.

Courtesy Valentine Museum.

The planned exhibition is firmly grounded in the institutional vision; rarely do museum goals dovetail so nicely with exhibition aims. Far too often exhibitions meander down paths that, while meaningful and exciting to the exhibit's curator, do little to enhance or accomplish broader institutional concerns. Such is not the case with the Richmond History Project. Ultimately, the Valentine Museum wants to "create a work of . . . historical synthesis accessible to a wide public" that assists the institution in implementing its long-range goals. All the ideas and decisions that shape the project are filtered through the prism of institutional needs and expectations. For this, the Valentine Museum deserves our applause. To accomplish these goals, the institution has developed innovative approaches to staff development, process, content and revision.

Staff Development

In one of its more important achievements, the Valentine Museum implemented an effective plan of staff development, an achievement that has significant, long-term ramifications for the museum field. Museums lag far behind the corporate world in staff development and aggressive institutional planning. Using its approach to team building, the Valentine Museum created an environment that effectively supports the development of the Richmond History Project, rigorous intellectual inquiry, and excellence in public history presentations.

The Valentine Museum recognized the need to develop both a broader, more inclusive approach to the creation of exhibitions as well as a plan for institutionwide team building. The Richmond History Project provided the opportunity to address this need. Beginning in 1985, the Valentine Museum embarked on an innovative course of staff development and enrichment that would ultimately make the Richmond History Project possible. Combining traditional practices such as participation in scholarly conferences and professional organizations with nontraditional elements like staff reading days, Jewell created a program to combat the problem that "some of the staff really did not understand the nature of the history that we will generate."

Like so many of the museum's endeavors, the goals of the staff development program were quite ambitious. First, staff would need to realize that each member had multiple responsibilities. While each was accountable for a specific program, collection, or area of scholarly expertise, each was equally responsible for assisting the museum in obtaining its broader, institutional priorities. The sense of subordinating individual concerns for the greater good of the institution is an important element in the success of any museum.

The feeling of the institution's greater good also breeds the sense of collaboration, community, and collegiality among the staff required to make the Richmond History Project succeed. Also essential was Jewell's desire to develop historical literacy among staff members that made them conversant with the scholarship of both urban studies and the "new social" history of the last twenty-five years. The staff could then share a language and a common intellectual framework that would spark more effective staff interaction, eliminate the feelings of isolation that often affect many museums, and encourage more creative tension and critical exchange in the development of the Richmond History Project.

The museum's staff development plan had four essential elements: staff reading days, staff seminars, a travel program, and a summer residency, all of

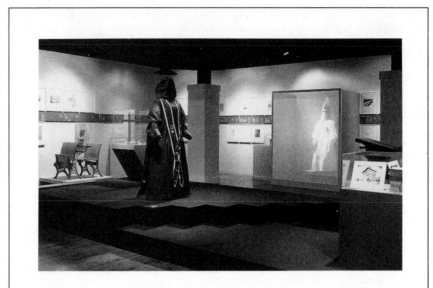

In 1989, the Valentine Museum mounted the exhibition, "Jim Crow: Racism and Reaction in the New South," which explored the origins and evolution of racism from the Civil War to 1940.

which were crafted to help shape the Richmond History Project. All too often, the press of meetings, collections and exhibit concerns, and the plethora of public and scholarly inquiries leave a museum's staff with precious little time to read. Thus, staying familiar with the changing currents of scholarly discourse is a difficult task for many museum professionals. The Valentine Museum sought to remedy that concern by creating staff reading days in 1988. Curatorial and public programs staffs are expected to use two reading days per month to remain current in their areas of interests or expertise. Reading days ensure that staff members are familiar with aspects of the history of Richmond and that they contribute to the success of the project.

The Virginia Foundation Residency Program offered museum staff additional opportunities for study. From 1986–89, the Valentine Museum, with the support of the Virginia Foundation for the Humanities and Public Policy, entered into a collaborative resident program with the University of Virginia. The endeavor allowed staff from the museum to attend a two-week program on the campus of the university. There, faculty such as Cynthia Aron, Edward

Ayers, and David Goldfield participated in formal presentations and informal discussions that highlighted the current scholarly debates and historical questions of their particular fields of study. Museum staff were immersed in such diverse areas as anthropology, trends in urban history, Southern history, women's history, and African-American history. Valentine staffers such as Gregg Kimball, curator of books and manuscripts, and Karen Luetjen, head of public programs, used their time in Charlottesville to shape the exhibition projects that they were working on for the museum. Clearly the program was an enormous success: pivotal members of the staff were not only aware of current scholarly concerns, but they had personal contact with many of the seminal figures in the field.

Staff travel to review other institutions and exhibitions also helped create a common intellectual base among staff members. The program provided the core staff of the Richmond History Project, along with members of the development and public programs offices, the opportunity to see the state of exhibition design nationally and to meet with peers to discuss the process and problems of exhibition development. The visits, funded in part by the museum and the National Endowment for the Humanities, provided not only a chance to evaluate the state-of-the-art but also encouraged the project team to develop a greater sense of comradeship and collegiality.

The final element, the Richmond History Project's staff reading seminars, is, in my mind, the most exciting aspect of the plan. Led by Marie Tyler-McGraw, the project historian of the Richmond History Project, the weekly seminars provide an opportunity for spirited yet supportive discussions among the project staff, the director, and representatives of the development and public relations staffs. Initially conceived by Jewell in 1985, the central focus of the seminar remains the discussion, led by selected staffers, of current books, articles or issues affecting the field. Many of the works discussed appear on a reading plan drafted by University of Virginia history professor, Edward Ayers, in 1987. The staff has debated readings as diverse as Wilbur Cash, *The Mind of the South*, C. Vann Woodward, *Origins of the New South, 1877–1913*, John Blassingame, *The Slave Community*, and Raymond Smilor, *Museums in Transition*.

In recent years, discussions during the seminars have shaped the ideas, content, and form of the exhibition. In seminars that I attended during my visits to the Valentine Museum, the staff engaged in lively discussions of the interpretive limitations inherent in an exhibition. Using a *New York Times* article about Michael Spock, the vice-president of public programs at the Field Museum in Chicago as a point of departure, Jewell led the staff through a wide-ranging discussion that touched on the "problem of 'theatrical' exhibition design," shifted to the use of audio-visual presentations in museums, and

292 / Lonnie Bunch

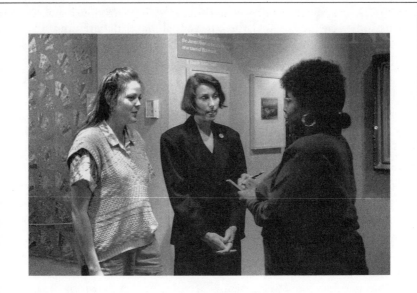

One of the strengths of the Richmond History Project is the notion of exhibits as works-in-progress. Here a staff member conducts an interview with museum visitors in order to evaluate the effectiveness of the exhibits.

Courtesy Valentine Museum.

crested with a spirited debate about "literalism." While there were over twenty staff members in attendance, the discussion was clearly shaped and limited by a few of the senior staff. Despite that concern, it was apparent that Jewell, Tyler-McGraw, and a few others attempted to use these seminars to stimulate the kind of creative tension that elevates good ideas into great exhibitions. At these discussions, one sees the passion and leadership of Frank Jewell. He is the professor, the gadfly, the rabble-rouser, and the final arbiter. Jewell challenges staff members, when necessary, to take their thoughts to a higher level, to understand scholarly nuances, to share his concerns and his vision, and to articulate their ideas in the face of withering debate. One comes away pleased by his commitment to building the team concept and impressed by his willingness to shake the intellectual and exhibition parameters of the profession.

What is less clear is the extent to which these programs stimulate and support middle- to lower-level staff members. While all echelons of the institution are encouraged to participate in these endeavors, it seems that senior employees dominated many of the meetings. Part of the answer lies in how successfully the museum balances staff needs with institutional concerns and how it ensures that the more dominant personalities do not inhibit the participation of the less-verbal or less-seasoned staff.

Team Process

What also helps to make the Richmond History Project so provocative is the Valentine Museum's commitment to the team approach of exhibition development. It is this practice that occasioned David R. Goldfield of the University of North Carolina at Charlotte to write that "one notices the extremely sophisticated and systematic manner by which the Valentine Museum developed the notions that shape the Richmond History Project." While the Valentine Museum is not the first cultural entity to champion the practice of team driven exhibition development, few museums have embraced this notion so passionately and expended such extensive intellectual, staff, and fiscal capital towards its implementation.

The team approach of the Richmond History Project owes much to the museum's commitment to develop common intellectual ground upon which all staff stand. It also demonstrates the museum's recognition that the shifting museum landscape as well as the rather ambitious nature of the project call for changing standards and practices in exhibition creation. Today exhibitions are expected to accomplish more than ever before. Presentations in museums are asked, I think quite appropriately, to aid in the development of new audiences, wrestle with more complex issues of race, class, and gender, incorporate new audio-visual technologies, and provide a forum through which the concerns of the academy and those of the museum are made accessible to a wide public. This is a great deal to accomplish in four thousand square feet.

To deal effectively with such external concerns and internal desires, the museum embraced the need for a sophisticated team approach that recognized the importance of shared leadership and specialization in the exhibition process. The museum rightly determined that the complexity of the project made the "traditional," single curator model obsolete. No one curator could develop the intellectual framework, oversee new collecting initiatives, respond to issues of audience and design, draft the label copy, work with an extensive network of consultants, and still manage the process efficiently. The Richmond History Project, therefore, brought together numerous staff members and consultants, each with specific areas of expertise and oversight. Additionally, the team is strengthened by the fact that a large percentage of the museum's staff, who received valuable training through the weekly Richmond History Project

American industry's newly developed techniques of mass production created the possibility of abundance for ordinary people during the decades after the Civil War.

This was a revolutionary possibility in human history.

Mass production demanded mass consumption. A new service industry — advertising — and new systems of corporate management, distribution, and retailing were needed to create and supply a mass market.

Advertising and mass markets stood traditional values on their heads and converted a nation of savers into a nation of consumers.

The tension between saving and consuming has troubled Americans for a century. Current trade and budget deficits and the lowest rate of saving of any western country have fueled a new contemporary debate.

Using Richmond's cigarette industry as a case study, SMOKE SIGNALS explores these themes and their effect on the local economy and values.

How to see the exhibition

This exhibition can be seen in several ways. The four section labels in larger type summarize the major themes of SMOKE SIGNALS. The next two levels of interpretive phrases and their grouped artifacts offer greater detail.

For more complete artifact identification, see the checklist at the end of the exhibition.

The SMOKE SIGNALS catalog contains an essay and selected objects from the exhibition. It is available at the reception desk.

Within the exhibition there is a study center with additional literature and audio-visual material. Please take time to explore these timely topics.

SMOKE SIGNALS is a "work in progress," one of an ongoing series of Valentine exhibitions that address neglected aspects of Richmond's history. The research products and artifacts from these exhibitions will contribute to a new interpretation of Richmond's past in the Tredegar Galleries on the James River in 1992.

To make exhibitions more accessible to both new and traditional audiences, the Valentine Museum creates text panels, like this one from "Smoke Signals: Cigarettes, Advertising and the American Way of Life," that explain how the visitor should view the exhibition and what additional information is available in catalogues or in audio-visual presentations.

Courtesy Valentine Museum.

seminars and other aspects of the museum's staff development program, are contributing, though, unofficial members of the exhibition team.

The constant and pivotal members of the exhibition team are the institution's director, Jewell, who is the project director and Tyler-McGraw, who is the project historian. The leadership provided by these academically trained historians speaks volumes about the scholarly direction and the idea driven bent of this project. While Jewell frames the broad institutional and intellectual agenda, it is the scholarship of Tyler-McGraw, shaped by information garnered from earlier "works-in progress" exhibits and from an array of consultants, that fuels the project.

Tyler-McGraw plays important and innovative roles. Often exhibit teams include a project historian (although it is sometimes a role assumed by the curator) who shapes the historical content of the presentation. Far too frequently the staff historian's expertise does not correspond to the project's needs. The institution then finds a consultant who will spend a few days providing a sense of the field and the issues that the exhibit should address. While the museum recognizes the central role that consultants play, the museum wanted a more frequent and consistent presence. Fortunately, they learned of Tyler-McGraw when she provided a seminar on the antebellum free black community of Richmond during the museum's two-week residency program at the University of Virginia. When Tyler-McGraw later joined the museum, the Richmond History Project had its much needed staff scholar.

The role performed by the project historian is central to the success or failure of the Richmond History Project. Tyler-McGraw's primary task is to draft an interpretive history of the city of Richmond from its inception to the post-civil rights era. This daunting task is all the more important because the document is the interpretive and contextual rudder for the project. The themes, discussions, and interpretive posture of the exhibition, and such ancillary products as a catalog, video presentations, educational materials, and public programs, all flow from Tyler-McGraw's manuscript.

Because the document is so crucial to the process, the project's weekly seminar have consistently reviewed and criticized the material. When Tyler-McGraw completes each new section, she presents her findings to her colleagues and submits drafts to a series of consultants who are expert in a particular aspect of Richmond history. She then incorporates suggestions and changes into the final draft.

Other members of the team perform tasks or exercise specific responsibilities designed to facilitate Tyler-McGraw's work and the successful completion of the project. Thus the project editor, Nancy Brooks, will assist Tyler-McGraw with the creation of the catalog as well as assume primary responsibility for drafting the exhibition script, with Tyler-McGraw reviewing and editing the final product. An exhibition coordinator oversees the project's administrative needs, while an evaluation coordinator works to ensure that the project is cognizant of the concerns of the audience. The team also consists of various humanities and museum consultants and numerous design, audio-visual, and audience advocates.

The use of the team approach by the Richmond History Project works because of several essential factors. One is the clear delineation of responsibilities, all geared to support the efforts of the project historian. The team members have a well-defined sense of their roles and their authority. Also, the success of the approach stems from the centrality of the project's interpretive history of the city and the project historian. Not only does the centrality of the interpretive history provide a sense of cohesiveness, but the accessibility of the document and of the project historian ensures more effective communication about the exhibit and its ancillary programs. Penultimately, much of the credit

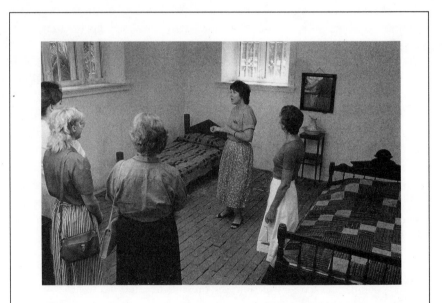

While the Valentine Museum has crafted a rich array of interpretive devices, the house tour is still an important part of the visitor's experience. Here a docent interprets the re-created room of a domestic slave in the Wickham House.

Photo by Doug Buerlein.
Courtesy Valentine Museum.

for the project's structure and approach belongs to the museum director. Jewell labored relentlessly and impressively to make team building central to the mission of the Valentine Museum.

Consultants

Finally, the Richmond History Project has reaped benefits from the effective and efficient use of consultants. The consultants are an essential and integral part of the exhibition team. As such, the choice and able use of consultants by the project deserves greater attention. Looking through the roster of consultants that the Valentine Museum has used since 1985, one is struck by the impressive array of talent that has developed an on-going relationship with the museum or with the Richmond History Project. At first glance, it seems that the museum follows the refrain often spoken by the prefect of police in the movie, *Casablanca*, "to round up the usual suspects." Upon closer examination, it is clear that while the institution does draw on many of the same scholars repeatedly, there are additions or deletions depending upon the immediate requirements of the project. Developing this scholarly bullpen is an important strength: consultants develop a better sense of the needs of museums and how their expertise might better serve these needs generally and of the specific concerns of the Valentine Museum. This scholarly bullpen, then, provides a flexible cadre of expertise that the project can marshall in any manner the staff deems appropriate. This practice eliminates, or at the very least shortens, the transitional period that often occurs when university scholars are asked to translate their expertise into the different and challenging exhibition medium.

Because of the fundamentally important role played by the consultants, the project's staff is careful in their selection and use. The staff identifies consultants through a variety of methods. Usually individuals come to the staff's attention as a result of their scholarly track records, something that is based primarily on the strengths of their publications. But scholarship alone is not enough to make one a project consultant. Often the staff asks the scholar to provide a lecture at the weekly seminar. The seminar is then a vehicle to ascertain how the staff feels about working with the individual. The project director and the project historian are frequently guided by the staff as to whether or not it is comfortable working with a particular scholar. It is rare that a consultant is added to the project without the complete assent of the central support staff.

The consultants chosen for the project are often the leading scholars in their fields. Obviously this ensures that the ideas that shape the project are undergirded by the best of current scholarship. Consultants are asked to assume several roles in the project. During the four meetings that the total team of

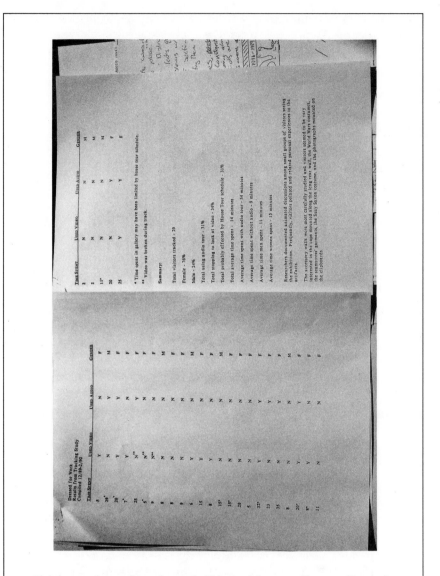

To help serve their audiences better, the Valentine Museum staff uses tracking studies to explore visitor preferences and experiences in an exhibit. The individual handwritten surveys are then compiled into a report that is used to analyze the current exhibit and inform decisions about future presentations.

Courtesy Valentine Museum.

consultants attends, much time is spent generating, shaping, and revising the exhibition's ideas. Each consultant is responsible for helping to develop ideas in their areas of specialization as well as commenting on issues outside their immediate realm of expertise. They are also expected to comment on and review the interpretive document drafted by Tyler-McGraw, present information at a weekly seminar, and evaluate the exhibition plans.

One of the best aspects of the Richmond History Project is the able manner in which the project staff employs its consultants. Too often consultants are expected to be expert on issues or areas outside of their expertise. The project clearly defines the scholar's roles and responsibilities so that no one is misused. The exchange between consultants and project staff works because much time is spent evaluating the type of relationship that is possible with each scholar. This extra effort creates an environment that allows scholars to develop a deeper relationship with the project staff. Consultants and project staff, therefore, see themselves not as disconnected forces that must coexist for several days each year, but as peers who support, stimulate, and encourage each other.

Exhibit Concept Development

Out of the relationship between staff and consultants comes the ideas that form the basis of the Richmond History Project's exhibition. The exhibit is unquestionably an idea driven project with themes stemming from the melding of the concerns of the scholarly consultants with the research and vision of the project's director and historian. To facilitate this melding, the Richmond History Project staff would meet regularly to discuss what it determined, based primarily on the work of the project historian, to be important exhibit themes.

During these discussions the project team was clearly, according to Jewell, "passionate about questions of race." The desire to explore issues of race in the exhibit grew out of both a recognition of the current scholarly interest in questions of Southern race relations and the staff's observation that interaction among the races in contemporary Richmond was nearly nonexistent after the end of the work day. Embracing, rather than marginalizing, a complex and painful subject suggests that the Richmond History Project seeks to do more than present an engaging and educational historical exposition. By filtering much of Richmond's past through the prism of race, the exhibit should raise questions that resonate with passion and a contemporary context.

To help inform these discussions, three consultants, Edward Ayers of the University of Virginia, David Goldfield of the University of North Carolina at Charlotte, and Christopher Silver of Virginia Commonwealth University, were asked to craft brief documents that outlined what issues they felt should be

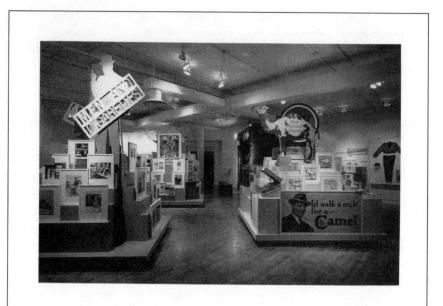

The 1989 exhibit, "Smoke Signals: Cigarettes, Advertising, and the American Way of Life," is an example of the willingness of the Richmond History Project to mount difficult or controversial exhibits.

Courtesy Valentine Museum.

central to the project's reinterpretation of Richmond's history. The project would then incorporate aspects of each author's vision and wed those to the project's interpretive posture, thus ensuring that the themes shaping the Richmond History Project reflect the best of current scholarship.

Ayers suggested that the exhibition present the history of Richmond from the perspectives of the Tobacco City, the Capital City, and the Southern City. Each perspective would incorporate an overlapping chronology that explores issues from the city's founding to its more recent past. In Ayers's scheme, the Tobacco City would explore Richmond's changing economic life by wrestling with such issues as the geography of Richmond and how that shaped its economic development, the impact of war and depression, the importance of tobacco culture, the composition and role of labor, and the post–World War II diversification, and corporationization. The Capital City theme would allow visitors to explore how much of the character of the city was shaped by its roles as the seat of power for both the state and the Confederacy. This aspect of the

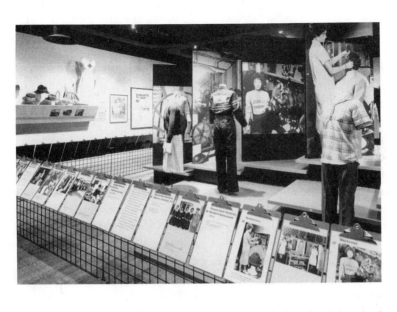

A display from the 1989 exhibit "Dressed for Work," which explored the role of women in work through costume.

Courtesy Valentine Museum.

exhibition would examine the city's role in the American Revolution, the secession crisis, as the capital of the Confederacy, the impact of the New Deal, and the changes generated by the civil rights movement. While the third area of the exhibit, the Southern City, would be where issues of race like slavery, reconstruction, outmigration, and civil rights would be explored.

Goldfield posited six themes that should inform the exhibition. Regionalism, the notion that Richmond was never separate or distinct from the surrounding countryside and that "the countryside blends into the city and vice versa in terms of commerce, culture, population, space, architecture, and technology," should provide a central framework for the exhibition. Additionally, Goldfield suggested that the project explore the area's cultural diversity, the impact of technological change—for example the automobile—the changing political culture, the role of entrepreneurs and the importance of "economic development in stimulating urban growth," and the importance and role of leisure.

Silver argued for a exhibit that explores the "urbanness" of Richmond by using the changing physical characteristics of the city as a means of portraying "its diversity, its complexity, . . . and its enduring contributions to the region." This would mean, according to Silver, that the exhibit would document the city-building process as well as examine how the development of Richmond compares with the process of urbanization regionally and nationally. Also, the exhibit would make a contribution if it explored the evolution of the downtown as a means to explore how communities change over time. Finally, Silver suggested that the show might also wrestle with such themes as race relations, economic development, changes in transportation, and suburbanization.

All the suggestions for exhibit themes were then evaluated at subsequent gatherings like the all-day planning meeting held in late 1989. At these meetings, the group discusses and reshapes the ideas presented. Ultimately the project incorporated much of the consultants' visions into five broad ideas that will shape the exhibition: (1) the urban ecology/the physical city, (2) power structures (including issues of race, gender, and money), (3) the city's self-identity, (4) the economy, business, trade, and industry, and (5) a brief look at the process of history.

The Richmond History Project staff has done an admirable job in developing the themes that inform the project. Its decision to place issues of race at the center of the interpretation of the city's history deserves admiration. As an exhibition that, in some ways, is completely determined by scholarly concerns, it runs the risk of its ideas exceeding the project's grasp. In the past few years, far too many exhibition projects have developed wonderful idea driven themes that made insightful monographs, but less than successful exhibitions. This is a pitfall that the project staff should be aware of as it moves towards its 1992 opening. A strong idea driven exhibition like that of the Richmond History Project, however, can be a liberating force that encourages a museum to wrestle with richer, more complex issues such as race and class, that more traditional, collections driven presentations might inhibit. Arguing for the primacy of ideas does not denigrate or undervalue the importance of the artifacts, rather, it simply changes the balance of the exhibition equation.

Though steeped in academic considerations, the Richmond History Project recognizes the need to ensure that its holdings support its interpretations. Since the mid-1980s, the Valentine Museum staff has scrutinized the institution's holdings and future collecting directions with the help of consultants like Barbara Carson and Linda Baumgarten. Since May 1989, the staff has conducted a complete survey of the institution's collections and shaped that information into a "intellectual inventory" that divides the holdings into groupings based on the exhibition themes developed by the Richmond History

Project. The survey also evaluated the three- and two-dimensional materials suitable for exhibit.

To ensure that the exhibition is more than a book-on-the-wall, the project has begun to develop a wish list of potential acquisitions. The project has sent out teams to survey the neighborhoods of Richmond, documenting objects in situ and identifying artifacts for possible collection. The process has enabled the museum to expand its holdings with findings such as machinery from the Tredegar Iron Works, a chinese laundry and a 1940's era black diner. The staff actually developed the wish list approach sometime ago. For previous shows at the Valentine Museum like "In Bondage and Freedom: Antebellum Black Life in Richmond, Virginia, 1790–1860," staff members have acquired objects that will be useful to the Richmond History Project, or they have developed ways of interpreting traditional artifacts in a manner that enlarges both the historical significance as well as their interpretive context. All of these efforts help ensure that the artifactual base of the exhibition is as strong as its intellectual foundation.

Works in Progress

The artifactual and intellectual underpinnings of the Richmond History Project are enhanced by an institutional philosophy positing the argument that much of the museum's prior and present efforts must be seen as "works in progress." This innovative notion argues that understanding the exhibit process, testing ideas, and determining the levels of audience engagement is ultimately more significant than the immediate end product. Few scholars could disagree with Jewell's belief that the "first draft is inevitably imperfect." This concept embraces the belief, long held in the academy, that true historical understanding comes from extensive discourse, the rethinking of prior interpretive postures, and an acceptance of the continual need to revise one's vision of the past.

While the works in process concept is a common practice among academics, museums rarely have an opportunity to revisit already trod exhibit territory. Since 1985, the Valentine Museum has crafted a series of exhibitions that were to be "dry runs" for many of the design, content, and collections issues that would eventually shape the exhibition crafted by the Richmond History Project. Everything from the type and color of label copy, to the effective use and placement of audio-visual components, and to the effectiveness of community driven collecting were tested. The Richmond History Project, in machine-gun-like fashion, spewed out nearly twenty exhibitions in five years such as: "Virginia Folk Art" (1985), "From Resistance to Renaissance: Race

Relations in Richmond Since 1945" (1985), "Free To Profess:The First Century of Richmond Jewry" (1986), "Elegant Attire, Genteel Entertainments: Leisure and the Elite, 1787–1830" (1987), "Why the South Lost the Civil War" (1988), "Dressed for Work: Women in the Work Force,1900–1989" (1989), and "Second Street: Business and Entertainment in Jackson Ward, 1900–1965" (1990). All of the exhibits serve as a proving ground and ultimately as the foundation for the final exhibition that will be installed in the Tredegar Iron Works.

The initial exhibits are more than simple trial balloons. The Richmond History Project staff views the exhibits as "complete projects in themselves . . . [that allow] the museum to test its arguments and designs, solicit additional information, and receive criticism." A prime example of the exhibit as experiment was "In Bondage and Freedom: Antebellum Black Life in Richmond, Virginia, 1790–1860," a show that was mounted at the Valentine Museum from February to September in 1988. One of the museum's first exhibits to receive national attention in both the museum and academic

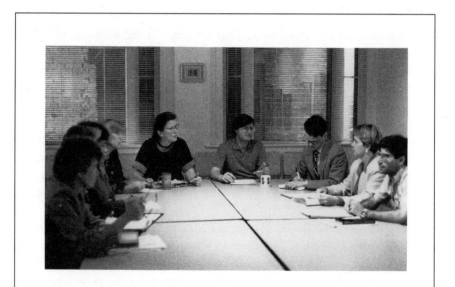

As part of the process of team building and staff development, the Richmond History Project conducts a weekly colloquium that discusses assigned readings, interacts with visiting scholars, or explores new directions in museum exhibits or interpretation.

Courtesy Valentine Museum.

communities, "In Bondage and Freedom" allowed the institution to test many of its notions about the effectiveness of a team approach, the balance between ideas and objects, and the role of educational and public programming.

The ideas and interpretive parameters of "In Bondage and Freedom" were crafted by a team of scholars led by Tyler-McGraw and Kimball, the exhibition cocurators. Benefiting from the participation of experts in urban history like David Goldfield and scholars of nineteenth-century black life such as James Horton and Edgar Toppin, the exhibit, using a wide array of two- and three-dimensional materials ranging from slave chains, estate inventories, illustrations from periodicals like *Harper's Weekly*, and blacksmithing tools, posited a series of innovative interpretations. "In Bondage and Freedom" sought to place the black presence within the context of expanding, ethnically diverse, industrial Richmond. The exhibit argued, quite successfully, that the labor of blacks—both slave and free—was central to the economic development of the city and that the nature of race relations in antebellum Richmond was fluid, with blacks and whites sharing public, semipublic and private spaces, a situation that precluded the rigid segregation that would appear throughout the postbellum South.

The successful marriage of academic scholars and museum professionals during the development of "In Bondage and Freedom" convinced the Valentine Museum of the feasibility of the team approach to exhibit development. It also allowed the institution to wrestle with the problem of a limited number of objects. Any future exhibit created by the Valentine Museum would have to face the problem of the paucity of African-American artifacts, an issue that plagued "In Bondage and Freedom." As a result of much discussion among staff and consultants, the exhibit team decided to reinterpret objects in light of new research in African-American history. Objects without specific African-American documentation, such as blacksmith tools, were reinterpreted as examples of African-American material culture because blacksmithing was a trade dominated by slaves and free blacks. This model of object reinterpretation, then, would be used to shape the artifact base in all future Valentine Museum exhibit. Each exhibit, each "works in progress," adds a new element or variable to the Valentine Museum's exhibit development equation. Each presentation is shaped and informed by the institution's prior efforts.

In order to reap the maximum benefits from these projects, the Richmond History Project has embarked on both traditional and nontraditional evaluation methods. Beginning with the exhibit, "In Bondage and Freedom" in 1988, leaders in the field of museum evaluation and audience advocacy, Harris Shettel and Randi Korn, have helped the project staff evaluate the products through such elements as audience surveys, unobtrusive observation of visitors, staff critiques, exhibit mock-ups of important interpretive or collection elements, and story boards for audio-visual materials.

The museum staff uses a more innovative method of determining the effectiveness of the exhibits in the use of "public editing." The practice stems from the idea, according to Jewell, that "our authority as historians is limited" and, therefore, the public must be allowed to help shape the content and form of the exhibition. These forums, in theory, bring together interested parties— from intellectuals to community activists to members of the corporate community—to discuss an exhibit and air their concerns, compliments, or criticisms. Held in the evening, these gatherings are peopled with invited participants and guests as well as being open to the general public. After brief remarks from the museum director or the exhibit curator that set the tone and the parameters of the evening's discourse, several invited participants deliver remarks that offer thoughtful critique and stimulate audience discussion.

During a recent public editing session sparked by the exhibit "Smoke Signals: Cigarettes, Advertising, and the American Way of Life," an audience of academics, advertising figures, and representatives of tobacco and antitobacco sentiments came together in a spirited meeting. While much of the discussion centered on political positions on smoking, the exhibit clearly stimulated vigorous and passionate debate. As with all the sessions, it was videotaped and will be used to help the project staff shape the manner in which it interprets similar issues in the 1992 exhibition.

While I strongly support efforts that make the work and process of museums accessible to a broad audience, it is unclear how effective the public editing sessions are—especially if their goal is to receive a wide array of concerns and comments. The staff must take pains to ensure that the speakers are not simply a reflection of extremes, those who come to praise or those who want to condemn. While a debate among extremes can be instructive, museums are better served if they tap into the middling core of our visitors who are interested in but not passionate about our endeavors.

In spite of this caution, there is much to applaud about the Richmond History Project's use of the works in progress notion. The earlier exhibits created a reservoir of expertise and experience that help to limit the project's missteps. By already surveying major project concerns such as the history of various elements of black Richmond or the changing roles and status of women, many of the themes and the intellectual constructs have been tested and are now subject to revision based on how successfully they were depicted in prior attempts. More importantly, the artifact and graphic support for many of the arguments has also been found. Therefore, the project staff has a sense of what different artifacts will be needed to convey the desired message. A prime example of this is how the show, "In Bondage and Freedom," has already wrestled with the problem of the paucity of antebellum black artifacts so that continuing exhibition can simply build upon that prior effort.

Also, there is now in place a network of internal and external scholars who can provide support in the process of clarifying exhibit elements and ideas. One of the real strengths of the works in progress idea is that the curators who developed previous exhibits lend their experience to and inform the Richmond History Project. Staff members like Kimball who cocurated "In Bondage and Freedom" and Karen Luetjen who curated "Second Street," can provide guidance on such diverse issues as appropriate objects or audience interest in certain aspects of Richmond history.

The impact of earlier pilot exhibits might be greatest in the area of audience and design concerns. After creating nearly twenty exhibits and encouraging key team members to visit almost forty other important exhibitions, the Richmond History Project has developed a philosophy that will help shape the final exhibit product. As a result of the initial historical presentations, the project has determined that its exhibit design must be sensitive to the needs of a highly diverse audience. The project staff has decided to incorporate various audio and audio-visual components in order to help orient the visitor and to service the visitor who is more attune to the sound bites of MTV than to the less immediate joys of reading. Additionally, the label copy of the exhibition will be tiered so that one level will provide a visitor with the basic information or themes, while other levels of text will provide greater depth of interpretation. Finally, the project seeks to develop environments and artifact groups that encourage visitor reflection and contemplation. Ultimately, what the Richmond History Project has learned about design issues is that there are no simple answers, but an exhibition is stronger if the team is aware and sensitive enough to ask the appropriate questions.

On the whole, the notion of works in progress serves the Valentine Museum and the Richmond History Project well. There are a few general concerns that might make the practice less appropriate to other institutions. The fact that the Valentine Museum is an institution in transition makes it easier to implement the concept. Rarely do museums have the financial resources or the institutional resolve to shape their exhibit agendas in so focused a manner. Also, the machine-gun-like exhibit schedule of the Richmond History Project is far too ambitious for many museums.

The rapidity of exhibit production is also responsible for the uneven quality of the Valentine Museum's exhibitions. Some exhibitions, such as "In Bondage and Freedom," innovatively wrestle with issues of object and design concerns. Presentations such as the Jim Crow exhibition and "Working People: Life and Labor in an Industrial City, 1865–1920" suffer from the lack of intellectual cohesion, modest design, and a dearth of artifacts. While many have been cutting edge presentations that wrestle innovatively with difficult issues, others are less successful as a result of subject manner, approach, or the limitation of staff expertise. Even when the presentations are successful, it is still unclear— and will remain so until the final installation—how the vast array of comments from the public editing sessions, visitor surveys, and new scholarly findings will surface in the exhibition when it opens at the Tredegar Iron Works. Yet, in spite of these concerns, this notion is an important factor in many of the successes of the Richmond History Project.

Conclusion

The successes and notoriety of the Richmond History Project lead many to promote the Valentine Museum as the model for historical museums in the 1990s, the latest museum messiah for a profession that traditionally revels in models and messiahs. While there is much to applaud about the accomplishments of the institution, it is less clear whether the successful programs of the Valentine Museum are an easily adaptable model for other cultural entities—or even whether the profession should continue its emphasis on discovering and disseminating transferable exhibit or administrative models. Rather than a model, the Valentine Museum must be seen as an institution that has clearly identified and aggressively articulated a set of assumptions and approaches that innovatively stretch the parameters of exhibit development and museum scholarship. The notions crafted by Jewell and the staff of the Valentine Museum offer insightful and provocative responses to the demands of a changing museum environment. There is little doubt that issues and questions raised by the Valentine Museum must be confronted by many of the nation's museums.

One of the most important issues facing museums today is the concept of multiculturalism. Museum periodicals and professional conferences explore ethnic diversity, cultural diversity, and cultural equity. At times, the overwhelming attention that these issues receive leave some individuals to wonder if such concerns are just the latest fad to sweep the museum profession. The Richmond History Project has struggled mightily to shape the museum through a commitment to multiculturalism. Such is not a fad to the Valentine Museum.

From the beginning of his tenure, Jewell has worked to alter the composition of the museum's audience so that it better reflects the racial and ethnic diversity of Richmond. "Museums choose their audience," Jewell argues, "and we have made a conscious decision to reshape ours." The decision to increase the black presence at the institution initially led to the loss of some of the museum's traditional visitors and funding sources. Nevertheless, the museum began to court its new audience by establishing new relationships with seminal institutions such as churches, sororities, fraternities, and alumni and business associations. When possible, the project staff has collaborated with African-American organizations such as the Virginia Black History Museum to craft exhibit projects such as "Second Street" or to uncover collections that had here-to-fore been ignored by the museum.

More significantly, the Richmond History Project has embraced racial concerns as a principal theme in all of its exhibition endeavors. Many of the project's most impressive achievements were exhibits such as "Jim Crow" and "Dressed for Work" that consciously wrestled with difficult issues of race, class, and gender. Multicultural considerations, therefore, are at the center of the project's interpretive agenda.

Too frequently, museums and exhibition development teams define and implement multicultural concerns too narrowly. I am concerned that many of today's institutions respond to these issues as if multiculturalism was the new "Plessy v. Ferguson," a Supreme Court decision in 1896 that sanctioned the idea that racial segregation was acceptable as long as it was "separate but equal." Museums must realize that embracing multiculturalism does not mean one simply develops segregated presentations about groups that are traditionally underrepresented in our cultural institutions.

While it is important to craft sensitive exhibitions like the National Museum of American History's "From Field to Factory: African-American Migration," or the Minnesota Historical Society's "The Way to Independence: Memories of a Hidatsa Indian Family, 1840–1920," it is incumbent on exceptional institutions like the Valentine Museum to work towards a new exhibition paradigm—one in which exhibitions transcend "separate but equal" presentations. It is essential for museums to create a new synthesis that allows visitors to see how diverse ethnic and racial groups in this society struggled and interacted with each other. This interaction, often violent and often contested, shaped and changed each group and the whole society. Creating such a synthesis and presenting it honestly—warts and all—is not easily accomplished. But it is a goal worthy of the effort. I am hopeful that the Richmond History Project will contribute much to this endeavor.

The Richmond History Project, then, is a complex undertaking that successfully grapples with issues that are at the heart of the museum profession. The unique circumstances of an institution in transition have allowed and encouraged the project to stretch the parameters of the exhibition medium and to develop an innovative approach to team building and exhibition development that is firmly ground in the best historical scholarship that the academy has produced. While the project's lofty aims are sometimes not achieved, the museum profession is truly enriched by their efforts. The Richmond History Project and the Valentine Museum have set a standard of creativity and innovation that few exhibition projects can match. This is a project fueled by scholarly excellence, a project fueled by passion.

Institutional Profile

Name: The Valentine Museum
Location: 1015 Clay Street, Richmond, Virginia 23219
Date of Founding: 1898
Number of Professional Staff: 29

Exhibition Data

The Valentine Museum has been included in this volume as an example of an institution that approaches all its exhibitions as "works in progress." You will not find an analysis of a single exhibition here, but rather a more holistic look at how one institution has approached exhibitions as a media for expressing and illuminating a city's history.

Examples of the Valentine Museum's exhibitions include:
"Free to Profess: The First Century of Richmond Jewry," Fall 1986–Spring 1987

"In Bondage and Freedom: Antebellum Black Life in Richmond, Virginia, 1790–1860," February–September 1988

"Jim Crow: Racism and Reaction in the New South 1865–1920," April–August 1989

"Dressed for Work: Women in the Work Force, 1900–1989," Fall 1989–Spring 1990

"Smoke Signals: Cigarettes, Advertising, and the American Way of Life," Spring–Summer 1990

Professional Journal Reviews

Lonnie G. Bunch, "In Bondage and Freedom: Antebellum Black Richmond, Virginia, 1790–1860," *Journal of American History* 76 (June 1989): 202–207.

Edward Chappell, "Valentine Museum's Jim Crow," *The Nation* 249 (17 July 1989): 102–104.

FINDING COMMON THREADS
An Afterword

Kenneth L. Ames

What can we learn from these studies? I thought it would be useful at the end of this book to draw together what seem to be some of the larger and more valuable lessons. Accordingly, I have combed the essays for major points, major insights, major conclusions that seem applicable to other situations, that seem pertinent to history museums in general. In the spirit of the Common Agenda, I looked for commonalities relevant to any history exhibition process. In the paragraphs below I share what I found. It turns out that, completely beyond any conscious intention on my part, the conclusions fall into eleven groups.

First, I was struck by the critical link between a museum's mission statement and its exhibition program. Staff working in institutions guided by mission statements that do not explicitly authorize and support interpretive exhibitions are on uncertain terrain when they propose interpretive exhibitions. Institutions whose mission statements do not endorse interpretive exhibitions may not, at some level, really want to do them. A very basic observation, perhaps, but an important one, for tortured and dysfunctional processes can often be traced to institutional failures to clearly articulate basic principles—as opposed to pieties—and traced to a confused or conflicted sense of purpose.

Part of the problem is that museum mission statements are too frequently larded with pieties that offer to museum staffs little in the way of direction. The chief purpose of such mission statements seems to be public relations. Considering museums' financial needs and social responsibilities, some recognition of community cultural and political values is both appropriate and necessary. But many mission statements are unnecessarily flat and banal, hardly charged or energized enough to power a program of distinguished interpretive exhibitions.

Some mission statements speak of promoting knowledge and appreciation of the past. But neither promoting knowledge, narrowly defined, nor appreciation automatically lead to interpretive exhibitions. Neither compels an institution to go beyond descriptive history. Most mission statements pay homage in some form to the museum profession's own trinity: collecting, preserving, and interpreting. Yet it is not clear that even this list is sufficiently empowering, since it places interpretation last, almost as an afterthought. A newer, alternative trinity—preserve, study, and communicate—still begs the issue of interpretation.

The place of interpretation remains unclear in part because many institutions have only a vague notion of what "interpreting" means. For many it seems to mean merely doing descriptive history or narrating stories. Stories can be important but to truly interpret something, to truly interpret that story, we have to dare to suggest what it means. To interpret something means ultimately to evaluate it, thoughtfully and critically. This means museums have to step outside their own culture and its prevailing wisdom to discover and evaluate the ramifications of whatever topics they study. It means they have to take an informed stand based on responsible and extensive analysis. Putting it in different terms, interpreting means demonstrating why something matters, how it has made a difference. Ideally, interpretation helps us gain not just knowledge but that rarer and more precious commodity, wisdom. Interpretation does not just inform us but pushes us to a deeper and more subtle understanding of some aspect of the world around us. Really interpreting is a difficult and challenging business. Only a few museums really grasp this. Only a few grasp it because most history museums still bear traces of their unreflective, celebratory origins. And regardless of their public posture, many museums still adhere to—or are trapped in—old ways, old assumptions, old values. I sympathize with museum staffs caught between their own desire to create interpretive exhibitions and very real pressure within their institutions to remain within a celebratory mode and endorse the status quo.

We often like to think that the factors hindering our ability to produce imaginative exhibitions lurk somewhere out there in the public realm. But the evidence of at least one of these essays suggests that much of the public is very open-minded about what museums might do. It is not the general public that requires us to conform to orthodoxies but our traditional visitors. The Brooklyn Historical Society found that the group *least* open to innovation, imaginative interpretation, and change of any sort were the museum's existing users, its regular customers. This is a depressing but eye-opening piece of news.

Following its implications, it is reasonable to suspect that much of the resistance to doing imaginative work actually comes from within institutions, from trustees, from management, from staff, from those we think are our best friends. Self-censorship is commonplace in the museum field. So is fear.

Therefore, it is not much of a surprise that some of the best interpretive work — understanding the definition of "interpretive" correctly — comes from institutions that have made pointed efforts to break with past understandings, to chart new identities and new directions for themselves. Sometimes a decisive break with an institution's past is necessary to signal to the outside world and to those within the institution that its purpose and its products will henceforth be different.

If institutions have difficulty mounting interpretive history exhibitions, they might consider re-examining their mission statements and the values, assumptions, and expectations that undergird those documents. For that matter, they might also look at their budgets to see how well allocations of funds conform to and support the institutional mission. If the products are not coming out, conflicts or contradictions within the institutional infrastructure are probably blocking them. And the institution is also probably not healthy.

My second observation is that exceptional exhibitions are distinguished by a clear sense of purpose. Finding a clear sense of exhibition purpose within an museum with a muddled sense of institutional purpose is not likely, which is why I placed my observations about mission at the head of this discussion. Like a well-run institution, a good exhibition seems to be characterized by focus, direction, an obvious sense of purpose, a clear vision of goals, and of end products. This clear vision is kept in view as the project evolves. Invoking Tom McKay's baseball analogy, in order to produce a quality product, the members of the exhibition team always have to keep their eyes on the idea.

On an intellectual level, this means continued attention to and reaffirmation of the exhibition's central message. At a more pragmatic level, it can mean that if an exhibition is meant to travel, that fact becomes integrated into the planning process. Situations where an exhibition that was great at one venue turns out to be disappointing at another can be avoided. To do so, exhibition planners need to consciously think about the limitations and opportunities associated with traveling a show. They need to think about and accommodate the special characteristics of various sites. They need to recognize that to travel a show may require radical changes to its physical—and therefore intellectual and affective—structure.

In actual practice, keeping an eye on the idea means that many people need to keep their eyes on the idea. They all have to share the same idea, the same vision. This is easier said than done. There is much talk within the museum community and in this book about the team system. Many who have used it endorse it. But they also acknowledge that sometimes willingness to be agreeable compromises a powerful vision, a exceptional idea. I suspect that there are many ways to unite people to create exhibitions. Egalitarian teams are one viable alternative but more hierarchical models, like those used in theater, movies, television, or in the kitchens of fine restaurants, are equally valid if less democratic. Regardless of the structure, however, the exhibition will probably not amount to much if, throughout the process, key people do not keep their eyes on the idea.

The third point may at first glance seem to contradict the above principle. For if it is necessary to keep focussed during the process, there is also a time when it is appropriate to let the focus slip. Up to a certain point, focus is premature. Good exhibitions seem more likely when the early stages of development are open and dynamic. Selecting a topic, an approach, an interpretive angle too soon can be counterproductive. Studies in this book demonstrate that much can be gained from unfettered and uninhibited brainstorming at the beginning of a project.

I recognize that sometimes the first idea really is the best idea and ultimately shapes the exhibition—but not usually. More often the first idea is just a starting point, just a formulation to organize and propel subsequent thinking. In brainstorming we cast the net widely and push out the limits that usually constrain our thinking. If we bring into the process people outside our typical working circle, we are likely also to bring in ideas and perspectives we ourselves could not have provided. Bouncing ideas around with an imaginative group of people usually improves the project. If the group is sufficiently diverse it can help museum people identify and deal with their own unexamined or unrecognized assumptions, biases, or blind spots.

Brainstorming is easier for some people than for others. It takes time, patience, and a tolerance for both ambiguity and digression. The major advantage of brainstorming is that it helps an institution identify a wider range of options than it might otherwise generate. Then selection of the final path is an informed choice, made with full awareness of the strengths and weaknesses, advantages and disadvantages of other possible paths.

Brainstorming works best where people are open and confident. People with open minds know that good ideas can come from anywhere. Only a very rigid—and foolish—person rejects a good idea because it comes from an unauthorized or threatening source, like a junior staff member, a volunteer, or a member of the public. Brainstorming works where people have the confidence to think big, to risk letting an idea spin out of control and take on a life of its own. It takes confidence to let exhibition explorations drift toward sensitive issues and topics. It takes confidence to travel beyond conventional truths, to re-examine assumptions, to reject prevailing wisdom. It takes confidence to ask the really big questions, the questions without answers, or the questions without happy answers.

It is true that much of what comes out of brainstorming sessions is eventually thrown away. Ideas turn out to be irrelevant, impractical, or politically impossible. In that sense, brainstorming is not an efficient process. Why bother with it? Because it has the potential to widen the scope of exhibition possibilities beyond what might be generated through more closed processes. In short, it is likely to lead to a better product.

The fourth point is congruent. For if exhibits are best when born from or tested in the expansive chaos of brainstorming, they are just as likely to be improved when the exhibition development process remains open and fluid for as long as possible. This is because creativity is an evolving process. Today's solution, today's vision gives way to tomorrow's. Each new set of ideas, each new group of objects suggests arguments or inquiries not visible at an earlier stage in the project.

Small organizations routinely work with great flexibility, making additions, adjustments, or corrections to an exhibition right up to the opening—and sometimes beyond. Think about the way the Stearns County Historical Society works. Larger institutions are necessarily much less flexible but will benefit from resisting rigidity and closure as long as possible. These essays show that it is possible to balance the needs of responsible management with the institutional mandate to produce the highest quality exhibition that time and resources allow.

Keeping the process open, putting off irreversible decisions for as long as possible, is not irresponsible. On the contrary, it is grounded in the critical realization that the process of developing exhibitions is an evolution. An idea takes on its own organic process of growth and expansion as new material and new insights are accumulated. An intelligent and flexible crew will be willing to let their project change its shape. They will embrace the little serendipities that come late in the planning process and often become the nicest moments within the exhibition. If they are really confident, they will even encourage situations of creative conflict, for conflict can push ideas and conceptions to higher levels. In short, a process that allows extensive and continuing exploration of options and alternatives, a process that supports a relatively long period of open creativity, is likely to produce superior results.

The fifth point follows logically and is also self-evident. A good exhibition requires adequate resources. One is time. Fast-track exhibitions sometimes succeed but most exhibitions require time to mature. I recognize that some institutions are so bureaucratically encumbered that nothing can be done swiftly or efficiently. I am not defending these institutions, nor do I endorse inertia or incompetence. What I am arguing is that quality exhibitions usually legitimately take time, particularly when staff and financial resources are limited. It takes time to develop ideas fully. It takes time to define goals and anticipated outcomes. It takes time to learn what collections are available and what objects must be borrowed. It takes time to determine what other institutions would be interested in collaborating. It takes time to locate the people who can help with matters of fact or interpretation. And there are many other parts of the exhibition development process that take time.

It is also painfully obvious that quality exhibitions need adequate funding. There is no all-purpose yardstick for measuring how much is required to achieve that quality. Each project has its own needs. Some exhibitions cost millions, others less than a thousand dollars. It is folly to attempt to create a costly exhibition with a beggar's budget. Good shows do not necessarily have to be expensive, but moving and insuring large numbers of three-dimensional objects, some of which may be delicate or fragile, quickly run to many dollars.

If an institution elects to raise money to fund its exhibition idea, time once again becomes an issue. It takes time to craft a compelling planning grant proposal. It takes time to locate the appropriate scholars and secure their participation. It takes time to put together a cogent implementation proposal. No matter how we look at it, good exhibitions require time and money. It is not always easy to know how much of each will be necessary but too easy to know when we don't have enough.

The sixth point I noted was that good exhibitions often came about when institutions played to their strengths. The Henry Ford Museum was able to develop an outstanding exhibition about the automobile in American life precisely because it has a world-class collection of automobiles. Minnesota Historical Society's exhibition about Hidatsa people was developed around a major but almost ignored collection. Brooklyn Historical Society more or less backed into the five major subject areas of its major exhibition by recognizing what elements it could not afford to leave out of that exhibition.

Playing to strengths makes the exhibition process easier. Time and energy are both finite. If an outstanding collection or major cache of documents are already available, no time is wasted trying to locate them. That time can be spent more productively on refining interpretive or design aspects of the show.

Playing to strengths also means recognizing both the potential and limitations of collections. In the current push to bring academic history into museums, some unjustified praise has been heaped on exhibitions that have been little more than books on walls or cases of written documents. These may be exhibitions of historical materials but they are not, to my way of thinking, the kind of exhibitions history museums ought to be doing.

One way to understand the meaning of playing to strengths, then, is recognizing that not all historic tales or all historic moments or all historic issues are equally accessible through material culture. What material culture of the past tells us about best is culture of the past. We need to accept the fact that some historical tales cannot be effectively conveyed by material culture. To plan an exhibition about such a tale is to set oneself a very difficult course. On the other hand, the chapters in the history of culture that can be effectively explored through typical museum collections are nearly unlimited. Some fine examples are discussed in this volume. They show the very real advantages that accrue when an institution sees the advantages of playing to its strengths.

Discussion of what it means to do history through objects leads directly to the seventh point: Good exhibitions are created by people who understand the medium. This is not an insignificant point. I am not at all convinced that many people working in museums really understand the strengths and weaknesses of the medium they work with. We are now all conditioned to reject book-on-the-wall exhibitions but I am not sure that we, as a profession, have grown much more sophisticated about the medium.

The best practitioners of the genre recognize that exhibitions are a dynamic synthesis of objects, words, and design. They also recognize, as authors in this book point out repeatedly, that of these three, words are the least effective component. Exhibitions are primarily nonverbal, sensory experiences. People may read the words we write, but they are more likely to be caught up in the multisensory experience we try to provide.

Good exhibitions are produced by people who accept this truth and exploit it. Really capable exhibition developers imaginatively engage all media appropriate to their subject. The exhibition at the National Afro-American Museum and Cultural Center, for example, makes music a central component, a decision that is affecting for visitors, historically justified, and enhances the exhibition's interpretive agenda. Look back at the essays and note how often these exemplary exhibitions have drawn on multiple media to enhance impact and enrich experience.

Our authors remind us that in exhibitions the sensory is more important than the cerebral. This realization has many ramifications. One is that interpretation has to be advanced more by sensory data and purposeful manipulation of media than by texts. The challenge is to help people *feel* the interpretation. This notion of feeling the interpretation is not as bizarre are it may seem, for we regularly describe ourselves as feeling one way or another about something. The challenge of history exhibitions is to evoke in people specific patterns of feelings about an event, a movement, a legacy of the past.

It therefore follows that design is critically important in exhibitions. This seventh point is both glaringly apparent and still insufficiently grasped. In recent times I have seen an exhibition about three centuries in the dynamic life of a major city and another about one of America's most painful and disruptive wars. In both instances, the designers seemed oblivious to the powerful dramas inherent in their subjects. Instead of helping audiences feel change and feel what that change meant, instead of drawing visitors into the powerful and engulfing affect that swirled around urban changes and the war, they offered elegant and tasteful installations of objects, elegant and tasteful installations that completely mitigated the extraordinary potential for touching people's emotions inherent in these two subjects. Instead of putting the objects into historical context, they took them out. Instead of varying design for dramatic effect, they homogenized it for aesthetic effect. Instead of inviting people to feel, they invited them to admire. Instead of doing history they did art.

As Lizabeth Cohen notes, there is a considerable difference between an effective art installation, the purpose of which is to promote contemplation and appreciation, and an effective history installation, the purpose of which is to promote thought and feeling. The best designers, the ones whose work we most admire, understand how design can enhance both the ideas and feelings that the exhibition wants to promote.

This is not easy. It requires an exceptional understanding of design, acceptance of the goals of the exhibition, and a willingness to be inventive, imaginative, and take risks in advancing those goals. Sometimes tasteful design works just perfectly. But sometimes tasteful design is absolutely the wrong thing and undercuts all the major goals of the exhibition. Design misunderstood kills exhibitions, and taste can be the enemy of passion.

The eighth point is that it takes talent to produce a great exhibition. Basically, you can't do great exhibitions without access to great talent. Museums that don't have that talent on staff need to find ways to get it.

The essays here present us with many ways of finding and using talent. All of these ways work, and all are worth trying. Planning grants, for example, are perfect for the early brainstorming phase of an exhibition. Regular implementation grants allow museums to augment their in-house talent by hiring consultants and project leaders with needed expertise. Borrowing sometimes works. Not every institution will be lucky enough to host Fath Ruffins or a scholar of her talent but there are ways for the imaginative and assertive to lure scholars into exhibition collaboration.

At the Valentine Museum, Frank Jewell developed what others have called a scholarly bullpen, a group of scholars on whom he routinely draws to provide expertise in given areas. But as his and other institutions have found out, sometimes these scholars are just as helpful outside their alleged specialties, adding to the aggregate of creative energy within an institution.

It should be obvious that to do good history exhibitions one needs access to good history. I say it should be, but it apparently is not. Some museums have produced shows of major historical significance but others seem to have been created in strange backwaters untouched by current or recent historical discourse. I do not want to be misunderstood here. I recognize that orthodox academic history is not necessarily what museums need, although they do need to get their facts and dates straight. But there are talented and open-minded academics in the arts, the humanities, and the social sciences who understand or want to understand the distinctive nature of exhibitions and are willing to participate in their creation. Too often museums pick the wrong academics to advise in a project, then write off all academics as unsuited for museum collaboration.

On behalf of the Common Agenda, in the spirit of cross-institutional collaboration, I urge museums to try again. Get on the grapevine and find out who has been good to work with. Call institutions that have been successful in the competition for NEH funds and ask them for candid recommendations. Skim the scholarly journals. Look at the programs of the annual meetings of appropriate academic organizations. Go to the meetings. Talk to people. The talent you need is out there. If it is not, then it is you who are on the cutting edge and in a position to lead.

The essays here document several instances of museums borrowing talent. But museums can also upgrade the talents of their own staff. The Valentine Museum is well known for its program of staff enrichment, although other institutions have comparable programs. The various forms of borrowing address short-term and often quite specific needs. Training its own staff may have more enduring value for an institution, since those with augmented talents presumably remain with the institution.

Regardless of the approach, the point to remember is that there is a direct correlation between the quality of the intelligence put into an exhibition and the quality of the result. And while I have been speaking of help for the academic side of a project, it is just as necessary and just as beneficial to seek additional expertise in design, education, connoisseurship of artifacts, and any other relevant area.

One of the major motivations behind the Common Agenda was to help history museums rise above parochialism. I believe one of the best ways to do that is to work with people who are both exceptionally capable and exceptionally well informed. If the essays in this book gloss over a point, it is about how critical the right people are to the successful completion of a project. Many people, most of our authors among them, work in situations where competence and talent are taken for granted. But not everyone is as fortunate. Despite all of our emphasis on process in this book, every process stands or falls because of the people involved in it. Talented people are the real magic that makes great interpretive exhibitions possible.

You cannot think about people in the abstract, creating ideal team diagrams and flow charts. All of the people who become part of your equation bring with them their own content expertise, their own priorities, their own prejudices. We don't work with a process, we work with people. Who those other people are and what talents they bring determine, more than any other factors, the quality of the final product. If you can't locate good people, even the best process won't be of much use.

The ninth point also concerns people. But here I speak not of the people who create exhibitions but of those for whom they are created. I mean the audience, the visitors, the public, those people who come to see what is going on in the museum. These essays suggest that successful exhibitions integrate expectations about visitors into the exhibition development process.

Until recent years, many museums had only impressionistic information about their audiences. They were also often naive and unrealistic, somehow expecting in an increasingly pluralistic society to create programs that would appeal to everybody. How many programs can you think of that actually attract a true cross-section of the many peoples and cultures of this country? Some of the most savvy museums have crafted their products knowingly for a specified segment of the population. They understand that while wanting to reach everybody is a noble and politically correct goal, it is not realistic. It may not even be desirable.

Awareness of audience takes many forms. One essay spoke of using focus groups, a system which can yield some very blunt and unsettling testimony. Some institutions involve people who come from within the culture that is the subject of the exhibition. The involvement of native Americans, for example, seems commonplace today. When museum staff and audience are from different cultures, the issue of voice often become problematic. Whose voice, whose view, will dominate the exhibition? Sometimes the decision has been made to let the other culture's voice prevail. Some exhibition teams have elected to allow multiple voices. Whatever the decision, responding to the question of audience may have a dramatic impact on the shape of the exhibition.

Thoughts about audience work their way into the structure of the exhibition in other ways. They prod us to wonder about the kind of relationship the museum wants to have with its audience, whatever that audience might be. Does the exhibition talk to the audience? Lecture? Preach? Does it make attempts to connect to experiences familiar to the audience? Does it ask questions? Does it invite or challenge the audience to puzzle some things out for itself? Does it do several of these things? Does it, like everyday reality, ask them to acknowledge the chaos, complexity, and contradiction that characterize the human condition? Does it treat its audience like children, even if they are adults? And there are many more questions that might be asked.

Reflections on audience lead to reflections on success. Success is often measured by gate. By that standard McDonald's is the best restaurant in America. And Domino's makes the best pizza. But we know that both are false. We also know that the relationship of quality to popularity is muddy at best. We have seen excellent exhibitions that were savored by a few. Execrable exhibits are sometimes wildly popular, for any number of bad reasons. But, finally, we recognize that counting a lot of heads is only one measure of success. In the end, in exhibits, as in teaching, having a powerful and lasting effect on a few people may be more beneficial and more influential than providing short-lived amusement and diversion for many. But then the question is, were those few people the ones you hoped they would be? Maybe the answer to that question is a key to understanding success.

The tenth point is: Understand your own process. If a rule is only a rule when people know about it, a process is only a process when people use it. Processes are developed in many different ways. Some grow and change organically, others are imposed by management mandate or as the result of recommendations from consultants. Whatever the case, a process can't work unless people know about it and follow it. All the players need to know the rules of the game.

Finally, the last lesson is that we need to build evaluation into the process. This can take many forms. Staff can themselves become better evaluators if they develop a high level of exhibition literacy. One way to do that is by visiting and critiquing exhibitions at other institutions. Being more alert to evaluation can lead to assembling a portfolio of ideas that work, whether culled from one's own exhibitions or from exhibitions in other parts of the country or other parts of the world. It can mean finding and recording ideas that work in the theater, in restaurants, at fairs, in store windows, at antique shows, in advertising, in open fields, in the stars.

Taking evaluation seriously can mean recognizing that the opening is not the end of exhibition development. A few institutions designate a portion of their exhibition budgets for corrections and adjustments after the show opens. Taking evaluation seriously can mean consistently and systematically soliciting feedback from visitors in many different ways and about many different dimensions of the exhibition, learning in the process what worked for visitors and what did not. And it can mean many other strategies to provide museums with the tools to produce more powerful and compelling exhibitions.

Few of these observations are new. But then, there is no necessary correlation between novelty and quality. In many cases, there is much to be said for the informed use of very old and venerable devices. For, in truth, what exhibitions are about, even if their subject matter is recent and their technology at the cutting edge, is the ancient goal of making a difference in people's lives. We want interpretive history exhibitions to affect the way people think and feel about a given phenomenon or issue. We want to give people an experience that is rich on sensory and intellectual levels. And, if we are honest about it, we want to change, albeit sometimes in very small ways, how people think about, feel about, or see the world around them. We want history museums to play more prominent, and by that we really mean more powerful, roles in American life.

And if that is really what we want, if we really want to be taken more seriously and wield greater power, we will have to gain greater mastery of the exhibition medium. If we want to become more prominent purveyors of the humanities in American life, we need to become more imaginative, more adept at manipulating this idiosyncratic form of humanistic inquiry.

This is a challenge that some institutions have met better than others. We asked our authors to examine a few of those institutions and tell us about the processes behind their exhibitions, for we recognized that product is inseparable from process. Each essay in this book analyses what took place at one institution over a finite period of time. Each essay presents a case study of institutional culture. In these few pages I have tried to summarize some of the major points made in the essays. I recognize, however, that there are many other significant points on which I have not commented. I hope only that my dialogue with the essays prompts other readers to recall others of the many helpful findings that enrich this informative and path-breaking book.

In this book readers can find some of the best insights into the process of creating interpretive history exhibitions available anywhere. This book provides commentary on all the major parts of the process that can be put into words. For it is true that in all artful work, some parts lie beyond the grasp of words. Those parts cannot be captured here. But most of the rest can. And that is considerable.

CONTRIBUTORS

KENNETH L. AMES is currently Chief of the Historical and Anthropological Surveys at the New York State Museum in Albany. Trained as an art historian at Carleton College and the University of Pennsylvania, Ames taught for many years in the Winterthur Program in Early American Culture, an American studies program jointly sponsored by the Winterthur Museum and the University of Delaware. He has written and lectured extensively about material culture and folk art. His most recent book is *Death in the Dining Room and Other Tales of Victorian Culture*, published by Temple University Press.

LONNIE BUNCH is the Assistant Director for Curatorial Affairs at the Smithsonian Institution's National Museum of American History. Prior to moving to Washington, D.C., he served as the Senior Curator of History at the California Afro-American Museum in Los Angeles. He has curated a wide range of exhibitions including "The Black Olympians, 1904–1984," "Land of Promise: America in the 19th Century," and "Go Forth and Serve: The Black Land Grant College." Bunch has written numerous monographs and articles such as *Black Angelenos: The Afro-American in Los Angeles, 1850–1950, The Black Olympians, 1904–1984, Visions Towards Tomorrow: The East Bay African American Community* (coauthor). Bunch is coeditor of a column of museum reviews and interpretation for the American Historical Association's periodical *Perspectives*. As a film maker, Bunch has produced and written several documentaries for the Public Broadcasting System including "The Black Olympians" and "Black Paths of Leadership."

LIZABETH COHEN is Assistant Professor of History at Carnegie Mellon University and a trustee of the Historical Society of Western Pennsylvania. She has worked on the staff of Old Sturbridge Village, the Fine Arts Museum of San Francisco, and the Camron-Stanford House in Oakland, California, and has served as a consultant to many museums and historical organizations including the Chicago Historical Society, the Illinois State Museum, and the Oakland Museum. She is the author of *Making New a Deal: Industrial Workers in Chicago, 1919–1939* (Cambridge University Press, 1990) and a number of articles on museum exhibitions and material culture.

BARBARA FRANCO, a graduate of Bryn Mawr College and the Cooperstown Graduate Program in Museum Studies, has been working in museums since 1966. She began her museum career as Curator of Decorative Arts at the Munson-Williams-Proctor Institute in Utica, New York, and then worked successively as curator, coordinator of exhibits, and assistant director at the Museum of Our National Heritage in Lexington, Massachusetts. Since January 1990 she has been Assistant Director for Museums at the Minnesota Historical Society with responsibility for the educational programs, exhibitions, and museum collections in the new History Center scheduled to open in the fall of 1992.

MICHAEL FRISCH teaches history and American studies at the State University of New York at Buffalo. He is the author of *A Shared Authority: Essays on the Craft and Meaning of Oral and Public History* (Albany: SUNY Press, 1990), which includes several essays on museum exhibitions and historical presentation. He is also editor of *The Oral History Review*, journal of the Oral History Association, and the author of the forthcoming *Portraits in Steel* (Cornell University Press, 1993), an oral history of steel workers and deindustrializations in Buffalo, New York, in collaboration with Milton Rogovin.

L. THOMAS FRYE is Chief Curator of History and head of the Cultural History Department at the Oakland Museum in California, where he has developed more than eighty permanent and temporary exhibitions, including the renowned "California: A Place, A People, A Dream." A pioneer in collecting and interpreting the twentieth century, Frye has recently published "Viewpoint: Collecting 20th-Century Objects and People," in *The Public Historian* and, with Nancy Kolb, "20th Century Collecting: Guidelines and Case Studies," a Special Report for *History News*. Frye is active in professional organizations in leadership positions including the Western Museums

Conference, for which he has served as president, the California Heritage Task Force, and the American Association for State and Local History. He has acted as a consultant to scores of historical organizations and frequently reviews grant applications for the National Endowment for the Humanities and private foundations.

MARY ELLEN HAYWARD currently serves as Grants Coordinator and Maritime Curator at the Maryland Historical Society in Baltimore. Since 1980 she has worked on a number of large-scale interpretive exhibitions, including the Baltimore City Life Museums's "Rowhouse: A Baltimore Style of Living" and "Maryland's Maritime Heritage" at the Maryland Historical Society. In 1986–87 she acted as project director for galleries at the MHS and is now in the process of developing a new Civil War exhibit. She received her M.A. from the Winterthur Program in Early American Culture and her doctorate from the American and New England studies program at Boston University.

MICHAEL HEISLEY is Curator of Folklore at the Southwest Museum in Los Angeles, California, where he develops public programs, exhibitions, and research projects relating to Mexican and Chicano folklore and folk arts. A native of Texas, he received his Ph.D. from the Folklore and Mythology Program at the University of California, Los Angeles in 1983. He has worked for the Smithsonian Institution's Festival of American Folklife in Washington, D.C., and for numerous public sector folklore projects in California. Heisley's publications include *An Annotated Bibliography of Chicano Folklore from the Southwestern United States* (1977) and "Sources for the Study of Mexican Music in California" (1988). A recent recipient of a Rockefeller Foundation Fellowship in the Humanities, Heisley is currently completing a book on the role of traditional songs and singing in the California farm workers' movement of the 1960s and 1970s.

WARREN LEON is Director of Public Education for the Union of Concerned Scientists. He previously directed the Interpretation Department at Old Sturbridge Village. With Roy Rosenzweig, he edited *History Museums in the United States: A Critical Assessment* (University of Illinois Press, 1989). Leon earned a Ph.D. in history from Harvard University.

CANDACE TANGORRA MATELIC is currently the Director and Professor of Museum Studies at the Cooperstown Graduate Programs. Before assuming her duties in Cooperstown, Matelic worked in the Education Department of the Henry Ford Museum and Greenfield Village, managing interpretive training, interpretive programs, and adult education, and as an interpretive specialist for Living History Farms in Des Moines, Iowa. She has been active in the history museum field and its professional organizations, and she regularly consults in the areas of interpretive planning, management, training, and self-study.

TOM MCKAY serves as Coordinator of the Office of Local History at the State Historical Society of Wisconsin. He heads a program that provides advice and assistance to 246 affiliated historical societies throughout Wisconsin. In this position, McKay served as coauthor and coproducer of the award-winning "Exhibiting Your Community's Heritage," an NEH funded, five-part instructional video tape series on planning and preparing interpretive exhibits. McKay has been curator for eight local history exhibits in Wisconsin, including "Beginnings: Community Formation in Wisconsin" and "Culture and Agriculture," both of which received AASLH Awards of Merit. Before working in Wisconsin, McKay held positions as historic sites administrator for the Iowa State Historical Department, director of the Lyme Historical Society in Connecticut, and research associate at the Schenectady Museum in New York. McKay's earned his M.A. from the Cooperstown Graduate Programs.

CLEMENT ALEXANDER PRICE is Associate Professor of History at Rutgers, State University of New Jersey, Newark Campus. He is the author of numerous publications on Afro-American history and race relations and is preparing a study of cultural diversity and the arts for the American Council on the Arts. His *Freedom Not Far Distant: A Documentary History of Afro-Americans in New Jersey* is a standard textbook. He is the former chairman of the New Jersey State Council on the Arts, a trustee of the Newark Museum, and a consultant to the Jewish Museum's exhibit, "Bridges and Boundaries: African-Americans and American Jews." Price earned his Ph.D. from Rutgers University.

CARROLL PURSELL is currently the Adeline Barry Davee Professor of History at Case Western Reserve University in Cleveland, Ohio. Before that he taught at the University of California, Santa Barbara, where he directed the Graduate Program in Public Historical Studies and edited *The Public Historian*. He received his Ph.D. from the University of California, Berkeley. From 1990-1992, he served as president of the Society for the History of Technology and in 1991 received its Leonardo da Vinci medal for lifetime contribution to the field.

CYNTHIA ROBINSON is Executive Director of the Bay State Historical League. She is also a principal of C&S Associates, museum consultants. She previously worked as education coordinator at the Worcester Historical Museum and as an interpreter and museum teacher at Old Sturbridge Village. Robinson hold an M.S. in education from Bank Street College.

PETER H. WELSH is Chief Curator and Director of Research at the Heard Museum, Phoenix, Arizona, where he supervises all collections, education, and exhibition activities. He received his Ph.D. in anthropology from the University of Pennsylvania. He has curated numerous exhibits, ranging from permanent installations at the Southwest Museum in Los Angeles to exhibits of painting and sculpture. His exhibit "Exotic Illusions: Art, Romance, and the Marketplace," received an award for excellence in 1989 from the Curator's Committee of the American Association of Museums.

INDEX